CALIFORNIA

The publisher gratefully acknowledges the generous contribution to this book provided by Stephen M. Silberstein as a member of the Literati Circle of the University of California Press Foundation.

AMERICA'S

HIGH-STAKES

EXPERIMENT

CALIFORNIA

PETER SCHRAG

University of California Press
Berkeley   Los Angeles   London

University of California Press, one of the most distinguished
university presses in the United States, enriches lives around
the world by advancing scholarship in the humanities, social
sciences, and natural sciences. Its activities are supported
by the UC Press Foundation and by philanthropic
contributions from individuals and institutions. For more
information, visit www.ucpress.edu.

University of California Press
Berkeley and Los Angeles, California

University of California Press, Ltd.
London, England

Library of Congress Cataloging-in-Publication Data

Schrag, Peter.
    California : America's high-stakes experiment / Peter
Schrag.
        p.   cm.
    Includes bibliographical references and index.
    ISBN 0-520-24436-2 (alk. paper).
    1. California—Politics and government—1951.
2. California—Social conditions.   3. California—
Economic conditions.   I. Title.

F866.2.S38   2006
979.4'05—dc22   2005023952

Manufactured in the United States of America

15   14   13   12   11   10   09   08   07   06
10   9   8   7   6   5   4   3   2   1

This book is printed on New Leaf EcoBook 60, containing
60% post-consumer waste, processed chlorine free; 30% de-
inked recycled fiber, elemental chlorine free; and 10% FSC-
certified virgin fiber, totally chlorine free. EcoBook 60 is
acid-free and meets the minimum requirements of
ANSI/ASTM D5634-01 (Permanence of Paper).

In memory of John Jacobs

CONTENTS

SOURCES AND ACKNOWLEDGMENTS

This book is based in part on work I've done for the *Sacramento Bee* and other publications over the past thirty years, in part on research and interviews aimed specifically at this project in both the United States and Mexico in 2003–2005. Many of the sources are quoted or cited in the text or in the endnotes; others are standard census and economic databases. (I should also point out that I've tried to combine and compress the notes as much as possible to minimize distractions in the text.) Of the sources not mentioned or not sufficiently recognized in the citations, I owe particular thanks to countless individuals at the office of the California Secretary of State; to Elizabeth Hill and her colleagues at the California Legislative Analyst's Office; to former California state librarian and California historian Kevin Starr for invaluable suggestions and wisdom; to Dean Misczynski and his colleagues at the California Research Bureau; to California Finance Director Tom Campbell and others at the California Department of Finance; to the staff of the National Governors Association in Washington and those at the National Conference of State Legislatures and the Education Commission of the States in Denver.

Also thanks to Bob Blattner, Paul Goldfinger, and others at School Services of California; Los Angeles community activist David Abel; Connie Rice and Molly Munger of the Advancement Project in Los Angeles; David Lyon, Mark Baldassare, Michael Teitz, Fred Silva, Joyce Peterson, Abby Cook, Hans Johnson, Kim Rueben, Deborah Reed, Jon Sonstelie, Heather Rose, and their colleagues at the Public Policy Institute of California; Carol Whiteside, director of the Great Valley Center in Modesto, and her colleagues, who shepherded me to some of the more remote locations of California's Central Valley; Senator Gil Cedillo and his communications director, Edward Headington, who provided an extended guided tour of his Los Angeles district; David Mas Masumoto for his peaches and hospitality; Severin Borenstein and his colleagues at the California Energy Institute; Sarah Lira, comanager of Ciudad del Sol, the Davis Migrant Housing Center; former California Assembly Speakers Robert Hertzberg and Antonio Villaraigosa (now mayor of Los Angeles); and former Senate Minority Leader Jim Brulte.

Also, thanks to Philip Martin of the Agricultural and Resource Economics Department of the University of California, Davis; Jack Citrin of the Political Science Department at the University of California, Berkeley; John Ellwood and Eugene Smolensky of the Goldman School of Public Policy at Berkeley; former Dean Tom Goldstein of both the Berkeley and Columbia journalism schools; Sylvia and Leon Panetta of the Panetta Institute at California State University, Monterey Bay; Wayne Cornelius of the University of California, San Diego; Belinda Reyes and Kenji Hakuta of the University of California, Merced; Mike Kirst of the School of Education at Stanford; Chancellor Charles Reed of the California State University; Richard Atkinson, former president of the University of California; and the late Clark Kerr for his constant generosity and perspective.

I'm also grateful for help from Manuel Orozco of the Inter-American Dialogue in Washington; Rafael Alarcón of the Colegio de la Frontera Norte in Tijuana; Angel Santa Ana and other agents of the San Diego sector of the U.S. Border Patrol for their special tour of the border; Alice Petrossian and her colleagues at the Glendale Unified School District; Garry South, Gale Kaufman, Dan Schnur, and Tony Quinn, political consultants and analysts extraordinaires; former California Finance Director Tim Gage; Don Villarejo and Rick Mines of the California Rural Studies Project; Angelo Logan of the East Yard Communities for Environmental Justice; the late Miguel Contreras of the Los Angeles Labor Federation; former California Secretary for Education Gary Hart; education consultant John Mockler; Joel Fox, former executive director of the Howard Jarvis Taxpayers Association; the California Taxpayers Association; Steve Levy of the Center for the Continuing Study of the California Economy; Harry Pachon of the Tomas Rivera Center; Jean Ross of the California Budget Project; Lenny Goldberg of the California Tax Reform Association; Mervin Field and Mark DiCamillo of the Field Institute; Dane Waters, founder and former director of the Initiative and Referendum Institute; and Bob Stern of the Center for Governmental Studies in Los Angeles.

In addition, I owe special thanks to Bruce Cain, director of the Institute of Governmental Studies at Berkeley; Mark Baldassare of the Public Policy Institute of California; and my longtime friend Susan Rasky at the Journalism School at Berkeley, for reading a draft of this book and for their valuable suggestions in getting (at least some of) the lumps out of it. Special thanks as well to my editor and friend Naomi Schneider for the same and much more; to Bruce Cain (again), Nelson Polsby, Jerry Lubenow, Liz Weiner, and others at the Institute of Governmental Studies for their help, smarts, and support over many years; to Russlynn Ali, the director of EdTrust-West; to Trish Williams, Mary Perry, and others at EdSource; to Pat Brown biographer Ethan Rarick; and to my colleagues and former colleagues and friends at the *Sacramento Bee*, the *Modesto Bee*, and the *Fresno Bee*; and particularly to Claire Cooper, Robert Mott, Mark Paul, Tom Philp, Jim Boren, Russ Minick, Judy Sly, Howard Weaver, Gary Pruitt, Susanna Cooper, David Holwerk, Pia Lopez, Jewel Reilly, Ginger Rutland, Debbie Meredith, Dan Weintraub, and the late John Jacobs, whose journalism remains a model for many of us and to whose memory this book is dedicated.

Finally, thanks to the wise and ever perceptive Trish Ternahan for countless insights, suggestions, and twenty years of love and encouragement.

INTRODUCTION

California has served multiple purposes as model and antimodel for the nation and sometimes the world. A half century ago its universities, freeways, water systems, and parks made the state an exemplar of enlightened government and progressive public services that became the envy of the industrialized world. Twenty years later it became ground zero for the national tax revolt and later for the campaigns against illegal immigration and affirmative action. Since then it has been dismissed as too liberal, too absorbed by its own insular concerns—gays, identity politics, environmentalism—too brown and Asian, too dominated by immigrants to remain the national trendsetter it was once supposed to be. Conversely it has been celebrated, for similar reasons, as the source of a new New Deal, the place where those immigrants were becoming the base of a revived and politically effective labor movement and were ushering in a new era of progressive politics. Until the 1992 election, California was seen as moderately (and more or less safely) Republican. After 1998, when Gray Davis became the first Democrat to win a gubernatorial election in twenty years, and particularly after 2002, when Democrats captured every statewide office, it was regarded as safely (and more or less indefinitely) Democratic.

Less than a year later, the widely disliked Davis was gone, removed in a historically unprecedented recall—only one other U.S. governor had ever been recalled, and that was in North Dakota in 1921—and replaced by Republican Arnold Schwarzenegger, an Austrian-born body-builder/actor who had no experience in politics and had rarely voted before he entered the sometimes goofy 135-candidate race to succeed him. The election brought countless consultants, scholars, and journalists to California, many of them from abroad, who wondered what was going on: Was this yet another turn in California's ever unpredictable hyper-democracy? Was it "circus democracy," as one Berkeley professor called it? What did it portend for other nations, some of which were just taking their first steps into democracy, or for those who, like the Dutch, were themselves contemplating wider latitude for voter referenda?

But all that attention, revealing as some of it was about the state's cultural, economic, and political importance and power, also ignored and maybe concealed the bigger California story and its potential as either an example or a harbinger for the nation and perhaps much of the world. The key element in that story is immigration and the huge array of questions it raises about the future. Shortly before the 2000 census was taken, California became the first large majority-minority state in the country. Anglo whites, while still constituting the largest single group of residents, were just another minority and within a generation would no longer be even the largest minority. And, provided that all the ethnic categories do not become hopelessly blurred by intermarriage and self-redefinition, by mid-century Latinos will become the state's absolute majority. And since California is only the first of many such states—in 2005 Texas also became a majority-minority state—and since the population of the nation itself was rapidly becoming increasingly Latinized, California's willingness and ability to accommodate its new residents, and their ability to assimilate to *it*, could well be important, and perhaps definitive, indicators for the nation.

The most obvious of those immigration-related questions, and maybe the most crucial, is how immigration, and especially Latino immigration, is changing California and affecting its willingness to invest in itself, as it did so lavishly and enthusiastically in the generation after World War II. Now that the state's future depends in large measure on the children of Mexicans, Salvadorans, Filipinos, Indians, Koreans, and Pakistanis, are the voters, who remain disproportionately Anglo white, willing to provide the schools, universities, and other services that they provided when the beneficiaries were the children of Iowans, Kansans, and Nebraskans? How much has changed—and why and how—since the voters and the beneficiaries of the programs they are voting on lived in the same house or in the homes of similar kinds of families, spoke the same language, and looked pretty much alike? Is it an ethnic issue at all or something relatively more benign? The contemporary debate is generally framed as one that's just about illegal immigrants, and for many Americans it probably is only that. But there is a powerful tendency on both sides to reduce the issue merely to immigration and assimilation. Can the nation's new immigrants be assimilated in the same way that European immigrants were a century ago? And that question brings a long list of others in its wake. What about preservation of language and culture? Melting pot or mosaic or fruit salad?

In the past thirty years, the period of the great spike in non-European immigration, Californians have increasingly relied on direct democracy—the voter initiative process particularly—to set state policy on everything from tax limitations and prison sentencing to affirmative action, gay marriage, and medical marijuana. Direct democracy, not representative democracy, now lies at the core of California government.[1]

The Davis recall was part of that, as is Governor Arnold Schwarzenegger's unprecedented use of voter initiatives in the governing process itself, creating what one scholar called a new "hybrid democracy." The result, and maybe the cause as well, has been the gradual replacement of the traditional communitarian ethic, in which all citizens shared the costs of public goods, by a proliferating market ethic that seeks to put an increasing share of the cost of public services—park fees; university tuition; roads, schools, sewers, and other infrastructure needed for new housing developments—on those who use or buy them. Similarly, the state's property tax structure, also created by voter initiative, taxes new owners of homes far more than their neighbors who've been there longer. In both cases, new residents pay proportionately more than their predecessors did a half century ago. To what extent are those two sets of developments—on the one hand, the rise in non-European immigration, on the other, the growth of the market ethic and the share of public services borne by the new kids on the block—related and, if so, how?

The Schwarzenegger victory, a victory in an election with 135 candidates that, despite its resemblance to a sort of electoral Oklahoma land rush, had three or four other plausible contenders, was impressive. It immediately prompted speculation about whether President George W. Bush, who lost California to Al Gore by 1.2 million votes in 2000, might be able to carry the state in 2004. That, in turn, opened not only the possibility that Republicans could own the White House for another generation but also that key members of the overwhelmingly Democratic California legislature might themselves be vulnerable. Schwarzenegger, playing both good and bad cop with the Democrats in struggles over the state budget, workers' compensation, driver's licenses for illegal immigrants, and other issues, certainly thought so. Others, including Republican senator Orrin Hatch of Utah, began a push to amend the U.S. Constitution in the (unlikely) event that Schwarzenegger might someday be elected president.

At the time of the California gubernatorial election, some scholars were even asking whether the recall set in motion an unprecedented populist fervor that would trigger state and local recalls across the nation wherever state constitutions allowed them. Was this another 1978, when the tax revolt that began in California rolled across the nation, shaping U.S. politics ever after? More positively, would the recall and the intense interest that it created, or that Schwarzenegger created, reenergize an apathetic public—bring them back to the voting booth and to a new political engagement? Was the recall the end of the old order in California's politics and perhaps in the nation's? California, caught between its unwillingness to raise taxes and its demand for the kind of services its people had once taken for granted, had run up multi-billion-dollar deficits, deficits so large that its bonds had been downgraded to just above junk status. Schwarzenegger promised to restore the old grandeur without raising taxes—indeed the first thing he did was to cut them by another $4 billion—but beyond promising "action, action, action," he never said how.

Even before he took office, Schwarzenegger warned that he would go to the shopping malls and the right-wing radio talk shows that had been so important in the campaign against Davis, and into the districts of recalcitrant legislators, whose collective approval ratings—at 19 percent—were even lower than Davis's had been, to urge his admirers to remind those legislators just who had won the election. In effect, he set out to do something that even Ronald Reagan had been unable to do, and which, probably, as a man already well past his movie fame, Reagan had been in no position to do: convert his Hollywood celebrity, the star power that brought the admirers and the cameras to any place there might be an Arnold sighting, into effective political power.

But beneath the singular event of the Davis recall and Schwarzenegger ascendancy, far more important things were taking place. In the preceding forty years, immigration, the global economy, and high technology had created a new California whose population, culture, economy, politics, and government were likely to have even more profound consequences for the nation and perhaps the world than Hollywood or Silicon Valley or tax revolts had in the recent past, or than the gold rush had in the distant past. In 2004, one of every eight Americans—some 36 million people—lived in California. The state, as its politicians constantly pointed out, had the world's fifth-largest economy (or perhaps the sixth, depending on how France was doing in any given year) and had become a state-nation with a population larger than that of Canada, and larger than that of Denmark, Sweden, Norway, and the Netherlands combined. By 2025, when it will have close to 50 million people, it will be larger than all but three or four western European countries.

Those factors alone—all predictions of the state's irrelevance notwithstanding—almost insured that, for better or worse, California would remain the nation's, and perhaps the world's, great political and social laboratory, the site of the ultimate test of whether a society so large and diverse could successfully integrate that diversity into an effective modern democracy in a postindustrial age. No nation had ever tried anything like it. California was a force, an indicator that, because of its sheer size alone, was impossible to disregard. The institutions of direct democracy that had brought the Davis recall, and which Schwarzenegger was trying to forge into an unprecedented instrument of governance, were themselves crucial in the context of the broader mistrust of representative government, the growing national backlash against immigration, and the growing orthodoxy of no-new-taxes.

No one can predict precisely what will emerge in California, much less the nature of its long-term effect on the nation. But the elements of that new entity are in place:

• The effect of Latino and Asian immigration. In 2005, more than 26 percent of Californians were foreign-born, the highest percentage in modern history. Since the early 1960s, when California, with some 17 million people, overtook New York to become the nation's most populous state, California's population has doubled in size. Of those additional 17–18 million people, nearly 80 percent are Latino or Asian, in part an unexpected consequence of the 1965 act of Congress abolishing national-origins immigration quotas, and in part an unintended consequence of more recent immigration policies. In recent years, more native-born Americans have moved out of California than have moved in from other states. In 2004, California became the first major state to graduate more blacks and Latinos than Anglo whites from its high schools.

• The globalization of California's economy and culture, some of it, like the continuing reliance on cheap Latino labor, long familiar, some altogether unprecedented. Among its elements: the dependence of Latin American and Caribbean economies on remittances from immigrant workers in the United States, remittances that in many countries constitute the largest source of foreign

revenues; the financial, technical, and entrepreneurial relationships between Indian engineers and computer experts in this
country and schools and new enterprises in India; the open intervention of the Mexican government in domestic U.S. politics and
its encouragement of Mexican identity for Mexicans living in the
United States; and the offshoring to India, China, and other parts
of Asia of an increasing number of technical jobs. California grew
great, in significant part, with the boom in high-tech and other
skilled industries but now faces the challenge of competing with
increasingly sophisticated foreign operations and of accommodating a large, unskilled immigrant population, a prospect that
will generate particularly difficult problems. And given the rapid
dispersion of those immigrants, it won't be California's problem
alone.

• The growing reliance of California voters on direct democracy
in the governance of the state, and, less noticed but not trivial,
the growing use of the initiative in local growth and planning decisions. Notwithstanding the fact that 35 percent of California
residents are Latino and another 12 percent are Asian, only 14
percent of the voters are Latino; nearly 70 percent are non-
Hispanic whites. The most reliable forecasts indicate that, while
the percentage of Latino and (to a lesser degree) Asian voters will
gradually increase, they will remain a minority for at least another generation. But because California's politically gerrymandered legislative districts are equalized by population, not by voters, the legislature's ethnic makeup more closely reflects the
population than the voters as a whole, who (now with the strong
involvement of the governor) use the tools of direct democracy to
trump the legislature on major issues. In surveys asking voters
which they trust more—the initiative or the governor and legislature—direct democracy wins by a wide margin. But given the im-
pulsive nature of the electorate and the ad hoc structure of the

process, the same voters who pass a measure seeking to end bilingual education one year and banning gay marriage in another will also approve initiatives to permit the medical use of marijuana, raise the minimum wage, mandate treatment rather than prison for small-time drug offenders, and pass massive bond issues to fund stem cell research.

• The instability of the state's fiscal and governmental systems, with their Rube Goldberg–like structures—partly the consequence of California's major initiatives—and the dysfunctionality and nonaccountability of the state's elected state and local governments. That in turn exacerbates the distrust of governmental institutions, the legislature particularly, and brings yet more ballot measures. As in Congress, the creation of politically safe districts either through bipartisan agreement, as in California, or through the exercise of raw partisan muscle, as in Texas, has effectively moved the choice of congressional and state legislative representatives into the primaries, where the most extreme partisans of the respective parties make the decisions. And it is those partisans to whom candidates appeal and who produce legislatures in which there are few moderates. Most of those who come to Sacramento from those gerrymandered districts have relatively few incentives to compromise and lots of rewards for posturing and resistance. Combine that with California's tight legislative term limits and the constitutional provision requiring a two-thirds majority in each house of the legislature to approve a budget or state tax increases and you have a formula for fiscal gridlock. Further confounding that is the question of whether California, in view of its sheer size and its deep divisions—regional, economic, and social—is one state at all.

• The national antitax orthodoxy, now driven by the militant and increasingly powerful Club for Growth and Grover Norquist's Americans for Tax Reform and the erosion of political certainties dating back to the 1930s, to the point where even Social Security has become a debatable issue. In effect, what was first sparked by California's Proposition 13 in 1978–79 and more recently reenergized by the Republican Party's ascendancy both in Washington and in most of the major states has now come back in its more blatant "starve the beast" version. (In California in 2002 and 2003, GOP legislative leaders, picking up the message from Norquist and Steve Moore of the Club for Growth, were warning that any GOP caucus member voting for a tax increase would be targeted for defeat in the primaries. Subsequently Schwarzenegger himself spoke of his vehement opposition to feeding "the monster.")[2] Unless that mood changes, both in California and at the national level, the deficits produced by heavy tax cuts and the lack of fiscal discipline will spawn even more severe fiscal difficulties likely to force still greater long-term reductions in public services and infrastructure.

For most of the generation since 1980, Democrats held majorities in the California legislature. The state constitution, however, requires a two-thirds majority in each house of the legislature to enact a budget, raise taxes, or approve any other spending measure, which gave Republicans an effective veto even when there was a Democratic governor and thus allowed them to exercise decisive fiscal power. In 2003, as California, one of a long list of states with major budget problems, sank into a multi-billion-dollar deficit, Norquist told *New York Times* reporter David Firestone that he'd like to see some state go bankrupt to set "a bad example." Polls indicated that Californians would be prepared to support some tax increases for designated purposes, but in 2003–04 voters in Alabama, Oregon, and other states overwhelmingly rejected such proposals. And they did so despite the warnings of political and business leaders—subsequently realized—that failure to increase revenues would result in substantial cuts in education and other crucial services.[3] Underlying the success of the Norquist strategy, at both the state and national

levels, was what Larry Bartels, a Princeton political scientist, called "un-
enlightened self-interest," the inability of voters to understand the effect
of hefty tax cutting, particularly for the wealthy, on the public services
and quality of life that they take for granted.[4] By 2005, Washington's
phase-out of the federal estate tax cut, part of which had gone indirectly
to the state, was already costing California $1 billion a year.[5]

All these things impinge on one another in complex ways, especially
considering the state's sheer size—its geography, population, and economy—as well as the diversity of its regions, native cultures, tongues, and
economic interest groups; the extremes of exurban wealth and urban and
rural poverty, especially in the Central Valley; and the state's twelve or
fourteen television markets. Is California, finally, really one state? What
beliefs or institutional structures hold it together? And (a recurring
question) is it governable at all? Historically, it was thought to be divided
between the water-rich north and the semiarid south. But for the past
generation, California's emerging politics have more obviously divided
the state along a line that, like the nation's sharp political divisions, runs
north and south, between the "blue" (liberal) coast and the "red" (conservative) inland. Those divisions are at bottom as much cultural as anything else—on issues of faith, family, and values; on guns and gays, affirmative action and abortion; on NASCAR dads and soccer moms, what
pollster Stanley Greenberg called the "F-You Boys" against "the Super
Educated women."[6]

Few Californians would fail to recognize the fact that the growing
presence of Latinos is having significant effects on communities, on politics, on ethnic relations, and, just possibly, in shaping the future of those
cultural politics. That increased presence is reflected in the size and
power of the legislature's Latino caucus, which in 2005 included 29 of the
120 members of the state senate and assembly, meaning there are proportionately more elected Latinos in the capitol than there are in the
electorate as a whole, among them Assembly Speaker Fabian Nunez, the
third Latino Assembly Speaker in less than a decade, and including Lieutenant Governor Cruz Bustamante, California's first Latino official to

win a statewide election since the nineteenth century. The Latino caucus was a major force in changing the admission process of the University of California to reduce its reliance on grades and tests, on which minorities as a group don't do well, and to place greater emphasis on "comprehensive review," which looks at each applicant's complete academic record, plus handicaps overcome, community service, and overall potential as a member of the community. The caucus was also instrumental in passing the bill in 2003 that would have given illegal immigrants the right to obtain California driver's licenses and which became a major factor in the recall of Gray Davis.

Inevitably, the growing political heft of California Latinos has simultaneously reduced the relative political visibility and power of California's African Americans—historically, and in many places still, *the* American minority. There are still a handful of blacks in elective California offices, but their numbers will almost certainly shrink as previously black districts become increasingly Latino or Asian. In Los Angeles, Representative Diane Watson's congressional district, once overwhelmingly black, has so many Koreans that she now deals with issues on the Korean peninsula that her predecessor never thought about when he was first elected a generation ago. In 2004, California also saw the election of the first Vietnamese American legislator in American history.

Conversely, there's the ongoing ambivalence about, and recurring backlash against, immigrants, and especially illegal immigrants, evidenced by ballot measures in California and other states—none with much practical effect—declaring English to be the state's official language; by California's vote for Proposition 187 in 1994, which sought to deny schooling and all other services to illegal immigrants and their children (most of which was declared unconstitutional by a federal court); and by the vehement reaction against the driver's license bill, which was repealed after the recall. In 2004, the Republican contender Bill Jones, unsuccessfully trying to beat incumbent Barbara Boxer in a race for the U.S. Senate, ran on a strong immigration-control platform. At the same time, conservatives were preparing a constitutional amendment that would forever prohibit undocumented immigrants from getting driver's licenses and would deny services to illegal aliens—a vaguely similar initiative was passed in Arizona in 2004. A few months later, Congress passed a bill, also triggered by the controversy in California, that in the name of national security seeks to bar any state from issuing driver's licenses, as a dozen or so states still do, to undocumented residents. The House also passed legislation to authorize bounty hunters to find aliens who had eluded deportation orders.

Beneath those immediate issues, there are deeper questions: How do the immigration ledgers balance? How crucial are immigrant workers to the economy? How much do those with limited education, most of them Latino, depress wages for other low-wage American workers—African Americans in particular—who, contrary to the frequent argument, might take many of the affected low-skill jobs if the wages were high enough? What's the effect of immigrants on population density, especially in big cities like Los Angeles, and on pollution, health, and other social conditions there? At what point do immigrants contribute more to the economy and to federal tax revenues (and ultimately to the states) than they cost in public services? A large share of the taxes paid by illegal immigrants goes to the federal Social Security Trust Fund. Because they'll never collect benefits, they're already subsidizing it to the tune of many billions of dollars. On the other hand, are states and local governments burdened unfairly? To what extent does the backlash, particularly against illegal immigrants and what some of the more vehement anti-immigrant voices call "Mexifornia," contribute to the voters' unwillingness to tax themselves for quality schools and other high levels of public services?

Those services are increasingly perceived to be going primarily to "them" by at least some, perhaps many, of the non-Hispanic white voters who are likely to dominate the California electorate for at least another generation, but who—because they're richer, older, and have fewer children—are far less dependent on the state and local public services than are immigrants and their children. Such issues in turn raise difficult questions about immigrant assimilation and political participation. Does the new generation of immigrants behave as its European predecessors did on the East Coast and in the Midwest a century ago? What does assimilation mean in the new context and, given the fear of some immigrants and some scholars that many children in the second generation assimilate *down* into everything from high-fat and high-sugar diets to drugs and gangs, to what norm are they assimilating?

The proximity of Mexico and—despite the frequent invocations of the virtues of diversity—the concentration of Spanish-speaking immigrants in Southern California, the Central Valley, and the Southwest generally, reinforce the belief among California conservatives and among many anti-immigration activists that Hispanics, with their own newspapers, two major Spanish-language television channels, and countless radio stations, churches, and other cultural institutions, as well as an internal economy that requires little English, sustain a Spanish-speaking culture that resists full assimilation. That belief has been reinforced by campaigns of some Hispanic activists for a multiculturalism that encourages the retention of Latino culture and Spanish language in the schools. Immigration opponents also contend that, unlike in New York or Boston in the years between 1860 and 1920, where immigrants of so many different backgrounds and languages were crammed together that at least rudimentary English became a high priority, the new immigrants in the Southwest are overwhelmingly Spanish-speaking and thus have less need for English or assimilation. Of the legal Mexican immigrants admitted in 1982, 22 percent had become American citizens by 1997; for immigrants from the Caribbean, it was 40 percent; for Asians it was over 50 percent.[7]

The fact that the country succeeded in assimilating millions of immigrants from southern and eastern Europe in the first half of the last century, when an industrial economy had ample numbers of reasonably well-paid low-skill jobs but virtually no public welfare system, and when (after the immigration acts of the 1920s) new immigration was highly restricted, might thus not be an entirely accurate indicator of future success or of public willingness to make the effort. What seems obvious is that the warmth of the country's welcome, while varying with the state of the economy, tends in general to be inversely proportional to the numbers, and especially to the number of aliens, that are to be welcomed. A variety of studies of other societies also indicate that, the greater a society's ethnic diversity, the lower its investment in schooling and other public goods.

Nonetheless, nearly every survey also indicates that, for today's immigrants, learning English, and learning it quickly, is as great a priority as it ever was. Of native-born Latinos, only 4 percent are Spanish-dominant. Immigrants—Latinos, Asians, Europeans—are forming businesses and buying homes at high rates, and the rate of intermarriage between Anglos and Latinos, and between whites and Asians, is at an all-time high and rising rapidly.

Third-generation Latinos still appear to lag behind their peers in rates of college attendance and graduation, a fact that will be of increasing concern for California and, ultimately, for the nation, although even those data are complicated and uncertain.[8] Yet despite residual resistance among some rural immigrants to higher education for daughters whose labor is wanted for the household (as was the case for some southern European households a half century ago), the demand for good schooling (and complaints about the lack of it) and university access for their children appears to be as intense among most immigrants as it is anywhere else: 82 percent of California Latinos and 83 percent of immigrants say they hope their children will finish college; many expect them to go to graduate school.[9] Already a significant majority of California's high school graduates belong to ethnic minority groups, and this proportion will continue to grow through the coming decade. This not only raises the stakes for California's economy and society but also increases the likelihood that the second generation will assimilate, though perhaps in unprecedented ways. Steve Levy, who runs the Center for the Continuing Study of the California Economy, pointed out that fears of—and resistance to—immigrants will decline as the sheer "physicality" in dress, language, and attitudes of the second generation merges with the mainstream.

In many respects, all residents of the state—those whose forebears came on wagons across the plains, the great waves of former GIs who came during and soon after World War II, the most recent arrivals from refugee camps in Southeast Asia—are now immigrants in the emerging society that California has become. As Joan Didion pointed out, it has always been one of the elements of California's political culture for each generation to regard each successive generation as despoilers of the pure California into which it was born or to which it emigrated.[10]

The stories of California's nativism and xenophobia, often tightly linked to the state's progressivism, are familiar—the rampant bias against the Chinese in San Francisco in the last years of the nineteenth century, the alien land acts, the attacks on Okies and Mexicans in the 1930s, the support for the internment of Japanese-Americans after Pearl Harbor, the latter-day anti-immigrant initiatives. But as minorities become majorities, and as globalization becomes an incontrovertible fact socially and economically, the norms of assimilation—indeed its very meaning— have changed. It's not simply that Americans have all learned to eat burritos and dim sum, or that within the next thirty years nearly half the country's Latinos (assuming that this is the way they choose to identify themselves) will be the children of mixed marriages, but that the classic influence of immigrant groups on mainstream culture will be amplified by the sheer power of numbers.

California, as Carey McWilliams said a half century ago, is "the great exception."[11] But in its high-tech economy, its lifestyles, its politics, and its Hollywood-influenced images of the good life, the state has also been the national model and worldwide magnet that it became even before the great rush of new migrants during and after World War II. Some of the very things recently cited as evidence of California's "left-out coast" irrelevance are also things that link the state so powerfully to a rapidly globalizing world: those economic connections with China and South

Asia; the state's emergent de facto bilingualism; and, through its diverse population and languages, its strong social and cultural commonality with Latin America and the Pacific Rim countries. It may be correct, as one British observer said, that California, perhaps because of its distance from New York and Washington, was less passionate about the war in Iraq, but in those respects also it was more global and perhaps more cosmopolitan than the rest of the country.

Ultimately, all these questions point to a central dilemma: the growing gap between the fundamentals of the twenty-first-century global economy to which California is so inextricably linked and the residual principles of nineteenth-century institutions of nationality, citizenship, and government. As Bruce Cain, director of the Institute of Governmental Studies at the University of California, Berkeley, pointed out, it's not likely that there'll ever be another period of immigration as low as the forty-year period after 1924, when Congress enacted the nation's tight national-origins-based immigration restrictions. Nor is it likely that the nature of new technologies and markets will ever again permit any major protectionist measures. A great many of the tensions in California, especially those regarding immigration control, job protection, and economic development, arise in that gap between the new realities and the old institutions and attitudes.

Many scholars contend that, despite the shortage of the well-paying factory jobs that helped earlier generations of newcomers into the middle class, succeeding generations of Latinos and Asians will become part of the American mainstream, just as all other immigrants have, either in California or in Arkansas or in Iowa or in any of the other states to which many of California's "West Coast Ellis Island" emigrants eventually move.[12] But given the economic and cultural globalism and, in California's case, the emergence of the transnational entity—a controversial word—straddling the Mexican border, that mainstream may be different from the traditional American pattern. California's gap between those in the top 10 percent of the income scale and the bottom 10 percent is wider than the national average, which is itself far greater than it was a generation ago and far wider than it is in any other modern nation. There exists at least a strong possibility that the economy will not generate enough high-wage jobs even for those with college training. Thus, conventional assimilation may become still more difficult and the possibilities for tension between haves and have-nots proportionately greater.

Those economic realities combine powerfully and sometimes explosively with California's political demographics, with the dysfunctional structure and endemic distrust of government, with the state's fiscal deficits, with the broader antitax mood, and with the pervasive market ethic in public services. Together they could well presage further deterioration in those services and in the communitarian principles that would generate support for them. That process—what I called "Mississippification" in a previous book—has been in place in California at least since the beginning of the tax revolt in 1978. Even during the boom years of the late 1990s, when the state's revenues rose sharply along with the spike in capital gains and other stock-bubble income, California did not manage to restructure its tangled fiscal system or restore taxes and other funding for schools and other essential services to the high levels of the decades after World War II—a period that even California's conservatives now evoke as the state's golden age.

Many center-conservatives, people like Bill Hauck, the veteran political operative who heads the California Business Roundtable and who has been deeply involved in a long string of high-level governmental reform efforts, believe this pattern won't change until the growth in state spending is constitutionally limited and until the legislature is reformed by changing the reapportionment process to create more competitive districts and instituting an open primary in which voters can choose among candidates of any party. Some of these ideas became elements of what the media called Arnold Schwarzenegger's "bold" second-year agenda. Such reforms, in the view of their sponsors, would produce more moderate and politically accountable candidates—people, in Hauck's words, "who are [in Sacramento] to solve problems, not just fuck around."[13]

But that's hardly all of it. Can public confidence ever be fully restored from the top down, or must it be built from the bottom up? Can it be done without first revitalizing the authority of local government, much of which was enervated and in some respects destroyed by the nearly absolute prohibition on local property tax increases and by the supermajority-vote requirements for other local tax or fee increases brought by Proposition 13 and its successors? That task of revitalization is further complicated by California's shrinking sense of community—by, on the one hand, the withdrawal of a large and growing number of residents into gated privatized residential enclaves and by, on the other hand, the global economic and social relationships in which growing numbers of "resident expatriates" with dual loyalties and, perhaps, dual citizenship now live. Many of the Indians and Taiwanese in the Silicon Valley have closer connections with Mumbai or Taipei than they do with the Mexican immigrants working in the kitchens down the street, who, in turn, are more closely linked to relatives in their native villages.

Making the task of restoring social morale in a single society still more difficult are California's seven thousand overlapping and sometimes conflicting jurisdictions: cities, counties, school districts, community college districts, water districts, fire districts, park districts, irrigation districts, mosquito abatement districts, public utility districts, each with its elected directors, supervisors, and other officials, a hyperdemocracy that, even without local and state ballot measures, confounds the most diligent citizen. It's hardly surprising, then, that the political structure, combined with a host of other governmental reforms of the past generation, has eroded accountability, distorted local growth and planning policies, and disconnected citizens from their local governments. (Most Californians believe that their property tax, now controlled by the governor and legislature, who allocate it according to their own priorities and snatch some of it when things get tight, still goes to local government.) The system is so convoluted that even the most involved voters (or journalists for that matter) don't really understand how the place works. Worse, there's a marked absence of the kind of strong civic leadership that has been crucial in other states. There is no effective California civic establishment, and hasn't been for thirty years. That, too, may be connected with California's mutable, diverse society.

In his first state of the state speech, Schwarzenegger promised not to simply move the "boxes" of government around but to "blow them up." And as some of his critics said, maybe it takes someone who doesn't really understand the magnitude of the problem to even try solving it. In Schwarzenegger's first months in office, there was a temporary sense—particularly among legislative Democrats—that the new governor, a social liberal who prides himself on his ability to sell anything (including, as he says, his really bad movies), and who, more than anything, seems to like being a deal maker, had shown more promise in mitigating Sacramento's partisanship than any of them had expected. But the mood didn't last long. Within a year, the governor, facing resistance in the legislature, was referring to Democrats as "girlie men," to his opponents as "special interests," and to three independently elected state officials—the treasurer, the attorney general, and the state superintendent of schools, all Democrats—who were campaigning against his second-year program, as the "three stooges."

Given California's monstrous continuing deficit and Schwarzenegger's own reliance on budget fudges and gimmicks not so different from those of his predecessors, it was always unlikely that even his "bold" proposals would work any quick changes in undoing California's divisions and its fundamental governmental problems. Indeed, some were more likely to compound them. The state's long-term debt and the nation's well-organized tax resistance made it more likely that the state would be unable, or unwilling, to finance the generous public services—high-quality schools and low-cost public universities, major expansions of public transit and other infrastructure, decent support for the arts and libraries, accessible health care for all low-income people—that Californians more or less took for granted forty years ago and that the new Californians now required.

This book is divided into five parts that try to address the questions facing the state and, in many of their implications, the country as a whole.

The first deals with the seismic changes in the state's population, economy, and circumstances, particularly in the years since California became the nation's first large majority-minority state. The second part is a compressed history of California politics and government in the half century after World War II: its great boom, progressivism, and public optimism in the generation after the war; and the gradual, and sometimes dramatic, erosion of that optimism that began in the mid-1970s and continues to this day.[14] The third part briefly tells the story of the recall and its possible significance for larger state issues. The fourth examines the first years of the Schwarzenegger era, including the "bold" and potentially divisive reforms of his second-year agenda. The final part is an attempt to look at how all these parts of the California puzzle and dilemma could, or might, be reassembled and, more important, a look at the question of whether, given the combination of California and national circumstances—demographic, economic, political—it's even possible. Can any state with California's global connections and environment build a successful society on the fragile, institutional base that California—and perhaps the nation—began the new millennium with? If not, what would it take to make it possible?

Robert Reich, secretary of labor in the first Clinton administration, talked about "snapping" in times of severe economic gaps and social dislocation. The choice, he said, is between snapping back with fundamental reforms, as in the Progressive era and the New Deal, and "snapping apart" into a segmented, resentful, defensive, and mutually distrustful Balkanized society.[15] The story in this book is incomplete, as all stories about democracy necessarily are. But it does, I hope, point to possibilities and alternatives, and it lists ideas and options.

There are all manner of projections about the effects of globalization that will become apparent during the coming generation, effects on the nation and more particularly on California, whose economy has been driven by the same high-skill technologies and industries now growing so rapidly in the Far East. But there is no question that to remain competitive and to support its dependent population—the retired, the young—California will have to rely heavily on the productivity of its immigrants and their children. "Providing sufficient human capital, rather than more physical capital," said David Lyon, the president of the Public Policy Institute of California, in the introduction to a sweeping set of projections of California's future, "could well be California's biggest challenge in the year 2025 and beyond."[16]

People like pollster Stanley Greenberg, who worked for Bill Clinton and a host of other political leaders in the United States and abroad, believe that Clinton, among others, persuaded the country that diversity is a source of national strength. And with the passage of time, Greenberg argued, the idea of equal opportunity has become more than just a euphemism for favoring blacks. On that score, it's encouraging that some demographic projections show that immigration has reached a plateau and that the percentage of newcomers—those here less than ten years—is declining. This will mean that, as one study showed, "the upward trend in poverty will be reversed." There is, as Hauck said, "a reservoir of optimism—reserves of intelligence, innovation and creativity. . . . People don't want government to fail." The state, said Mark Baldassare, the survey director of the Public Policy Institute of California, is at a critical stage but not yet in a crisis.[17]

But none of those things are certainties. The only reasonably sure thing is that something altogether new is emerging in California—the outcome of an intense and very fundamental demographic, political, and social process likely to define citizenship and community differently from what they were perceived to be in the gung ho 1950s and 1960s. The result may be no less creative, even visionary. But it will be a test for a nation, much of which is not so different, only a generation or two behind, and for a world that has never seen anything like it. We are, to repeat, all immigrants in this new society.

1

THE NEW CALIFORNIA

No one will ever know what particular event did it—maybe the birth of a Latino boy or a Korean girl or the arrival of an immigrant—but sometime in the fall of 1999 the statistical counter clicked and forever changed California's demographic landscape. That it happened almost precisely on the 150th anniversary of the gold rush, when the settlement of California really began and when the seventeenth-century Spanish explorers' dream of El Dorado seemed momentarily to be realized, was only coincidence. As late as 1960, California had been so Anglo, what the U.S. Census Bureau later came to call non-Hispanic white, that the primary language of foreign-born Californians, most of whom had come from either Canada or Great Britain, was still English. In the 1950s the annual Fourth of July All States Picnic in Ontario, east of Los Angeles, attracted as many as a hundred thousand people, who gathered at huge "tables" designated according to the states they came from—Iowans, Kansans, Okies—to reminisce about the old place and reflect on the new. In those years Los Angeles was the most WASP city in the nation.

With the 2000 census, a short forty years later, California, whose population was then close to 34 million, officially became the nation's first large majority-minority state, although Texas was not far behind.[1] Anglos were still the largest single ethnic group: by 2004 they constituted roughly 46 percent of the population. Latinos were second with 35 percent, up from 11 percent in 1970. Asians were third, with some 11 or 12 percent, and African Americans, still regarded as *the* minority in much of the rest of country, were fourth, with about 6 percent. The decline in the numerical importance of blacks was itself freighted with social and political consequences.[2]

But even those numbers are changing at a dizzying pace. Shortly after 2010, Latinos—primarily people of Mexican and Central American descent—are projected to become the state's largest minority. And of the 51.5 million Californians projected by 2040, nearly 30 million (58 percent) will be Hispanics; 6.5 million will be Asians, partly as a result of immigration but largely through natural increase. There will also be 2.5 million *fewer* white Anglos than there were in 2000. Beginning in 2001, according to David Hayes-Bautista, a medical sociologist at the University of California, Los Angeles, more than half the babies born in California were Latino. (All told, 46 percent of California babies born in 2002 were born to immigrant mothers.) In the Southern California region that includes Los Angeles, Orange, Ventura, Imperial, San Bernardino, and Riverside counties, Hispanics already outnumbered Anglo whites, who constituted barely 39 percent of the region's population. "The Latino majority," said Hayes-Bautista, "has emerged."[3] But since a rapidly growing percentage of children are born into mixed marriages, the categories will get fuzzier and the count itself will depend as much on self-identification as on any objective criteria. Nearly three of every ten marriages involving a Latino or an Asian is an interracial or interethnic marriage.[4] Among the third generation, 57 percent of Latinos and 54 percent of Asians marry a person of some other ethnicity. By nineteenth-century standards of racial purity in this nation—which in many cases were still being observed well into the twentieth century—that's what the writer Gregory Rodriguez, in a sardonic reference to a century-old racist scare phrase, has called "Mongrel America."[5]

Of the 34 million Californians in 2001, almost 9 million, or 26 percent—among them the man who would become governor in 2003—

were foreign-born, giving the state far and away the highest percentage
of immigrants in the country. (New York was second with 20 percent.)
Of those foreign-born Californians, 37 percent entered the United
States between 1990 and 2000, at least a third of them illegally, and by
some estimates many more. (All told, according to the Urban Institute,
of the nearly 9 million California immigrants, 2.4 million were undocumented, the majority of them from Mexico.)[6] Although many people regard the high percentage of the foreign-born as alarming, it's lower than
the post-gold-rush record of 38 percent in 1860 or the 30 percent in
1890. The growth in the percentage of the state's foreign-born appears
to have slowed and will peak within the next generation, at about 29 percent, and then decline. In the meantime, the percentage of newcomers,
as opposed to "settled immigrants," is declining.[7] But because the rate of
change in the generation after 1980 was stunning—by 2004, sixty California cities had populations of which more than half were foreign-born,
the majority of them Latino—the backlash (denying driver's licenses to
illegal aliens or declaring English the state's official language, or seeking
to deny illegal aliens even emergency medical services) was not altogether surprising.[8]

In 1962, when California surpassed New York as the most populous
state in the union, it had just under 17 million people, of whom nearly
83 percent were non-Hispanic white. Between then and the first years of
the twenty-first century, California's population doubled, but of the additional 17 million some 85 percent were something other than white
Anglos. Currently, in public school enrollment, Latinos are already close
to a majority; Anglos compose barely a third. One-fourth of California's
schoolchildren come from homes where English is not the primary language. All told, some 11 million people born in Mexico—10 percent of
the Mexican population—live in the United States. Of those, nearly half
are in California. According to the Census Bureau, in 2001 residents in
some 39 percent of California homes spoke some language other than
English. In communities where the majority population has long been
nonwhite, what does assimilation or integration mean?

The California landscape—physical, economic, cultural—tells part of the story. In large parts of the state, *bilingualism* means that a person speaks English as well as Spanish. But in Silicon Valley or San Francisco, an immigrant is more likely to be an Indian engineer or a Pakistani entrepreneur or even a Mexican engineer on an H-1B visa—a *cerebrero*—than a Mexican farmworker. (Of all Mexicans with Ph.D.s, about 30 percent work in the United States, itself a major issue in Mexico.)[9] When the high-tech boom fizzled after 2000, one of the places hard hit was the East Bay city of Fremont, where engineers and technicians had sparked a shadow boom in Indian restaurants and shops. In the little city of West Sacramento, there are three Russian communities—Orthodox, Baptist, and Pentecostal. Given the enormous ethnic differences and, more important, the huge class differences, not to mention the differences between recent and settled immigrants, legal and illegal, there is no typical California immigrant.

In the Central Valley—places like Fresno, Sacramento, and Merced— there are some seventy-five thousand Hmong, Southeast Asian hill people who had no written language, as well as other Laotians, Thais, and Cambodians, with thousands more arriving periodically from the refugee camps in Thailand where they, or their parents, have been since the Vietnam War. Some become small farmers or janitors, but as rural hill people who'd never seen a kitchen or a toilet and who had no written language, they've had particular adjustment problems. In Fresno, the Lao Family Community, a social service organization, offers a free umbrella stroller or a free car seat to parents who attend just one parenting class. "They come," said Pao Fang, the organization's executive director, who is himself a refugee, "with no resources, no skills, no nothing." As among the Cambodians in Sacramento, there are high rates of depression and suicide. And while many of the kids have become valedictorians, joining the great march into the mainstream—and some are now doctors and engineers—some assimilate downward into drugs and gangs so, as Pao Fang said, they can feel safer: "They want to be protected." They fight the Hispanic gangs even though their own English is laced with

Hispanic inflections. Conversely there have also been adjustment problems for county welfare, medical, and child protection authorities, who had no protocols on how to deal with their new arrivals' arranged marriages for their thirteen-year-old daughters or their deep beliefs in the spiritual basis of illness and how to treat it.[10]

In Orange County, once regarded the most solidly white-bread Republican place in the country, Santa Ana, the county seat and its largest city, is now 76 percent Hispanic. Its congresswoman, Representative Loretta Sanchez, a Latina, and her sister, Representative Linda Sanchez, who represents a nearby part of Los Angeles County, are the only pair of sisters in the House.[11] In Little Saigon, which straddles the Orange County cities of Garden Grove and Westminster, and which in 2004 elected a Republican lawyer named Van Tran as the first Vietnamese legislator in the country, the phone book has more Nguyens and Trans than Smiths and Joneses.[12]

In Glendale, northeast of Los Angeles, sometimes described as a melting-pot suburb, one-third of the city's thirty thousand public school students are classified as Middle Eastern, most of them Armenians whose families, having fled the Turkish genocide of 1915–16 or the repression of the Soviet era, ended up in Iran, which they fled after the overthrow of the Shah in 1979. (There was still another generation, refugees of the devastating Armenian earthquake in 1988, which killed forty-five thousand and left another three hundred thousand homeless.) When Glendale school administrators like Alice Petrossian, an assistant superintendent, speak about multilingualism, they are as likely to mean Russian or Armenian or Farsi—which many of the district's counselors must be able to speak—as Spanish. Arlette DerHovanessian, a counselor at the district's Welcome Center, speaks Farsi, Russian, Armenian, and a little Arabic and Turkish.[13] All together, according to Petrossian, who makes occasional trips to Armenia as part of various aid programs, the district's students speak so many primary languages—sixty-four in all, from Bengali and Korean to Russian and Tagalog—"that we're going crazy with all the dialects." People in Glendale are certain that its fifty-two thousand

Armenians make it the world's second-largest Armenian city, after Yerevan.[14] Of the Iranians in Southern California, significant percentages are Jews who, like the Armenians, fled after the Islamic revolution in 1979.

In the strip malls of the Central Valley, as in many parts of California's cities, you're likely to see the Muebleria Morales next door to Bombay Cuisine, which is a door or two away from the Inthavong Oriental Market, La Bola de Oro, Billar Familiar, and the Barnwood Arms Indoor Shooting Range. In the smaller cities, the marquees outside the schools are likely to have the school calendar in English on one side and Spanish on the other. On the freeways the ambulance-chasing *abogados* advertise (in Spanish) on huge billboards, saying that if you have an accident, just call the number because they're ready to help.

In Representative Diane Watson's Thirty-third Congressional District, in central Los Angeles, where blacks replaced Jews in the 1960s, and which still has an African fashion district along Crenshaw Boulevard and in parts of the surrounding 90008 zip code, blacks are themselves being replaced by Latinos. The district also includes the "Miracle Mile" of Wilshire Boulevard, the city of Hollywood, and (another) Little Armenia. And there's Koreatown, whose voters are significant enough that Watson, an African American, sponsors seminars for Korean immigrants and runs bills naming post offices for Korean activists. At the same time, there are now so many Latinos in and around the fringes of Koreatown that Korean retailers are renaming their outlets La Baratita and Playas Azules.[15] Or take Gil Cedillo's California Senate District—the Twenty-second—which sits almost squarely in the middle of Los Angeles, straddling an area that stretches from the exclusive precincts of San Marino on the northeast, to the working-class neighborhoods of Boyle Heights where Cedillo grew up, to that same Koreatown on the west and the Civic Center, the heart of downtown Los Angeles, and skid row. Like all California senate districts, it has some nine hundred thousand residents, which makes it larger than any congressional district.

It also includes substantial parts of largely Hispanic East Los Angeles and its jewelry manufacturers, and "Toy Town," which grew around

Hong Kong immigrant Charlie Woo's Megatoys import and distribution business (mostly of toys made in China), as well as the city's garment district. The twenty-block garment industry area on the edge of downtown is said to include the largest concentration of sweatshops in the country, many of them owned by Asian immigrants employing illegal Latinas, who are powerless to demand decent wages and conditions.[16] So while Cedillo's description of the place as "the world" may not be literally accurate, it's close enough; the area is as close to a cross section of the new California as you're likely to get in one place.

Cedillo is the author of a string of bills that have sought to restore to illegal immigrants the right to obtain driver's licenses, a right they had until 1994. People at the state capitol sometimes call him "one bill Gil" because of his relentless push, some would say obsession, to get that bill passed. California voters, including many Latinos, oppose such a measure by a margin of some 60 percent, but in Cedillo's district, it would almost certainly go the other way. In 2004, when Cedillo toured the sprawling lofts housing the American Apparel plant in East Los Angeles—it employs some twenty-five hundred people in the production of T-shirts and other sportswear, most of them Latinos, but many Chinese workers too, many of whom now speak Spanish as well as (and sometimes better than) English—he was cheered wildly. Workers wanted to have their pictures taken with him, they applauded, they hugged him. The plant pays good wages and benefits—the owner, a Canadian immigrant Jew named Dov Charney, who calls his place a T-shirt kibbutz, boasts that it's "sweatshop free"—though probably not one in ten of those workers is a U.S. citizen, let alone a voter. But Cedillo obviously represents them as much as he does those who do vote.[17] Like many of his fellow legislators, following his election Cedillo himself went to a language institute in Mexico to learn the Spanish he never learned as a kid.[18]

But what makes the district most representative is that it defies almost any generalization. Even narrow ethnic labels conceal as much as they reveal. "Asian" is a grab bag that includes everything from those Indian and

Pakistani engineers and programmers to those newly arrived Hmong—Korean architects, Sikh farmers, Chinese physicians, Vietnamese entrepreneurs—but it generally doesn't include Filipinos, who, with nearly seven hundred thousand immigrants, constitute the second-largest group of foreign-born Californians and supply a large percentage of the state's nurses.[19] The Network of Ethnic Physician Organizations in the state includes nearly fifty groups, from the Afghan Medical Association, the Armenian American Medical Society of Northern California, and the Association of Black Women Physicians, to the Western Chapter of the Thai Physicians Association and the San Diego Vietnamese Physicians Association. In Los Angeles, one of the many Chinese newspapers publishes two editions, one for readers from mainland China, another for the Taiwanese. Everybody wants the hometown news.

At the University of California, Asians, who make up a disproportionate part of the student body, have long ceased to be counted as a minority. The same is true for Filipinos. UC's diversity agenda focuses only on "underrepresented minorities," meaning Hispanics, African Americans, and American Indians. At Montebello High School in Los Angeles County, as at many other schools, the students, 93 percent of whom are Latino, divide themselves sharply between recent immigrants who call themselves "TJ" for Tijuana, whose primary activities are *folklorico* and soccer, and "Senior Park," those who speak English comfortably and have assimilated to American sports, music, and institutions, some of whom never spoke Spanish at all.[20] These divisions, too—divisions of culture, of class, of loyalty—reflect similar splits within the larger Latino community and, indeed, within other American ethnic communities as well, just as they have through much of the nation's history.

Or consider the thirty-five-year-old Charney himself, who started his career hawking T-shirts (brought in from Vermont) on the streets of Montreal and now operates in an industry notorious for its exploitation of immigrant workers and its race-to-the-bottom search for the cheapest overseas producers. But Charney doesn't outsource, not because he's being a good guy keeping jobs at home, but because he believes that having his goods made in China is too slow and cumbersome and, he said, getting more expensive all the time. In his operation he can begin with an idea on Monday—as he said, "this is LA," where fashion trends are spawned—and have the garments in the stores, many of which he owns, by the end of the week. He is "*in* the market" and the culture that shapes it. And, he said, he has "a continuous stream of motivated workers." As for the illegal immigrants, "they're paying the Social Security for all those retirees." The highest skilled workers in Los Angeles, he said, "are falsely documented Mexican engineers. . . . Los Angeles would be a dull place without immigrants." A few years ago, he marched with his workers in a demonstration for immigrants' rights under the banner "Legalize L.A."[21]

Yet even strong advocates of immigrant rights—people like Assemblyman Juan Arambula, a Harvard-educated former Fresno County supervisor—have acknowledged that, while immigrants and especially illegal aliens get, or ask for, few public services, the high rate of in-migration of low-skilled agricultural workers, many of whom are illegal, depresses the economy and stresses the public resources of the agricultural communities of the Central Valley. (Of all U.S. workers without a high school education, nearly 40 percent are immigrants.)[22] The high poverty levels in California's rich agricultural belts, Arambula said, are having a "horrendous effect" on local communities.

The stress is particularly acute because most of the taxes illegal aliens pay, particularly sales tax and Social Security—taxes from which, as illegal residents, they'll probably never benefit—go to the federal or state governments, not to the local government. And since work in the Valley is seasonal—meaning that unemployment rates in the winter reach regional averages of 20 percent and, in Valley towns like Parlier, 30 to 40 percent—the problems are compounded. Given the fact that the Valley still lacks even a semblance of a diversified economy, there are few other jobs. "Successful people," said a former mayor of Fresno, "don't want to come here." Even successful businesses in California's Central Valley have difficulty attracting and retaining capable managers. In comparison to workers in similar jobs in Mexico, immigrant farmworkers in California are well paid. By U.S. standards, they represent cheap labor doing the backbreaking work that has made the Valley what it is.

They've had another major effect as well—helping to shrink the United Farm Workers, Cesar Chavez's old union, to a sad shadow of its former self. The union was once a major force, morally and economically, in California agriculture and in the national imagination. The union, run since Chavez's death in 1993 by Arturo Rodriguez, Chavez's son-in-law, is now engaged in a dozen other enterprises, some operated by a spin-off called the National Farm Workers Service Center directed by Chavez's son Paul. Among them: the Chavez memorial and visitors' center in Keene, a health plan, a pension plan, twenty-seven hundred low-income housing units in rural towns and cities, and the nine broadcasting stations called Radio Campesino that were created to increase the political awareness and social coping skills of immigrant workers and their families. But the membership of the union itself has dwindled from the 80,000 it had in its heyday to perhaps 12,000 (of some 500,000 peak-season workers) and perhaps many fewer. The union, which has only a handful of contracts, claims 27,000 members, although in its official reports to the Labor Department it declares only about one-fourth that number. "My dad was criticized for not running a union," Paul Chavez said. "But he was running a movement."

Rodriguez disputes the connection between the decline of the union and illegal immigration, and he's partly right. Organizing seasonal workers has never been easy, and while the state's Agricultural Labor Relations Board under Democratic governor Jerry Brown strongly favored Chavez's cause in the 1970s, it tilted sharply toward the growers after Brown was replaced by Republican George Deukmejian in 1983. Equally important, perhaps, labor contractors are now dominant in supplying workers to growers, which means the growers don't need to deal with the union at all. But Rodriguez also acknowledged that the composition of the farmworker population has changed. In the 1970s, when the United Farm Workers union flourished, and when the union, like the rest of organized labor, supported tight immigration restrictions, a large proportion of farmworkers were U.S. citizens or longtime residents—Mexicans, blacks, Okies—who weren't vulnerable to immigration crackdowns and didn't have to compete with an endless stream of new immigrants ready to work longer hours and for less money. The founders of the United Farm Workers, as Rodriguez pointed out, were themselves born in the United States. Now Rodriguez seems to pin his hopes on the growing political power of immigrant Latinos, both in California and in Washington.[23]

Nonetheless it would be hard to imagine the Valley without those farmworkers. For most people in coastal California, the place is all but invisible—a hot dusty no-man's-land to cross on the way from the Bay Area or Los Angeles to Lake Tahoe, Yosemite, or Kings Canyon. But in its four-hundred-mile stretch along I-5 and California Route 99, its main drag, from north of Chico south to Bakersfield—through Sacramento, Lodi, Modesto, Fresno, Visalia—the Valley is the richest and most diverse agricultural region in the world: acre upon acre of rice and tomato fields; nectarine, plum, citrus, peach, and almond orchards; vineyards; feed lots; cotton fields; wheat fields; and fields of a hundred other commodities, nearly all grown on irrigated land, commodities which, the roadside signs from the agricultural associations remind you, would wither away without plenty of water (meaning water subsidized by the federal government). "Water, Wealth, Contentment, Health," says the historic gateway arch into Modesto. And dotted among those fields: the wineries, canneries, grain elevators, packing plants, food processors, and implement dealers (and, plunked next to a truck rental yard just south of Fresno, the gleaming golden domes of a Sikh temple) that make the Valley a center of industrial agriculture, not a conventional farm region, and the base of the state's most powerful ag-biz dynasties: Boswell, Salyer, Gallo. At the same time, it is still suffused with Dust Bowl culture—the Oklahoma accents, the social conservatism, the gun culture, the religious fundamentalism.

The establishment in 2005 of a University of California campus at

Merced, the first new UC campus in nearly forty years, is seen by its local promoters as a great boost for business (especially businesses depending on the biological sciences) and, of course, for real estate development. Initially, at least, the school is likely to struggle to "serve the survivors of a terrible education system," said Professor Kenji Hakuta, a distinguished Stanford linguistics scholar who now heads Merced's division of humanities and social science. The university, in order to draw academic talent, is also laying out a housing development near the campus that could well become another segregated community. But as Hakuta said, the university could also "raise the level of aspiration" of the region's high schools, their students, and the students' parents and, more generally, bring the glare of modernism to a region that, in many places, has remained fearfully immune to it.[24] In the Valley, a lot of people use the same image when discussing schools: the kids would rather have a pickup truck than an education. When UC Merced enrolled its first class in 2005, only 38 percent of the students were from the Valley.

The Valley—indeed all of California agriculture—will badly need that modernism and the diversified economy it could bring. In the coming years, California agriculture, still first nationally in many of its commodities, will almost certainly face mounting challenges in a globalized economy dominated by a dozen large corporations buying from increasingly efficient producers of homogenous crops who can grow and ship at ever lower costs. The state is already feeling the competition, either in the United States or in foreign markets, from foreign producers—Turkish raisins; Chinese garlic, asparagus spears, mushrooms, and processed tomatoes; Mexican, Chilean, and South African grapes; Mexican melons, zucchini, and sweet onions; Spanish olives; Iranian pistachios. In Delano, Pandol Brothers, once a family of small farmers, has grown into a multinational import-export enterprise in an industry where growers are also becoming processors, shippers, and global traders. "Agriculture in California," said Mechel Paggi, the director of the Center for Agricultural Business at California State University, Fresno, "is under tremendous pressure."[25]

The homogenization of crops and, often, the need for imperishability has produced the tasteless tomatoes, peaches, and other produce that many people are all too familiar with, leaving a niche for specialty organic growers like David Mas Masumoto of Del Rey, south of Fresno, who sees his work not as a business but as a cultural responsibility. "When did you last have a great peach?" he asked. "When does the memory of a good tomato go?" Masumoto grows great peaches and grapes on the same eighty-acre place where his father grew them, where the grapevines are almost a century old, and he hires the same workers every year, part of whose wages go back home to "to help build a village in Mexico." His immigrant grandparents, he said, probably pruned these vines. Farming is about physical relationships: "It's about sweating the small stuff, it's the core of what it means to be human." Masumoto said he talks to his trees.[26]

But Masumoto is a rare exception in the Valley's industrialized agriculture. The sooner the valley can break the lock of its monoculture, therefore, the healthier it will be. (One possibility being promoted by people like Mark Drabenstott, director of the Center for the Study of Rural America of the Federal Reserve Bank of Kansas City, is the cultivation of pharmaceutical crops—"farmaceuticals"—genetically engineered corn, for example, to produce a protein for a drug to combat symptoms of cystic fibrosis.)[27] For the immediate future, however, the Valley's economy, like California's hotel and restaurant industry and much of its construction business, will depend on low-wage immigrant workers, most of whom are undocumented. "Without them," Arambula said, the small farm towns, many of which have lost most of their Anglos, wouldn't be able to survive. "They'd blow away like tumbleweed."

Demographer William Frey has described California as the "West Coast Ellis Island." It is the entry point through which the new waves of immigrants, especially those from Mexico and Central America, are increasingly moving beyond California and beyond the long-standing Latino immigrant centers like Houston, El Paso, Tucson, and Chicago, into the rest of the country, particularly Nevada, Arizona, Georgia, and the Carolinas—what Frey called "the secondary foreign-born migrant magnets."[28] Some are also moving to take jobs in the beef packing, poultry processing, and construction industries of the Midwest. (The University of Northern Iowa now has a New Iowans Program to orient communities to the new arrivals, which, the university said, the state badly needs if it's not to shrivel from its declining population.)[29]

Yet while California is still far and away the state with the largest number and the largest percentage of U.S. immigrants, and while the total number of the foreign-born in California remains roughly the same, at about 8–9 million, the state's share of the nation's foreign-born population began to decline in the 1990s. Moreover, California's share of the nation's rapidly growing number of illegal immigrants plunged from 45 percent in 1990 to 24 percent for the period 2002 to 2004.[30] Those changes alone are indicators of a much more fundamental change in the U.S. economy, which is increasingly dependent on immigrants. According to one major study, immigrants made up 60 percent of the growth of the U.S. labor force between 2000 and 2004. "At no other time in U.S. history," the report said, "has the U.S. been so dependent on foreign immigrants for our growth in labor force and employment." Of the 1.3 million new jobs created by the U.S. economy in 2003–04, more than 28 percent went to recent immigrants.[31] For most of those immigrants, the fields, orchards, restaurant kitchens, and sites offering day-labor construction jobs are still the first stop.

Some 95 percent of California's agricultural workers were born in Mexico; 63 percent are undocumented; 26 percent have been in the United States less than a year. Advocates of tighter immigration restrictions like Mark Krikorian, the executive director of CIS, the Center for Immigration Studies, argue that if the flow of immigration were reduced, wages would rise and Americans would be found to take many of those jobs. Reducing immigration would also intensify the mechanization of agriculture, he believes, which is already highly developed in the Valley, thus creating better jobs and increasing the efficiency of the industry.

For a variety of political and economic reasons, this hasn't yet hap-

pened. Virtually every attempt to reduce or control illegal immigration
has either hit a stalemate in Washington or, where reforms have been instituted, has backfired (as explained more fully below). In effect, as noted
in a paper presented at a Labor Department conference, "The U.S. agricultural labor market is already, in many respects, a binational one." Between 1990 and 2002, as the economy grew and then boomed, the share
of undocumented Central Valley farmworkers doubled, from 30 to 63
percent.[32] But Philip Martin, an agricultural economist at the University
of California, Davis, and a student of immigration, pointed out those
numbers may be driven in part by immigrants' first steps up the economic ladder. "The kids [most of whom were born in the United States
and thus are citizens] don't follow their parents into the fields." About
one hundred thousand farmworkers leave the fields annually, "and that
sucks in more immigrants. Tomorrow's farmworkers are growing up outside of the United States."[33]

                                    II

In important respects, California is not a single state at all and hasn't been
for years. For much of the twentieth century, it was represented as being
split between the water-rich north and the semiarid south, and by the associated water battles among the various interests: urban dwellers and
their powerful water agencies; farmers, represented by their equally muscular irrigation districts; and the increasingly powerful environmental
groups. But it's now easier to see California with a different axis. It's a
blue state along much of the coast, though not all of it, and a red state
once you get thirty miles inland. (Republicans who can see the water, said
Bruce Cain, director of Berkeley's Institute of Governmental Studies, are
more moderate than those who can't.) California has a dozen major
media markets, where few newspapers and even fewer TV stations recognize the rest of the state, much less pay much attention to it. For most,
excepting there's a scandal, some major act of collective nonfeasance, or
(of late) an Arnold sighting, Sacramento might as well be on the moon.

In the 1990s, when Stan Statham, a state legislator and TV broadcaster, promoted a series of nonbinding votes in Northern California counties on the advisability of splitting the state in two, virtually every county voted for it. Since, as noted earlier, California is more populous than Canada and has a gross product roughly equal to that of France, it often looks and acts more like a nation than like one of the fifty states. This is the state where a former governor, Jerry Brown, proposed his own space program and where, most recently, voters approved a $3 billion bond to establish the state's own stem-cell research program—one far larger than the crimped programs funded by the George W. Bush administration.[34]

And what's true for the political culture is equally true for the extremes in the state's topography, its climate, and, of course, its seismic instability. It *is* (usually) wet in the north and dry in the south. Thus despite California's elaborate water engineering—the dams, levees, dikes—the balance between drought and flood in low places like the Sacramento Valley is so delicate that the engineers who run those systems are often hard put to decide whether to release water in a storm and thus reserve dam capacity for the next downpour or to store it for next summer's dry season when the farmers soak it up. When serious flooding is imminent or levees are endangered, the engineers also must decide which weirs to open and which riverside region to inundate. California has the highest point in the continental United States—Mount Whitney—and, less than a hundred miles away as the crow flies, the lowest, Death Valley. For miles along Route 86 near the Imperial County city of Brawley (altitude: minus 119 feet), there are barns and silos with horizontal lines painted thirty or forty feet above ground marked "sea level."

The state's growing social and economic extremes easily match its extremes of topography and climate. In Marin County—across the Golden Gate from San Francisco—where the *average* price of a home in 2003 was $927,000 and where per capita income was over $60,000 (household income: $147,000), California has one of the nation's wealthiest counties. In Imperial County (per capita income $13,000), and a few others like it, it also has some of the poorest. That should hardly be surprising in a nation which has the world's largest income and wealth gaps, but California's gaps are considerably larger than those in the nation as a whole. California stands fourth among the states, after New York, Louisiana, and Texas. By a different analysis, between the late 1970s and the late 1990s, the income of the poorest fifth of California households (in inflation-adjusted dollars) decreased from $14,860 to $14,050. The income of the top fifth increased from $112,300 to $154,300.[35]

In the beachfront city of Malibu, where the median home price in 2004 was $1.8 million, up $153,000 over 2003, the Parks and Recreation Department offers courses in feng shui and horseback riding and one titled "[TV] Commercial Class for Children Ages 3 to 6 Years" ($120 for eight classes), designed to teach "what it takes to be in a commercial [and which] includes audition process, how to handle copy[,] . . . and how to be professional and natural in front of the camera."[36] In San Francisco, Palo Alto, and many other Bay Area cities, schools can't keep teachers because home prices are out of reach for anyone on a moderate income who doesn't want to share a flat or who wants to raise a family. For the same reason, Bay Area cities are losing school enrollment: families can't afford to live there, and places like San Francisco have been talking about leveling underused schools and replacing them with moderate-income homes for teachers. California, once near the national average in home ownership, now ranks near the bottom among the states. Its housing prices are among the highest.[37] As in the nation as a whole, the California middle class is being hollowed out, only at a faster rate. As one Republican legislator said, in California it's increasingly tough to be middle class.

At the lower end of the spectrum stands the City of Commerce on the east side of Los Angeles County. Where the little homes off Washington Boulevard back against a vast rail yard, the toxic fumes from the diesel engines transferring freight from the Los Angeles ports is so thick that many parents have to make weekly trips to the emergency rooms with their children. During a port strike in 2003, they literally breathed sighs of relief because, for a week or ten days, the kids weren't getting sick.[38]

The City of Commerce lies near the center of the "hollowed out" parts of Los Angeles, where warehouses have replaced the dead factories of the now-bygone industrial age, the hole in the regional donut. Residents of the City of Commerce are among those paying the price of having booming Los Angeles ports twenty miles to the south.

In parts of the San Joaquin Valley, which some have called "California's Appalachia," immigrant farmworkers crowd, often six or eight to a room, in anonymous "back houses"—garages, sheds, cabins—that don't appear on any official register, and third- and fourth-generation Okies live almost as primitively as the Joads did when they first arrived from the Dust Bowl in the 1930s. The tent cities are gone, but the rest is mostly unchanged. Among the crumbling house trailers and little cabins that replaced the tents, their paint peeling, their roofs badly patched, the kids play in dusty yards among the rusty junk cars, the abandoned tires, and the feral cats. Despite the Valley's sumptuous agricultural productivity, 26 percent of San Joaquin Valley children live below the poverty level; not surprisingly, the Valley also has one of the highest teen pregnancy rates in the country. "Poverty feels different here," said Carol Whiteside, who directs the Great Valley Center in Modesto, which has been the Valley's most vigorous voice on the region's common problems. "It's not like Los Angeles. People are more isolated. It's easier for them to be invisible."[39]

In the Monterey Park Tract, a little cluster of rural homes not far from Modesto, where most of the residents are black, nitrates contaminate the community well. In the dying southern San Joaquin Valley town of Alpaugh, one of the places where those Okies originally settled and which is now largely Hispanic, arsenic contaminated the water in such high concentrations that residents had to go to Corcoran, ten miles up Route 43, or to Delano, to get their drinking water. When the land around Alpaugh began to fail and Pirelli closed the Armstrong Tire Plant in Hanford in 2001, many of those Okies moved back to the Ozarks, where their people had come from. Word had arrived that a cement plant in Mountain Home, Arkansas, paid ten dollars an hour, and so, as an elegant piece in the *Fresno Bee* put it, "the Dust Bowl migration kicked into reverse."[40]

The reverse migrants, some of them encouraged with transportation and resettlement money from Valley counties eager to be rid of the costs they imposed on public services, were part of a statistic showing that in the 1990s the white population in California had declined.

Yet while California defies efforts to characterize it as a single state—even as you describe it, it seems to obey some geographic uncertainty principle, and changes—it has also become an integral part of an increasingly globalized economy, particularly engaged with the Far East, Mexico, and Central America. The neighboring container ports of Los Angeles and Long Beach are now the third busiest in the world—lagging behind only Hong Kong and Singapore, and the largest in the United States. Forty percent of all U.S. imports pass through them, which, of course, is what generates the pollution around the rail yards in East Los Angeles, where those containers are transferred from trucks to trains and vice versa. In the post–Proposition 13 tax-limitation era, and particularly since the legislature started snatching local property taxes to balance its budgets, said Steven P. Erie, director of the Urban Studies Program at UCLA, the cities of Long Beach and Los Angeles "turned to the ports to balance their own budgets." But the real benefits of the ports are dispersed, while the environmental costs are concentrated, creating a deep conflict between the ports and the communities lying along the Alameda Corridor railroad link, through which the goods from the ports are moved inland.[41]

The globalization of California's economy is a complex two-tier, or perhaps multitier, phenomenon. The North American Free Trade Agreement (NAFTA), one of its prime institutional incarnations, has been widely (and perhaps justly) criticized for its negative effects on both sides of the border. The agreement boosted some Mexican wages in the decade after 1994, when it went into effect, but it left average wages lower and drove more Mexicans off farms that can no longer compete with large U.S. producers of corn and other products. At the same time, as noted above, the increasing globalization of corporate agriculture has put increasing pressure on U.S. growers.[42]

But either way the links are real enough: in the burgeoning $18 billion trade between California and Mexico—already the prime destination of California exports—and the countries of the Pacific Rim; in the growing crossborder investment; in the thousands of Mexicans who cross daily to work in U.S. border cities; in the thousands of Americans who go to Mexican border towns where drugs and dental work are cheaper than at home;[43] in the integration of multinational corporations based in Southern California and the huge maquiladora plants—Delphi, Ford, General Electric, Hitachi, Samsung, Siemens, Sony, and Yazaki North America, among many others—in Tijuana, Mexicali, Juarez, and other cities on Mexico's northern border. The Mexican maquiladora manufacturing operations receive machinery and other capital equipment from their parent companies and send finished goods back across the border. The parent companies pay no import duties on those goods and, of course, take advantage of the cheap Mexican labor now crowded into the *colonias* that the workers have erected on nearby vacant land, eight people to a room, without running water, proper sewers, or other basic services.

In recent years, the maquiladoras have been under pressure from competition in China—"that great Chinese sucking sound"—where labor is even cheaper and production is getting more efficient every day. But maquiladoras appear to be adapting by trying to make higher-end products, and still employ some 1.2 million workers.[44] (In the meantime, the Chinese are said to be looking at investment in maquiladoras to get around some U.S. trade restrictions.) In addition, there are the increasingly close relations between the cities in northern Mexico and their U.S. neighbors. For many purposes, most are already single cities with common, and sometimes competing, economic, safety, health, water resource, and environmental concerns. There are, in addition, hundreds of crossborder businesses, art exhibits, and commercial associations, countless academic, health, scientific, technological, environmental, and cultural commissions, compacts, associations, and study groups, many of them with ambitious agendas, high-level leadership, and substantial budgets.[45] Through these and many other relationships, the border has itself become a major institutional entity.

There are also the growing cross-Pacific connections in organizations like the Brain Gain Network, which is trying to create a replica of Silicon Valley in the Philippines. Indian, Chinese, and Taiwanese engineers and entrepreneurs in Silicon Valley companies, some of which were originally financed with Asian capital, are involved in schools, high-tech enterprises, and research facilities in Bangalore, Mumbai, Shanghai, and Taiwan's Hsinchu region and in multi-billion-dollar Indian companies like Wipro and Tata. Professional consultants like Atul Vashistha specialize in the outsourcing of technical jobs. Vashistha, who heads a firm called neoIT in the East Bay city of San Ramon, said he has outsourced fifty thousand jobs to India and the Philippines, part of a process by which Indian and Taiwanese entrepreneurs "have built social and professional networks to support American ventures[,] which they use to accelerate the formation of new firms [in the home country] as well." There's even a journal, whose name, *Siliconindia*, pretty much describes it.[46]

Many of those engineers have since returned home to Asia's rapidly growing high-tech centers—in 2004 it was estimated that there were thirty-five thousand "returned nonresident Indians" in Bangalore alone. However, they continue to live in the same international culture, through university alumni associations, financial and professional relationships, and other connections, that they did in the United States. In Bangalore a group of Indian repatriates have settled in a gated community where the homes, with their wide front lawns, red-tiled roofs, and two-car garages, form a perfect replica of an upscale California suburb. In either country, said Aneesh Aneesh, a sociologist who teaches in Stanford's Program in Science, Technology, and Society, "they miss the other. . . . They want to be in both places at the same time." In this "transnational condition, you're always where you're not." They are, in his view, prime examples (as are Mexican engineers and many other professionals) of the rise of the "emergent transnational elite," the professional and entrepreneurial global class often holding dual citizenship that, however much it longs for the place where it's not, is far more rooted in the community of its social peers than among its fellow citizens of other ranks. In effect, said Aneesh, "the so-called brain drain from India and China has been transferred into a more complex two-way process of 'brain circulation' linking Silicon Valley to urban centers in those countries."[47]

But the prime examples of the emerging transnationalism—a word that is itself controversial—are the crossborder connections of first-generation, and occasionally second-generation, Mexicans, Salvadorans, and others with relatives and hometowns south of the border. The connections may be transient, or they may be long lasting, but they've been growing. In 2004, remittances sent by Mexican workers living in the United States, the largest number of them in California, topped $17 billion (just ahead of remittances to India in total dollars); a year later they were estimated at $19–20 billion, topping oil exports, which until then had been the largest source of foreign income in Mexico. For Latin America and the Caribbean as a whole, the Inter-American Development Bank put the total at $45 billion.[48] In every small Central Valley town and on every other block in East Los Angeles and in scores of other cities, there are money transfer offices ("Money Orders to Mexico: Pay Only $3 Commission for Each $100") through which farmworkers, busboys, hotel maids, and construction workers send between $100 and $300 a month to families south of the border, a huge sum considering the modest wages many of them earn. In addition, banks and construction companies solicit U.S. immigrants to buy home-building materials for themselves or their families in Mexico, where there is no workable mortgage market, where most banks don't grant small local loans, and where, despite globalization and the maquiladoras, endemic corruption remains a major impediment to economic development.

In El Salvador, which appears to be even more dependent on those revenues, 28 percent of all households receive remittances. Nearly 30 percent of Nicaragua's gross domestic product takes the form of remittances; in El Salvador it's 14 percent. According to one study, "in Honduras, Nicaragua, El Salvador and a few other of Latin America's poorest nations, remittances may be more than doubling the incomes of the poorest 20 percent of the population." The bulk of those remittances go directly to families for consumption, though Manuel Orozco of the Migration Policy Institute, an authority on remittances, believes that at least a small percentage, perhaps 5 or 10 percent, is invested in land or farm equipment or perhaps in small businesses, and thus those remittances "constitute key building blocks of economic growth and subsistence in many countries." He cited a study showing that "remittances were responsible for 27 percent of the capital invested in micro-banks and other micro-enterprises in Mexico and 40 percent in the major remittance-receiving areas."[49]

Remittances, a stable and growing source of foreign income in the Third World, are themselves a major element in economic and social globalization, and probably a stabilizing political influence in Latin America and the Caribbean—maybe even what a report from the Pew Hispanic Center and the Multilateral Investment Fund calls "a fuel pump." "Families linked by remittances," the report said, "are quintessential players in the era of globalization. Like entrepreneurs who seek out markets, capital and labor around the world, they too hop borders in search of competitive advantage. The United States may be a better place to earn wages; Mexico may be a better place to raise children."[50]

In many cases, children are being raised on both sides of the border, going to school in California or elsewhere on the migrant trail during the spring, summer, and fall, then in Mexico during the off season in the winter. In some instances, California schools have changed their calendars to accommodate the patterns, greatly extending their winter breaks, when families return to Mexico, but starting school in mid-August or even sooner and running until the very end of June. In others, school districts like Woodland or Dixon, working through the Binational Support Teacher Program, arrange for independent study by immigrant children during the off-season breaks, supervised by Mexican teachers who've been trained in the California curriculum. The U.S. districts provide the materials and orient the binational Mexican teachers. Part of the task, said Ernesto Ruiz, who runs the federal Migrant Education Program in Northern California, is simply to get Mexican schools to let children who arrive after the normal start of classes go to school at all. Another part is to increase articulation between the school in the United States and the Mexican school.[51]

There are other connections as well. For much of the past century, Mexican migrants, taking advantage of their "social capital," have followed well-trod networks: from a particular village in Guanajuato, Jalisco, Michoacan, or Zacatecas to communities in the Salinas Valley or the San Joaquin Valley or to neighborhoods in Los Angeles (or Chicago or, now, New York), where already-settled relatives and acquaintances can help with housing and jobs. The Bay Area cities of East Palo Alto and Redwood City have hundreds of residents who came, or whose forebears came, from the village of Aguililla in Michoacan, the first ones as braceros, the later ones in the wake of the original migrants. In Berkeley, said Rafael Alarcon, a scholar at Tijuana's Colegio de la Frontera Norte (and himself the holder of a doctorate from the University of California, Berkeley), many restaurant workers came from Tepatitlan in the state of Jalisco; many of the workers at Spenger's fish house were mestizos from Chavinda in Michoacan. The process develops a self-reinforcing dynamic that links particular communities on both sides of the border which Alarcon calls *nortenizacion.*[52]

It's also through such networks that many California farm labor contractors, some of them with databases of fifteen thousand or more worker names, get their people. Drive through the Salinas Valley or the San Joaquin Valley and you see their white Blue Bird buses parked on farm roads at the edges of the fields. Often the Mexican relative in Fresno or Merced becomes the recruiter for his American employer or, if he's in business, maybe for himself. He also becomes the exemplar of success and maturity: "In [Mexican] communities where foreign wage labor has become fully integrated into local values and expectations, people contemplating entry into the labor force literally do not consider other options; they expect to migrate frequently in the course of their lives and assume they can go wherever they wish. As migration assumes a greater role in the community, it becomes increasingly important as a rite of passage for young men, providing an accepted means of demonstrating their worthiness, ambition and manhood to others."[53]

That statement was written in 1994, before the increased patrols at the border and other checks on illegal immigration made border crossings more difficult, dangerous, and expensive and, paradoxically, resulted in a sharp increase in the number of permanent undocumented workers in the United States by discouraging the circular flow of illegal workers, particularly during the off-peak seasons, that had been a common pattern in the old days. The emigration also drained many Mexican towns of labor and economic energy, leaving ghost villages of the old, the infirm, and those who tried but didn't make it into the United States.[54] But despite the recent dispersion of immigrants into other regions, creating new networks in new places, the old networks and relationships between communities remain pretty much the same.

California, Illinois, and New York, among other places, are dotted with hundreds of hometown associations (HTAs)—social clubs made up of Mexicans or Salvadorans, most of them immigrants—which serve as orientation, social welfare, and networking centers. There are some 275 HTAs in Los Angeles alone, sponsoring soccer leagues, dances, beauty pageants, and fiestas and raising funds to help build or repair churches, playgrounds, schools, bullrings, and other facilities in the Mexican villages their members came from and to which many legal U.S. residents regularly return: the Oaxacan Indigenous Binational Front, the Federation of Jalisco Clubs, the Federation of Zacatecan Clubs of Southern California, the United Community of Chinameca (in El Salvador), and countless others. The funds are delivered to affiliated clubs in the home communities, which monitor how the money is spent. Alarcon suggested that, given the difficulties immigrants face in integrating into American life, it's often easier to participate in development in their home communities. But the second generation rarely participates in hometown associations and contributes almost nothing to them. The children born in the United States, and most of those raised here, said Alarcon, won't go back.

The hope, of course, is that the money will go to economic development and not merely to enhance dependency on still more remittances. A road or school is generally productive infrastructure, but a sports team or a bullring? Efrain Jimenez, who runs the Zacatecan federation from an unmarked East Los Angeles storefront, said his clubs—there are some eighty-two of them—had shifted their priorities from social to infrastructure projects—sewers, roads, and electrical distribution networks—and were making efforts to create minibanks to lend money to small businesses and bring in investors to commercialize guava packing and processing and develop peach and chili bean packing and processing. In the five years between 1999 and 2004, they'd raised some $50 million for twelve hundred projects in their home state.

In Atacheo, in the Zamora region of Michoacan, residents invested their remittance money in raising turkeys. In other places the money went to start nurseries or to develop little businesses exporting avocados, mangos, and other produce. Willy-nilly, such investment has also brought smudge pots and, at times, drip irrigation techniques from Napa to Zacatecas. But overall, while the economic effect of the remittances has been huge, the effect on development appears to be marginal at best. In general, in the view of some U.S. scholars, migration, by drawing the most ambitious and creative workers north, may do more to freeze development than foster it. If the United States really wanted to reduce immigration, Jimenez said, it would take some of the billions now being spent on building walls at the border and hiring ever more U.S. Border Patrol officers and use the money as matching funds for productive, job-generating investment in Mexico.[55]

For most club members, the remittances have always been intended to make life more comfortable at home, either for relatives or for the immigrants who plan to return, as many initially say they do, rather than to foster economic growth—or, as in much other philanthropy, to enhance the prestige of the givers. One of those givers, Andres Bermudez, who came to California in the 1960s from his native Jerez as an illegal immigrant in the trunk of a car, is now a successful tomato grower near Winters. Having become a prominent donor to his home city, in 2004 he got himself elected mayor of Jerez (population forty thousand) with the promise that, using his American know-how, he would bring in more investment capital. In his campaign, he called himself "the Tomato King."

He wasn't going for glory, Bermudez said as he prepared to take office, sounding ever more like an American politician; he was going to help clean up Mexican politics. "I'm not interested in being a power guy. My reason is to help the Mexican people in my village, my town. I want to put Jerez on top of the world." But his election campaigning relied, as two observers reported, on "traditional methods of Mexican patronage [including] offering gifts, including refrigerators, stoves, and other household appliances, to supporters at campaign rallies[, suggesting] he may have been less intent on democratizing the political culture than on replacing the local authoritarian regime with his own."[56] At almost the same moment, Jesus Martinez-Saldana, a professor of Chicano studies at Fresno State and a longtime activist seeking political rights for migrants in Mexico, became a candidate for the legislature of his native state of Michoacan, to which, as a member of the Party of the Democratic Revolution slate, he was subsequently elected. (In 2004, he quit his Fresno State job to devote all his time to his new political job.) Among his objectives, he said, was to get the government to pay more attention to its diaspora and to raise the status of migrants at home. Like others, he also hoped that the influence of migrants could lead to the democratization of Mexican institutions.[57] But clearly the greater challenge was to increase the development payoffs of Mexican migration, and on that score the prospects remain marginal at best.

A number of labor-exporting countries have tried to institutionalize and exploit their foreign workers: the Philippines, for example, requires mandatory remittances—not always successfully—regulates overseas employment agencies, allows dual citizenship, and allows overseas absentee voting. But no country has been more vigorous than Mexico in its efforts to cultivate its expatriates in the United States. Mexican governments, state and federal, have encouraged the contributions of the hometown associations by offering matching funds, sometimes two dollars for every dollar contributed, sometimes three. Mexico has extended dual citizenship to expatriates, sent high government officials to meet with hometown associations, and, through the strenuous efforts of President Vicente Fox and others, lobbied hard for the rights of the 11 million Mexicans in the United States. Most prominently, and most controversially, it has lobbied for the "normalization," if not the legalization, of illegal immigrants, and it has at least gone through the motions of making it easier for Mexicans in the United States to vote in Mexican state and federal elections.

No Mexican president had ever campaigned as vigorously as Fox did in the months before September 11, 2001, to get the U.S. government to agree on some kind of amnesty for the estimated 3 million illegal Mexican immigrants then living in the United States, a figure that was almost certainly too low. (By 2005, the number of illegal aliens in the United States, from all countries of origin combined, was estimated to be 10 million, with 24 percent of them in California alone.) Fox, "the Coca-Cola cowboy . . . who could express in English his wish for a borderless future," said essayist Richard Rodriguez, "is the first Americanized president of Mexico."[58] At some point in the 1990s, wrote California historian Kevin Starr, "California had experienced a transformation of value and attitude. It now knew itself to be, in significant measure, a Mexican American commonwealth, linked to Mexico by economic ties, by trade and commerce, but also by the even more binding ties of shared culture and bloodlines. Mexico and California, along with the other states of the border, now shared a people in common. In turning against Mexico, if that ever happened again, or against the Mexican people, California would be turning against itself."[59]

III

All of that, needless to say, is controversial. Even leaving aside the poor communities in places like California's Central Valley, do immigrants contribute as much in taxes and to the economy generally as they cost in public services—for schools, health care, and public safety? Would there be a school overcrowding problem in California were it not for the children of aliens, illegal aliens most egregiously? Do they take jobs from American workers and depress wages for legal residents, as Mark Krikorian of the Center for Immigration Studies and his colleagues believe? Does their presence dampen the willingness of Californians to support high levels of public services? Whenever there's a report about the need for more classrooms or teachers, there are letters and e-mails to the media and public officials declaring that there'd be no problem were it not for those illegal immigrants, if not all immigrants. Could states like California, indeed all of America, absorb immigrants at the current rates and maintain their standard of living and their environment? Conversely, would the economy be severely hobbled without those workers?

Both sets of concerns, the economic and cultural, are generating great accumulations of studies and reports, some solid and defensible, some tendentious, some vituperative. Among them are well-documented complaints from local officials stating that hospital emergency rooms and clinics are stretched to the breaking point in part by illegal immigrants who rarely have any other kind of resources for health care. And there are complaints from state officials who assert that a considerable part of the prison population is composed of illegal aliens who are truly the responsibility of the federal government, given that it failed to protect the borders, and for whom it is paying only a fraction of the costs of incarceration. In addition there is a long string of reports from organizations like the Center for Immigration Studies and the Federation for American Immigration Reform concluding that the costs of immigration, legal and illegal, both to public services and to American workers, are intolerable. George Borjas, a Harvard economist and prolific writer on the negative economic effects of contemporary immigration, calculated that, by "increasing the supply of labor between 1980 and 2000, immigration reduced the average annual earnings of native-born men by an estimated $1,700, or roughly 4 percent[, and that] among natives without a high school education, who roughly correspond to the poorest tenth of the workforce, the estimated impact was even larger, reducing their wages by 7.4 percent."[60]

A lot of economists believe those conclusions are unfounded. Some argue that, by lowering wages, immigrants lower prices and keep the economy competitive.[61] But there's little dispute that most of the growth both in the U.S. and California labor forces since 2000 has been the result of immigration, as have been most of the gains in employment. Steven A. Camarota, research director for the Center for Immigration Studies, using census data, calculated that between 2000 and 2004 "the number of *unemployed* adult natives increased by 2.3 million, while the number of *employed* adult immigrants increased by 2.3 million" (his italics). This, in general, is similar to the findings of Andrew Sum and others at Northeastern University's Center for Labor Market Studies, which show that 60 percent of net labor-force growth in that period was composed of immigrants. Sum and his colleagues concluded, more softly, that, "in a period of higher unemployment and little net job growth, increased employment of immigrants appears to be displacing some native born workers, including teens, young adults without college degrees, and Black men in the nation's central cities."[62] But in many places, the effect is broader: "I have no problem competing against anyone on a level playing field," said a Sacramento-area construction worker whose income had steadily declined. "They're doing nothing but trying to provide a better life for their family. . . . But the contractors know most of these guys are illegal, and they exploit them at every turn. . . . The jobs that are being lost with our no-prosecution immigration policies aren't [just] picking lettuce. I need my job and I'd like to keep it."[63]

But what's the connection among unemployed and underemployed native Americans, depressed wages, the growth of lower wage industries, and newly employed immigrants? Which comes first? As anyone who's ever read *The Grapes of Wrath* will know, poverty in the Central Valley was widespread long before foreign immigration began to spike. Similarly, as Harry Holzer, professor of public policy at Georgetown and former chief economist for the U.S. Department of Labor, pointed out, in the late 1990s the nation had a robust job market and rising wages despite two decades of rising immigration.[64] Recent reports have also shown that even the numbers for employment growth in the recovery after the post-2000 recession may be misleading, because the new jobs being created pay less on average than the jobs lost.

In a survey released in June 2004, the liberal Economic Policy Institute found that the average wage in growing industries in the nation was $35,400; the average wage in contracting industries was $44,500. Among the greatest gaps are California's: $34,700 for the state's growing industries, as opposed to $57,800 in the contracting ones. In the same period, real weekly earnings for the United States as a whole declined from $530 in November 2001, the month when the recession officially ended, to $525 in June 2004.[65] The employment growth has been in retail merchandising, food services, cashier jobs, customer services, the "hospitality" industry, meaning primarily hotel and restaurant workers, and other lower-end jobs. Yet even the Economic Policy Institute, in explaining growing wage inequality, acknowledges that, along with the weakening of the trade unions and the declining value of the minimum wage, globalization and immigration have played a role.[66]

Most of the hospitality industry can't be outsourced, nor can the bulk of other retail service jobs. But much else can, and as globalization proceeds, not least through agreements like NAFTA, the pressure on American workers and industry can only increase. By now, the shift of manufacturing to Mexico, China, and elsewhere, and the offshoring of operations like computer-support services and code-writing to other countries, is a familiar story. In the coming decade, another 3 million white-collar jobs—engineering jobs, design jobs, jobs in medicine, jobs in accounting—will be moved to India, China, and elsewhere, "with the information technology industry leading the migration."[67] The economic earth, as *New York Times* columnist Thomas L. Friedman said, is flat. For many native-born American workers, outsourcing and immigrant labor are often two sides of the same coin. Those shifts may or may not have a deeply corrosive effect on the U.S. economy, but they certainly have major consequences for displaced U.S. workers, shrinking wages, and the politics of trade and immigration. One of the promises accompanying NAFTA was that it would boost the Mexican economy, thereby reducing immigration pressure. So far, it seems to have had few such benefits. If anything, its effect has been the reverse.[68]

The questions about the effect of immigrants on public expenditures and revenues are even more difficult. There's not much doubt, as Juan Arambula learned in his years as a Fresno County supervisor, that low-wage illegal immigrants in California's San Joaquin Valley and in other poor areas place an enormous burden on communities and particularly on schools, emergency rooms, and law enforcement. The most comprehensive study, published in 1997 by NRC, the National Research Council, concluded that, over all, immigration benefits the economy and has little effect on native-born Americans other than those without a high school education. But the report also found that in California in 1994–95, the latest year for which the panel had data, immigrants were imposing "a net fiscal burden of $1,178 per native-headed California household."

Given the great increase in immigrants since then, that fiscal burden may well be higher now, despite the intervening effects of federal welfare reform, which cut benefits for legal immigrants. James P. Smith, the Rand Corporation economist who headed the NRC study group, said, "The vast majority of Americans are enjoying a healthier economy as the result of the increased supply of labor and lower prices that result from immigration." But the NRC panel also concluded that, while "the majority of new immigrants and their descendants will add more to government coffers than they receive over their lifetimes," residents of states like California, with high numbers of new immigrants, most of whom pay lower taxes because they have lower incomes, "will bear long-term costs that are concentrated at the state and local level of government."[69]

Although the panel warned that its numbers shouldn't be used to estimate the cost of admitting future immigrants, its findings were reinforced by a report which concluded that "California's native households provide net surpluses to all three levels of government[,] while foreign-born households are a burden on the federal, state, and local governments." Because "foreign-born households contain more children[, they] consume a greater share of state and local spending on both kindergarten through twelfth grade (K–12) and higher education. This difference in education benefits accounts for nearly the entire relative deficit for foreign-born households at the local government level."[70] State and local taxpayers were effectively subsidizing the low prices of goods as well as the growers, contractors, restaurants, big-box retailers, and the other employers of low-wage workers, native and immigrant, that produce them.

At the same time, however, national data also indicate that illegal immigrants are heavily subsidizing the surpluses of the Social Security system, contributing as much as $7 billion a year—roughly 10 percent of the 2004 surplus—most of which they'll never get back.[71] Put all that data together and you seem to have a picture showing that, while state and local jurisdictions bore the lion's share of the short-term burdens, the long-term effects on the economy were positive, and the federal treasury and especially the Social Security Trust Fund were big gainers.

William Frey's data showed that California in recent years has been the nation's largest gainer of new immigrants and the largest loser of both native residents and "the established foreign born," those who arrived before 1990. In the 1990s, according to Frey's data, California gained college graduates, but it also lost 1.5 million native-born residents and 865,000 "established foreign born residents" and added nearly 3.3 million "recent foreign-born"—most, though hardly all, with low levels of education. Frey called it "the flight of the struggling middle class" to places where life is cheaper and simpler and where, at least for a time, the labor markets are friendlier.[72]

More encouragingly, demographer Dowell Myers and others at the University of Southern California have found that California's balance between "new" and "settled" immigrants—those who have been in this country a decade or more—and, of course, between immigrants and their native-born children and grandchildren, has begun to change and will continue to do so at an accelerating rate in the coming decades. While the Hispanic share of the population, as noted earlier, will continue to grow rapidly, by 2010 there'll be almost three times as many settled immigrants as new immigrants. In the meantime, the state's share of new U.S. arrivals has declined from 38 percent to 25 percent. Which is to say that the clock counting down to the time when the proportion of benefits, relative to the costs of supporting a growing number of immigrants, turns positive has begun ticking. The poverty rate among Hispanic immigrants who arrived in this country between 1995 and 2000 runs to over 30 percent. For those who arrived before 1980, it's less than half that—still too high, but a sign of progress. Myers and his colleagues also believe that the troubling generational data on education and other measures of social progress is somewhat questionable, since, among other things, many third-generation Latinos, some born to mixed marriages, no longer identify themselves as Latinos at all. They're the ones, of course, who are likely to be the most assimilated.[73]

In either case, there's no question that the combination of Latinos and Asians, who have made up more than half the state's high school graduating classes for nearly a decade, will soon also come to dominate the state's labor force. Latinos, reflecting that change, have also become the core of a reenergized urban California labor movement concentrated largely among Los Angeles hotel and restaurant workers, janitors, and other low-wage employees. Notwithstanding the decline of the United Farm Workers, those unions, all part of the Los Angeles County Labor Federation under the remarkably creative Miguel Contreras, who saw the possibilities of the immigrant-union alliance, have become a growing factor in the state's liberal politics, particularly in Southern California. And, in a pattern that echoes that of an older period, the unions have also become the training ground of some of the state's leading Latino politicians. Assembly Speaker Fabian Nunez was the political director of the Los Angeles County federation; L.A. City Council member and former assembly Speaker Antonio Villaraigosa was an organizer for the teachers' union; Gil Cedillo was an official of the Service Employees International Union. All have run with strong support from the Labor Federation. In 2005, Villaraigosa, enjoying broad support across a broad political spectrum—he got 59 percent of the vote against an unpopular incumbent—became the first Latino mayor of Los Angeles since its earliest days.

Whether the Latino-labor alliance will remain an effective political and economic force under the increasingly tough conditions of a Wal-Martized retail environment is hard to predict.[74] Nor is it at all clear that in the years ahead Latino politics will be cast in a liberal-labor—or indeed, in any—mold. Despite the driver's license bill and the continuing attempts of the legislature's Latino caucus, aided by other Democrats, to weaken the state's laws curtailing bilingual education and affirmative action, Latino politics in California are probably less overtly ethnic than the Italian or Irish ward politics of New York and Boston circa 1906, and they are sometimes surprisingly pro-business in their orientation. But there's no doubt that, in the not-too-distant future, California's immigrants and their children will be the majority of the state's workforce.[75] Both the state's economy and the pensions and living standards of retirees, the vast majority of them white Anglos, will depend in considerable part on their productivity.

The toughest questions of all, however—and those that clearly trouble middle-class intellectuals most—are the cultural ones. Is the state, and part of other states as well, turning into what Victor Davis Hanson, a historian and classicist at Fresno State, has called "Mexifornia"? What's the justification for putting the newly arrived children of illegal immigrants—or any of the nation's millions of new immigrants, most of them Hispanic—in the front of the line in affirmative action programs that, if they are still appropriate, were designed to mitigate the effects of historic discrimination against blacks and, inferentially, American Indians? Is multiculturalism, as the historian Arthur Schlesinger Jr. put it, sinking the country into too much *pluribus* and not enough *unum?* There is an accumulation of such questions, some of them from the most well-pedigreed quarters: "Unlike past immigrant groups," said Harvard political scientist Samuel Huntington, "Mexicans and other Latinos have not assimilated into mainstream U.S. culture, forming instead their own political and linguistic enclaves and rejecting the Anglo-Protestant values that built the American dream. . . . Demographically, socially and culturally, the reconquista of the Southwest United States by Mexican immigrants is well under way."[76]

Huntington's argument, which quickly generated a furor—one conservative reviewer called a major part of it "thunderously wrong"—was that unlike the great wave of European immigration at the turn of the twentieth century, which was genuinely diverse, the new immigration is so overwhelmingly Hispanic and so culturally irredentist that it defies traditional assimilation.[77] Where those previous immigrants—Poles, Greeks, Irish, Italians, Russians, Hungarians—almost necessarily had to learn English and accept what he calls the nation's Anglo-Protestant culture and traditions, the latter-day Hispanics constitute such a large bloc that they can live in their own sprawling enclaves, watch Spanish-language television, listen to Spanish-language radio, and ignore, if not aggressively reject, the mainstream culture that underlies the nation's unity and success.

Hanson made a similar argument but tied it more explicitly to California—to the poor condition and performance of the schools, to the state's budget deficits, to the costs for more prisons, to the need for remedial college courses, and to a host of other problems—all "to meet the challenges of millions who continue to arrive illegally from Mexico."

I fear [this new Mexifornia] would turn into an apartheid state that
even the universal solvent of popular culture could not unite; an en-
trenched though shrinking white and Asian middle and upper class; a
buffer group of assimilated and intermarried Mexican-Americans,
whites and blacks; and dwarfing both of these, a large unassimilated
and constantly growing younger cohort of Mexicans, at odds with
inner-city African Americans. . . . Our multicultural state would have
the veneer of a new alternate identity; but in fact, it would combine
the worst attributes of both nations.[78]

There's evidence to support some of those concerns: the growing gaps
between people in the highest 20 percent in income and those in the lowest; the rejection of traditional family values and the *downward* assimilation
into drugs and gangs among some immigrant teenagers; the interethnic
conflict over public service jobs and political power in communities for-
merly dominated by blacks and now being taken over by Latinos; the tensions and occasional violence between Korean shop owners and their black
and Latino neighbors; and the small "hot spots" in Los Angeles that, according to veteran civil rights lawyer Connie Rice, even the cops don't
venture into, but which, without attention, could well metastasize into
something much worse. According to reports of the Inter-American Commission for the Control of Drug Abuse, organized by the Organization of
American States in 2005, the *maras*, the drug and smuggling gangs that
originated among Central American refugees in the United States and
then spread back into Mexico and Central America, have over a hundred
thousand members.[79]

More prosaically, there are the relatively, and sometimes depressingly,
low rates of high school graduation and college attendance among third-
generation Latinos; the large immigrant neighborhoods, especially in
Los Angeles, where English is rarely spoken and where the lingua franca
among many younger people and often whole families is Spanglish
(which is now slowly migrating into the mainstream, as have other hy-
brids before it);[80] and the uncertainty among some immigrants—Indian,
Mexican, Chinese—about where they really belong and the evolving

morally inferior, and were inclined to rabbitlike fecundity and thus would soon overwhelm the nation's Anglo-Saxon stock and start a downward spiral from which the nation's civilization would never recover. In 1891, Representative Henry Cabot Lodge of Massachusetts declared:

> Immigration to this country is increasing and . . . is making its greatest relative increase from races [particularly Italians] most alien to the body of the American people and from the lowest and most illiterate classes among those races[,] . . . half of whom have no occupation and most of whom represent the rudest form of labor [and are people] whom it is very difficult to assimilate and do not promise well for the standard of civilization in the United States. . . . Most of the Italians, Poles and Hungarians have no money at all. They land in this country without a cent in their pockets. The condition of the Russian Jews . . . is even worse. [The kind of immigrants] who come to the United States, reduce the rate of wages by ruinous competition, and then take their savings out of the country, are not desirable. They are mere birds of passage. They form an element in the population which regards home as a foreign country, instead of that in which they live and earn money. They have no interest or stake in the country, and they never become American citizens.[84]

Those sorts of sentiments fueled a eugenics movement led by some of the nation's best and most progressive people, among them Stanford University's president, David Starr Jordan, who believed that "race and blood" was the chief, if not the only, determinant of human character, talent, and social condition. Combined with phrenology and a lot of other junk science, the movement sparked nearly a half century of eugenic sterilizations, at least thirty-six thousand altogether, and perhaps as many as sixty thousand, of which a third were performed in California.[85] The movement also led to the adoption of the Immigration Act of 1917 and the immigration law of 1924, which set national origins quotas and which remained on the books until after World War II.

Much of the Huntington-Hansen case is overblown and in some instances flat wrong. If there is one thing Latino parents—like all other im-

migrants—wish, it's for their children to learn English as fast as possible,
to finish school, and to succeed. Huntington himself cited the many surveys indicating that Hispanics feel that "teaching their children English
was by far the most important thing that schools do." He cited the story
of the poor and working-class Latinos who in 1996 boycotted their children's Los Angeles elementary school to protest the poor education the
kids were getting in their bilingual classes. He quoted Alice Callaghan,
the community activist who organized the boycott, who stated, "Parents
do not want their children working in sweatshops or cleaning downtown
office buildings when they grow up. They want them to get into Harvard
and Stanford." (More recent polls also showed that Latinos are no different from other Americans in their high educational expectations for
their children.)[86] Huntington expressed dismay that Hispanic politicians
and leaders of Hispanic organizations persuaded (as he saw it) 60 percent
of Latinos to vote against Proposition 227, the initiative sponsored by
Silicon Valley millionaire Ron Unz that severely circumscribed bilingual
programs.[87] But what seemed remarkable in that story was the boycott
itself, which as much as anything sparked Unz's campaign, and the willingness of immigrants, some of them probably also undocumented, to
take the risk associated with participating in such a protest and keeping
their children out of school.

The numbers bear out the Latino parents' desires. Of foreign-born
Hispanics, according to a survey by the Pew Hispanic Center, 72 percent
use Spanish as their primary language. Among native-born Latinos, it's
4 percent; 61 percent are English-dominant; and 35 percent are bilingual. Beginning with the third generation, no one is Spanish-dominant,
and 78 percent, perhaps regrettably, speak no Spanish at all. An analysis
of census data conducted by Richard Alba and others at the State University of New York, at Albany, came up with almost the same numbers.
Nor did the pattern seem to be changing. "The very high immigration
level of the 1990s," they concluded, "does not appear to have weakened
the forces of linguistic assimilation. Mexicans, by far the largest immigrant group, provide a compelling example. In 1990, 64 percent of

third-generation Mexican American children spoke only English at home; in 2000, the equivalent figure had risen to 71 percent." While many second-generation kids spoke Spanish, they found, 92 percent spoke English "well" or "very well."[88]

The Pew survey also showed that, while Latinos in general were more likely to identify themselves at one time or another by their country of origin—for example, as Mexican or Cuban—than as American (88 percent versus 53 percent), by the third generation 97 percent identify themselves as American, although, like other Americans, they also may identify themselves by ethnicity or by their forebears' country of origin. Also contra Huntington, the survey warns that Hispanics are in no sense a monolithic group, that first-generation immigrants regard themselves as Mexicans or Puerto Ricans and say they share little common culture with other Hispanic groups.[89] In Fresno and Imperial counties, there are "Hispanics"—grape pickers in the Coachella Valley, for example—who speak only an indigenous language and no Spanish. Part of the mission of Leonicio Vasquez, who runs the Oaxaca Binational Center in Fresno, is helping indigenous people from the Oaxacan region—Mixtecs, Zapotecs, and Triques—get prenatal care and other basic health services. He hoped to get them involved in their local communities, but he had to provide translators not only of Spanish but also of indigenous languages. The United States, Richard Rodriguez said, created "Hispanics." It's only in the United States that Hispanics are a formal entity.[90]

By now it's hardly news that immigrant Latinos tend to be more conservative than Anglo whites on social issues like gender roles, divorce, abortion, and homosexuality, and that immigrants work harder in uglier jobs than Americans generally. But it's also apparent that the attitudes of English-dominant Latinos and native Latinos tend to look more like—though they still do not match—the attitudes of other Americans, which, of course, is one of the reasons Republicans, stressing family values and other conservative social issues, are hopeful that they can take an increasing share of the Hispanic vote away from Democrats. The problem is that Latinos are more prone to supporting higher taxes and better government services than non-Hispanic whites or even African Americans (though here, too, native-born Hispanics begin to look more like non-Hispanic whites).

Indeed, on virtually every measure of trust in government rather than private institutions, the attitudes of later generations of Hispanics seem to approach those of other Americans.[91] Gregory Rodriguez, a senior fellow at the New America Foundation, pointed out that in Los Angeles, "home to more Mexicans than any other city in the United States, there is not one ethnic Mexican hospital, college, cemetery or broad based charity. . . . Places like south Texas have had majority Hispanic populations for years, and separatism—political, cultural or economic—is nowhere to be found." Paul Chavez, Cesar's son, said his four older siblings—Linda, Fernando, Celia, and Eloisa—all got Hispanic names. Paul and his younger sister and brother, Elizabeth and Anthony, got Anglo names. Paul learned his Spanish as an organizer in the fields, not at home. "The first thing that goes," he said, "is language. The last thing is food."[92]

And like other immigrants, Latinos look ever more like other Americans in their activities and behavior—and in their looks. Of the Latinos who came to this country before 1980 and stayed here, 55 percent own their own homes, which is almost the state average.[93] By the turn of the twenty-first century, one-third of all businesses in Los Angeles were minority owned, some of them billion-dollar enterprises. In California as a whole, according to the California Hispanic Chambers of Commerce, there were some 600,000 Latino-owned businesses with roughly $80 billion in receipts. One-third of all companies in Los Angeles, said urbanist Joel Kotkin, were minority owned; nearly 60 percent were either minority or women owned. Most, needless to say, were small manufacturers and retail and service businesses—bodegas, *carnicerias, supermercados, mueblerias,* taquerias, restaurants, construction firms, gardening businesses, car repair shops, real estate firms, law firms, accounting firms, and franchises of one sort or another. But they also included the businesses of people like Arturo Moreno, a near-billionaire as a result of his outdoor advertising business and the owner of the Anaheim Angels baseball team (now renamed the Los Angeles Angels of Anaheim); the Molina Health-care clinics, an $800 million HMO catering primarily to immigrant Medicaid recipients in California and four other states; and the Ruiz fam-ily, owners of Ruiz Foods in Dinuba, the nation's largest producer of frozen Mexican food—taquitos, tamales, quesadillas, burritos. Ruiz, which sells its products under the El Monterey label, grew in classic American fashion, beginning in 1964 with Luis Ruiz's grocery delivery truck and what the company said were his wife's recipes, through three generations of Ruizes, to become the eighteen-hundred-employee oper-ation it is now.

Or, similarly, there are the Cejas, the Robledos, the Renterias, and others who first came to the Napa Valley from Mexico as grape har-vesters, some as braceros in the late 1940s, some much more recently, many knowing not a word of English when they arrived. All now own their own vineyards and wineries and market chardonnay, cabernet sauvi-gnon, and pinot noir under their own labels. Most Central Valley and Salinas Valley farm labor contractors or "custom harvesters" are former farmworkers; many, like Bermudez Brothers, run by "Tomato King" An-dres Bermudez and his son in Winters, or Escamilla and Sons in Salinas, which runs 140 buses to get its workers to the fields, are large enter-prises.[94] In 2004, some 13.9 million people lived in households where ei-ther the head or the spouse was an illegal immigrant. But those house-holds also included 3.2 million U.S. citizens, many of them children, and millions more who were legal residents (a pattern that Roberto Suro, di-rector of the Pew Hispanic Center, said is "one of the thorniest dilem-mas in developing policies to deal with the unauthorized populations"). Contrary to the general assumption, one-fourth of those illegal aliens have at least some college education; another quarter have finished high school. But nearly half have less than a high school education.[95]

Despite the apparent—and puzzling—lag in college attendance rates among second- and third-generation Latinos, there are now so many Latino (and, of course, Asian and black) lawyers, doctors, college professors, accountants, and city and county officials and so many corporate executives of Fortune 500 companies—not to mention the nurses, dental technicians, teachers, journalists, and social workers—that the changing face of the state's (and, not far behind, the nation's) professions and corporate leadership, which would have been remarkable forty years ago, and might still be in some parts of the nation, is now largely unnoticed. Even the parade of capped and gowned graduates across the platform at Berkeley and UCLA commencement exercises and the names in the accompanying programs defy spot categorization: Chinese, Korean, Cuban, Mexican, Chilean, Pacific Islander, Iranian, Saudi, Palestinian, Israeli, Filipino, Vietnamese, Thai, Russian, Polish, American Indian, West Indian, Anglo American, African American, North African, East Indian, Pakistani. Which are what? Which names and faces are combinations? What languages did their parents or grandparents speak? Which of those forebears had fought one another in the old country—or maybe were still doing so?

As the nation's largest and fastest-growing minority, Latinos, by 2004 the target of $3.7 billion in TV advertising alone, are generating frenzied interest from marketers, complete with burgeoning firms of advertising agencies, researchers, consultants, market survey groups, and all the rest. *La Opinion*, the successful, long-established Los Angeles Latino daily headed by Monica Lozano, the granddaughter of its founder, is now beginning to face serious challenges from the *Chicago Tribune* and other major media conglomerates launching their own Spanish-language papers. With a circulation of over 130,000 subscribers earning an average household income of $42,000, and an estimated readership three or four times that, *La Opinion* is the largest Spanish-language daily in the nation. Those readers, Lozano said, don't want to carve out a separate culture, nor do most feel they're under attack: "They share the American dream and are grateful for what this country has given them. It's the second and third generations that begin to lose their belief in success. But Latinos are not the problem. It's the institutions that don't respond."[96]

NBC—which bought Telemundo, the nation's number two Spanish-

language TV network, for $2.7 billion in 2001—and Clear Channel
Radio, the country's largest radio chain and probably its most conservative, recognize the opportunities, and perhaps more. In 2004, Clear
Channel, many of whose stations cater to the fundamentalist right, announced plans to convert as many as 25 percent of its twelve hundred stations to a Spanish-language format, a reflection not just of the growing
market but of the rapid dispersion of Hispanics into states that until recently attracted few Latinos and the economic harvest they potentially
represent. In a number of major markets—Miami, Los Angeles, New
York, Houston—the Spanish-language network Univision claimed that
its TV stations draw larger audiences for their early evening news than
any competing channel.

NCM, the San Francisco–based New California Media, in its comprehensive compilation of ethnic print and broadcast outlets, lists nearly
seven hundred non-English-language newspapers, magazines, and
broadcasting stations in California, roughly 35 percent of the national
total, ranging from the *Afghan Journal* to the *Zhong Guo Daily*. California, said Sandy Close, who runs NCM, an association of some five hundred ethnic news organizations and the Pacific News Service, from
which it sprang, "is the epicenter of a nationwide explosion of ethnic
news organizations."[97] A survey commissioned by Close's organization
in 2005 reported that more than one-fourth of Hispanics preferred
Spanish-language papers to the mainstream papers. But Close also believes that, rather than furthering the balkanization of the society, the
"explosive growth" of the new ethnic media represents both "a hunger
for voice and visibility" and a major link between immigrant groups and
the larger society. Their audiences want to know about bank loans for
small businesses, home mortgages, and H-1B visas, but they're also looking for "opportunities to break out of their cultural silos and become
larger civic players." Communication, she said, has replaced community
as a source of belonging, not just for immigrants but also for youth and
other groups.

The presence of foreign language media is hardly new in American

history. In the 1920s, there were nineteen daily U.S. newspapers in Polish alone (one with a circulation of over one hundred thousand), plus
sixty-seven weeklies and eighteen monthlies. Close pointed out that, like
them, today's ethnic media begin with the neighborhood (and the neighborhood often includes the home country) and move from there to the
larger society—the reverse of large mainstream papers and broadcasters.
But she also pointed out that many mainstream papers started the same
way. Herman Ridder launched what became the Knight-Ridder media
empire as the publisher of a German-language paper in New York at the
turn of the last century (Joseph Pulitzer began his newspaper career as a
reporter for a German-language paper in St. Louis), something Close
saw as a natural evolution as ethnic media reinvent themselves in English
"to reach new audiences, expanding the notion of 'ethnic' beyond race
and national origin to lifestyle and identity." Along the way, they can become major political forces, as Chinese newspapers and radio stations became in energizing the Chinese community in defense of the Los Alamos
scientist Wen Ho Lee, who was accused of stealing nuclear secrets, and
who was subsequently cleared, with a judicial apology, of all but a minor
charge.

Similarly, *La Opinion* and other Spanish media have become major
factors in encouraging their readers to vote for school bonds and other
measures to enhance their children's education, and, in 1994, in activat-
ing Latinos against Proposition 187, which sought to deny schooling
and all other services to illegal immigrants and their children, and in the
naturalization and voter registration drives that the initiative helped
spark. On Proposition 187, the Hispanic "no" campaign, which included protests in Los Angeles where demonstrators waved more Mexican than American flags, backfired and almost certainly increased
support for the measure, perhaps even among Hispanic voters. On naturalization, voter registration, and the "Adios, [Governor] Pete Wilson"
refrain that accompanied the opposition to 187, it was a huge success.
Win or lose, those are things that *Americans* do. California added 1.1
million voters to the rolls between 1990 and 2000, nearly all of whom

were Latinos. That still left Hispanics with just 14 percent of the electorate in 2000, but that was up from the 9 percent of a decade before.[98]
Even the campaign against ethnic preferences that culminated in Proposition 209 and similar initiatives in other states was a reflection of the
rapid browning of a society—Asian-Indian-Mestizo-Hispanic-Polyne-
sian-Iranian-Afghani-African—long past the era when that society could
simply be divided in the old binary way, between whites and blacks.[99] By
2005, 29 of the 120 members of the California legislature were Hispanics (nearly all of them Democrats), a proportion of Hispanics that
was still smaller than the percentage of Hispanics in the state's population, but considerably greater proportionately than there were Hispanic
voters.

V

Among the great ironies of the immigration drama of the past generation
is that almost every effort to control the flow of illegal aliens into the
country—indeed, almost every discussion of it—has had perverse effects.
IRCA, the Immigration Reform and Control Act of 1986, the result of a
compromise negotiated between interest groups, traded amnesty for
nearly 3 million illegal immigrant workers, half of them in California—it
essentially allowed them to become legal residents—for what were to be
tighter restrictions on new immigrants, including sanctions against employers who hired illegal workers. But the sanctions didn't work, in large
part because the black market made bogus documents widely available,
and in part because political and economic pressure from employers persuaded the feds that they didn't "want to have a negative impact on the
production capabilities of these companies."[100] Nor was there any serious
enforcement of wages, hours, or other labor codes that might have dis-
couraged sweatshops and other exploitive employment (and thus, perhaps, employment of illegal aliens generally). And while the IRCA rules
seem to have lowered wages, they haven't reduced the employment of illegal aliens. Employers, said sociologists Douglas Massey, Jorge Durand,

and Nolan Malone, "simply transferred the costs and risks of [hiring the undocumented] to the workers themselves in the form of lower pay."[101]

Because employers preferred to avoid the additional IRCA-required paperwork, the law also spurred the use of the labor contractors in gardening, construction, and especially agriculture, where they helped undercut the ability of the United Farm Workers union to organize in the fields. At the same time, legalization and the accompanying SAW (Special Agricultural Worker) program, which was included to satisfy growers and which allowed three hundred thousand more farmworkers into the country, generated a new wave of illegal immigrants, many of them replacing the newly legalized farmworkers, who could now pursue better jobs. Many of them were the spouses and children of SAW workers and of the newly amnestied—what Massey and his colleagues called "a new feminization" of immigration.[102] Similarly, in 2001, when the administration began to discuss with Mexican president Vicente Fox some new "regularization" for 3 million undocumented Mexican immigrants, and when the subject was raised again in 2004, it triggered yet another wave of illegal immigrants hoping to come under the next legalization umbrella.

As noted earlier, IRCA, combined with the intensified controls at the border—the fences in California and elsewhere and the beefing up of the U.S. Border Patrol—paradoxically increased the number of undocumented Latinos in the United States. Altogether, Border Patrol staffing quadrupled between 1980 and 2000 and the agency's budget increased roughly twelvefold. Yet even with more agents and infrared scopes, electronic sensors, and high-tech communications, especially on the traditional south-north routes that cross the border at San Ysidro, south of San Diego, at Calexico, and at the Arizona border, the traffic continues. In San Ysidro, residents in the comfortable middle-class homes looking across the border sometimes find crossers hiding in their backyards. In Calexico, where the homes on First Street are no more than fifty feet from the fence separating it from Mexicali, its Mexican twin, some residents, nearly all of them Hispanic, lock their doors against the crossers who cut through the fence or climb over it and then melt into the bushes behind them. Others help the crossers, either out of sympathy or because they're paid by smugglers.

Further east, in 2005 a group of volunteers calling themselves Minutemen, some of them armed, spent a few weeks patrolling the Arizona-Sonora border in a declared effort to deter or report illegal border crossers to the feds and, a few months later, launched a similar operation at the California border (which was quickly swamped by much larger numbers of counterprotestors).[103] Another group, calling itself Save Our State and seeking high-profile confrontations—what its twenty-nine-year-old leader, Joseph Turner, described as "aggressive activism"—staged a protest at a controversial Southern California monument that seemed to celebrate the region as it was before Anglos arrived. In calling the monument "seditious and anti-American," the group drew a hot counterprotest and cops in riot gear. They've also picketed Home Depot stores in Southern California for allowing Latinos seeking day work to congregate there, and, along with others, protested billboards advertising a Spanish-language TV station referring to the nation's second-largest city as "Los Angeles, Mexico."[104] In both instances, said Richard Rodriguez, part of the impulse seemed to be avoidance of the sense of our proximity to the South.

The Border Patrol agents say that sometimes they catch the same people three or four times, and sometimes they run into them in Mexico, where, as one agent said, "they'll call me out." It's all a cat-and-mouse game, the agents said. "They know the agents," said one, "and know their habits, especially the older ones, who don't like to get out of their cars." And like the Border Patrol, the coyotes who smuggle people across the border have their own intelligence network. Agents like Angel Santa Ana understand that it's all a balance between effectiveness, safety, and politics. "Sometimes when I take people back to the border, they say, 'See you tomorrow.' " Sometimes, the agents said, Mexican Army patrols cross the border to protect the coyotes. The U.S. agents are instructed to avoid incidents.[105]

In making it more difficult to cross into the United States, the increased enforcement has tripled or even quadrupled the prices the coyotes charge to take people across. And along with the accumulating fatalities that occur during crossings through the desert and mountains of Arizona, the tougher border enforcement in effect has trapped illegal aliens in the United States by discouraging them from returning home. According to the best estimates, more than twenty-five hundred people died trying to come north between January 1995 and March 2004, an average of nearly one a day, some of dehydration or heatstroke, some by asphyxiation, some by drowning in the All-American Canal, which runs along the north side of the California-Mexico border. In response to the dangers, in 2004 the Mexican government printed 1.2 million copies of a thirty-two-page booklet of survival tips for illegal crossers, generating a small uproar in the United States. Critics complained that, rather than helping the United States to control illegal crossings, Mexico was encouraging them as part of its larger effort to dump its surplus workers.[106]

But the far bigger effect of the tougher border enforcement lay in its deterring illegal aliens from going back to Mexico. In the two decades before IRCA was passed, said Jorge Durand, Douglas S. Massey, and Emilio A. Parrado, "some 27.9 million undocumented Mexicans entered the United States and 23.3 million returned to Mexico, yielding a net increase of just 4.6 million persons." But "by significantly reducing the probability of return migration," they said, "the post-IRCA regime of border enforcement dramatically increased the ultimate size of the Mexican population in the United States, raising it by a factor of nearly four!"[107]

> Post-IRCA immigration policies have failed to stop undocumented
> immigration [said Massey, Durand, and Malone], and they have pro-
> duced a host of negative consequences for immigrants and natives
> alike; they have spread these unfortunate effects as widely as possible
> throughout the country; and they have maximized their negative im-

pact by transforming a permanent flow into a permanent settlement
that includes increasing proportions of dependents rather than productive workers. If this were not enough, the post-IRCA regime . . .
has actually encouraged additional immigration from Mexico to the
United States. By sponsoring a massive legalization campaign and
pushing Mexicans decisively toward naturalization, U.S. policies
have sowed the seeds for an even larger migration in the future. . . .
If the United States had set out to design a dysfunctional immigration policy, it could hardly have done a better job than what it did
between 1986 and 1996.[108]

While that may sound apocalyptic, there can't be many people in the
immigration debate, left or right, who'd challenge Massey's conclusion
that the real issue "is not *whether* Mexico and the United States will integrate—we are already well down that road. The only real issue is *how*
the integration will occur"[109] (his italics). California, for better or worse,
is as far down the road as any place and, as recent political and social circumstances in the state make clear, quite confused about where it is, and
even more confused about where it wants to go. Many of those issues are
federal concerns and out of the state's control, but many aren't.

Which brings the story back to the question of assimilation and, more
broadly, to what assimilation means in twenty-first-century California
and, ultimately, in the nation. Richard Alba of the State University of
New York, Albany, and Victor Nee of Cornell contended that if the history of American assimilation is stripped of its myths, the process today,
with one or two major exceptions, is not all that different from what it
was a century ago. The historic experience showed that "racial/ethnic
boundaries can blur, stretch and move. . . . Indeed, were it not for the flu-
idity of boundaries [of how race and ethnicity are defined], there might
be no racial/ethnic numerical majority in the United States today.
Only between a quarter and a third of the population can trace some an-
cestry to Protestants from the British Isles, the former 'majority' group.
Thus, were the ethnic definition of the majority group limited to the

original Anglo-American core, it would already have become a minority of the population; only because of past assimilation can one say that an ethnic majority, in any sense of that term, exists in the United States today."[110]

The stretch goes in two directions, or maybe in three or four and, as Alba and Nee saw it, always has, changing the mainstream even as it changes those entering it, both through intermarriage and through the assimilation of countless cultural ideas and practices. As Hayes-Bautista pointed out, not all assimilation is positive: Because of good dietary habits, he said, first-generation Latinos are healthier than U.S. natives, despite the poverty of the first generation and its lack of medical resources. The second and succeeding generations are far more likely to be overweight and to be less tied to traditional family practices and social institutions. There's also evidence that, as Margaret Gibson, who's done extensive research on the school careers of immigrant children, put it, "the children of immigrants who remain strongly anchored in their home culture/language/identity, while also adapting to life and schooling in the United States, often fare better in school than those rushing to assimilate, especially if their parents are not assimilating at the same pace."[111]

A broader and perhaps more worrisome aspect of assimilation is that some at least become assimilated to what Robert Hughes called "the culture of complaint." Or as Peter Skerry of the Brookings Institution put it, "Mexican Americans have assimilated into an array of post–civil rights political institutions that encourage them to define their interests in terms of the aggrieved racial minority perspective forged in the turbulent 1960s and their aftermath. [They] do not push for affirmative action and the Voting Rights Act in Mexico; they push for them after they have come to the United States and gained an understanding of contemporary political institutions," which is to say that some (though perhaps very few) assimilate the wrong way. Nonetheless, Alba and Nee are probably correct that, despite major differences in the cultural and economic environments that could slow assimilation, "today is more like the past than it is different."[112]

As in the past, the churches function as bridges, but often in new and unexpected ways, fostering what a report from the Center for Religion and Civic Culture at the University of Southern California called "segmented assimilation," where "religious institutions, rather than merely incorporating people into the American mainstream, serve the dual functions of preserving traditional identities and aiding incorporation."[113] Many churches still provide translators, adult classes in English, and information on medical, social, and other services. Like other churchmen, Cardinal Roger Mahony of Los Angeles, who as a young priest in Fresno was a friend of Cesar Chavez, has been vocal in his criticism of Border Patrol arrests of illegal aliens on the streets of Los Angeles and other inland cities. He has often called on the president to support amnesty for all illegal workers and for immediate citizenship for all immigrants who serve with U.S. forces in Iraq. Mahony has recruited priests from Mexico and insists that all seminarians in the Los Angeles archdiocese show competency in Spanish.

A lot of churches, especially in Southern California, have also created multiple congregations inside the same church, holding services in different languages, accommodating "niche congregations" (for example, of Vietnamese), and networking with churches and other organizations in their parishioners' home countries. In the Los Angeles archdiocese, 196 of 287 churches hold masses in Spanish, many of them said by immigrant priests. And, of course, there are new institutions in the mix—Pentecostal churches, Sikh temples, little Korean denominations (of which there are several hundred in Los Angeles) that serve a spectrum of Asian worshipers; mosques where Muslims from different, sometimes antagonistic, nations find common ground; old seminaries now filling their classrooms with Koreans eager to become missionaries. Often the churches are heavily engaged in trying to help parents hold the line with their children for strong moral and educational values and against the rampant consumerism and unchecked individualism that they fear all around them.[114]

Is that assimilation or not? Francis Fukuyama, in a review of Huntington's book, echoes those fears. The problem, says Fukuyama, is not that Mexican and other Latino immigrants come with the wrong values, but rather that they are corrupted by *American* practices. Many young Hispanics are absorbed into the underclass culture of American inner cities, which has then re-exported gang violence back to Mexico and Central America; or else their middle-class leaders have absorbed the American post–civil rights era sense of victimization and entitlement. There is a sharp divide between elites—organizations like the National Council of La Raza, or the Mexican-American Legal Defense Fund—and the general population of Hispanic immigrants. The latter, overall, tend to be socially conservative, want to learn English and assimilate into the American mainstream.[115]

The parents' boycott at the Ninth Street School in Los Angeles in response to the school's failure to teach their children English (or indeed much else) was a revolt against those elites.

Whether assimilation comes in good ways or in bad, however, it's now impossible to imagine American culture without the rich and vast spectrum of food, music, dance, design, dress and hair styles, architecture, religion, literature, art, and language absorbed from people once regarded as inassimilable aliens—and, of course, from slaves and former slaves, who, as Richard Rodriguez reminds us, stole the English language, learned to read against the law, and "then transform[ed]the English language into the American tongue."[116] The kosher burrito is now old news in Los Angeles and elsewhere in the Southwest, but what of kosher Thai fish sauce; or the kosher Thai recipes you can find on the Web; or A Touch of Thai, the kosher Thai restaurant in Beverly Hills (yes, there's another one in Tel Aviv); or Szechwan guacamole; or the growing popularity in school cafeterias of fruit-flavored tortillas and of burritos made with whole-wheat fat-free tortillas from La Tapatia's Tortilleria in Fresno? In restaurant kitchens, said Victor Valle, director of the American Communities Program at California State University, Los Angeles, "Latinos are making every kind of ethnic food—Chinese, Russian, nouvelle cuisine."[117] In the recording studios and the clubs, they are making the equivalent in pop music—styles like reggaeton, hip-hop with a mix of Spanish and English lyrics and spiced with Caribbean rhythms. Although reggaeton began in Puerto Rico, it's since swept much of the Southwest and seems to reflect some new impulse to assimilate by moving both poles closer together. "They're trying to blend in," a youth-market researcher told the *New York Times*, "by making the mainstream more like them."[118]

California, which always tended to be culturally inclusive because its elites are socially tolerant, has been the door to a lot of that. In 2000, the Los Angeles County Museum of Art mounted a huge and monumentally ambitious show called Made in California: Art, Image, and Identity, 1900–2000, which included absolutely everything from high art to kitsch: paintings by Richard Diebenkorn, David Hockney, and David Park; reproductions of Diego Rivera murals; Ansel Adams and Carleton Watkins photographs; Arts and Crafts bungalows and furniture; Frank Gehry architectural designs; Chicano street paintings; pottery, lamps, and glassware; rock-band psychedelics, bathing suits, orange-crate labels, glitzed-up car bodies, Barbie dolls, film clips, protest posters, movie placards, promotional postcards, magazine covers—all of it loosely organized not by form but by twenty-year periods.

The show, in its emphasis on the sordid and surreal in contemporary images and symbols, left out a lot of distinguished California art that didn't fit its strongly political themes: the paintings and monoprints of Bay Area artist Nathan Oliveira; Roy DeForest's happy Edenic funk art animal send-ups; the work of Christopher Brown, once a student in the fine arts department at the University of California, Davis, where DeForest and Robert Arneson, another distinguished California artist, taught. Even so, the museum show reflected an aesthetic and cultural tolerance and energy that was far ahead of (or beyond) California's politics and governmental institutions. "Think of the giant flea market at the Rose Bowl," said *Los Angeles Times* art critic Christopher Knight, "albeit sifted and sorted and endowed with pretensions."[119]

The Finnish-born conductor-composer Esa-Pekka Salonen, a musi-

cian trained in the classical European tradition, said much the same
thing, though a bit more positively, about his own experience when he
came west to be the music director of the Los Angeles Philharmonic:

> I came here and I realized that, in this kind of amazing melting pot
> of cultures and people, my list [of canonical works] is no more valid
> than anybody else's list. And this was a big shock. . . . I haven't given
> up on the idea of the importance of Beethoven in everybody's life, by
> any means, but I have realized that things are not that simple. And
> that was quite a wonderful experience. I sort of woke up one morn-
> ing—it wasn't quite that dramatic, but almost—I woke up one morn-
> ing and I looked around and I saw myself in the mirror, and I said,
> "You're free. You can do whatever you like."[120]

He could now compose, experiment, and program new music as he never
felt he could before. (He also had an exciting new venue in which to do
it, the Walt Disney Concert Hall, designed by Frank Gehry.) Los Angeles, said the Austrian-born painter Gottfried Helnwein, "is a city without a memory—it's only now . . . the best place in the world for art. . . .
There's no organized art scene. It's out of control. It's a kind of peaceful
anarchy."[121] In that sort of climate a lot of weird and tasteless things
might be celebrated, and often have been, but a lot might also be accomplished. And as with the Jews and other groups in New York or
Chicago, the movement of the tectonic plates of cultures produced yet
another wave of distinguished immigrant and first-generation writers:
Maxine Hong Kingston, born in Stockton of Chinese immigrant parents; Amy Tan, born in Oakland of Chinese immigrant parents; Chitra
Banerjee Divakaruni, born in India, who has a Ph.D. from Berkeley and
whose stories are set largely in Northern California, where she lives; novelist Bharati Mukherjee, a professor at Berkeley; novelist and memoirist
Khaled Hosseini, born in Afghanistan, now a resident of Fremont;
Richard Rodriguez, son of Mexican immigrants in Sacramento—all exploring the space, or lack of space, between those plates.

Nor is it possible to imagine today's America, and certainly not today's
California, without its almost unconscious acceptance of the influence of

Buddhism or Japanese architecture or Latino attitudes toward race or life generally. "There is something of inevitability," said Rodriguez, the Sacramento boy who, along with Joan Didion, also from Sacramento, is among the nation's most elegant essayists, "in what I begin hearing in America from businessmen—a hint of Latin American fatalism, a recognition of tragedy that is simply the verso of optimism, but descriptive of the same event: *You can't stop them coming* becomes *the necessity to develop a Spanish language ad strategy*" (his italics).[122] Rodriguez, like Ward Connerly, the black businessman (also from Sacramento) who wants to prohibit racial categorization in most official government counts and documents, is keenly sensitive to four centuries of racially based cultural segregation and resents how he himself is now shelved in the bookstores—not with the writers he loves, but set apart as Hispanic. "The most important theme of my writing now is impurity," he said. "My mestizo boast: As a queer Catholic Indian Spaniard at home in a temperate Chinese city in a fading blond state in a post-Protestant nation, I live up to my sixteenth-century birth."[123]

Mexico, Rodriguez pointed out, has no notion of multiculturalism. "Most Mexicans are some blend of races, usually a blend of the Indian and the Spaniard. But many of us also are African. We are totally all of that—we are that before anything else."[124] The inference, of course, is that, in another forty years, a lot of America will be like that, too. "It is your job," he told a group of California librarians, "to introduce California to itself, and we don't have a vocabulary yet. You don't have a vocabulary yet to even talk about what California is. This place is not simply this little neighborhood over here and that freeway exit over there. Something else is going on here." As to the conventional meaning of "diversity"—that's not diversity in any real way. That's "brown, black and white versions of the same political ideology." Even as the universities have engaged in a serious commitment to "diversity, they have been thought prisons."[125] In California and much of the Southwest, the brownness of Mexican Americans, combined with the high rates of ethnic mixing, itself a Mexican norm, is not only changing the shade of what qualifies as American, it's also undermining the nation's centuries-old binary black-white racial structure.

The success of contemporary assimilation, according to Alba and Nee, depends largely on voluntary, almost inadvertent, choices by new groups "as part of a strategy intended to improve their own life chances or those of their children. (Assimilation, one could say, is something that frequently enough happens to people while they are making other plans.)" It's not inevitable—as it wasn't for Asians for an entire century, and as it still isn't for many blacks from Africa and the Caribbean. Nor does it usually take when it's coercive. But Alba and Nee also made clear that, despite the similarities, there are still real differences between the classic era and the present, in part because there were no immigration restrictions before 1917. Among many contemporary groups, "illegal status frequently drives immigrant parents into a social and economic underground, where they are afraid to insist on the rights that legal residents and citizens see as their due." They also pointed out that, in the four decades after tight immigration restrictions were instituted, there were few newcomers to absorb, giving both immigrants and the larger society breathing space to let the process work.[126]

To this, add one other important element: The classic era of assimilation occurred when there were few welfare programs, no Medicaid, and few other social services (other than schools) whose problems could be attributed to the immigrant burden, and when most jobs didn't require high levels of education and no one worried about dropouts. Finally, there was the incalculably important integrating force of World War II, when, with well-known exceptions, men of a wide spectrum of ethnic and national backgrounds and from every section of the country served together and depended on one another in the military, and were linked as fellow Americans by films, radio, and wartime propaganda. Hollywood made certain that in every war movie the platoon (or the sub or the B-17 crew) had a Lombardi, an O'Brien, a Rosen, a Gomez, a Miller, and a Kosciusko.[127]

Alba and Nee recognized that transnational connections are much

easier to maintain today, that they sometimes produce social and economic benefits and thus "are sufficient to ensure pluralist outcomes for
some portions of the current second and third generations." But they also
contended that most of the insular ethnic niches in the economy offer so
little mobility that continued ethnic self-segregation is likely to be limited for U.S.-born generations. Most important is the relative decline of
race (that is, being white) as the sine qua non of Americanness. In a state
like California with its shrinking non-Hispanic white minority, it's virtually impossible to equate whiteness with Americanness. In a study conducted in 2002, PPIC, the Public Policy Institute of California, also
found that, contrary to Huntington's assumption, California's neighborhoods, as measured by the proportions of the major ethnic groups, were
significantly less segregated in 2000 than they had been in 1990. (A totally segregated neighborhood was one with only a single ethnicity; a
perfectly integrated neighborhood was one where people of every major
ethnicity had an equal share.) Rural Northern California, where the only
nonwhites were a small percentage of Indians, and exclusive enclaves like
Newport Beach remained all white. East Los Angeles was overwhelmingly Latino. "Nonetheless," the study concluded, "the patterns suggest
that increases in residential mixing that began in earlier decades, partly
as a result of civil rights initiatives and changing attitudes, continued in
California in the 1990s."[128]

But when it comes to education and income, it's a different story. The
large gains for second-generation Hispanics in both education and income are obvious enough. Roughly 44 percent of new Hispanic immigrants lack a high school diploma. Among their U.S.-born children, that
goes down to roughly 30 percent, a fact reflected in their gains in income
over those of their parents. On average, they have three and a half years
more schooling than their parents, a difference that undercuts all the data
that lumps all Hispanics together. But after the second generation, the
gains virtually seem to stop. Academic achievement in the third and later
generations, other things being equal, should—but does not appear to—
match that of other native-born Americans.[129]

Nor does the performance of third-generation Mexican American students appear to match that of their peers among other Latino groups, much less that of Asians, who tend to outperform everybody. ("Intergenerational progress for Mexican Americans," according to an analysis by Jeffrey Grogger of UCLA and Stephen J. Trejo of the University of Texas, "appears to stall after the second generation, with only modest improvement in educational attainment and no wage growth observed between the second and third generations.") Mexican American adults, ages 25–59, in California average 12.4 years of schooling in the third and later generations; Anglo whites average 14 years; and blacks average 13.3 years. Some 19 percent of the Mexican Americans in the so-called three-plus generation (those in the third and later generations) have less than a high school diploma, compared to 5 percent of Anglo whites, perhaps because, as Monica Lozano said, "in the third generation they lose their belief in success." Mexican Americans, in the words of a report from the Federal Reserve Bank of Dallas, "assimilate not to the national schooling average but to the Hispanic average."[130]

But the verdict on the slow progress of the three-plus generation is not unanimous. When the proper generational comparisons are made, said Rand economist James P. Smith, "the concern that educational generational progress among Latino immigrants has lagged behind other immigrant groups is largely unfounded." Unlike many researchers who compare today's third generation with today's first and second generations, Smith uses the first generation of a half century ago—in theory the real grandparents of today's third generation—as the base, which shows much greater gains. Where Latino immigrants born in the early 1920s had an average of 7.91 years of schooling, their grandsons two generations later averaged 12.4 years. The gap between the education of the grandsons of the 1920s immigrants and that of third-generation Anglos had shrunk to 0.71 years. Thus, said Smith, the fears that Latinos are not assimilating "are unwarranted." (The other problem in this definitional and statistical maze is determining which parent or grandparent is the immigrant or even determining the ethnicity of the third-generation off-spring of mixed marriages.)[131]

Victor Davis Hanson contended that "a tacit alliance of Right and Left has created an open borders policy."[132] In fact what's been created is a policy no-man's-land that relegates a large and ever-growing part of the U.S. population to the legal and economic shadows while doing nothing that effectively reduces that growth. Governor Pete Wilson's controversial (and memorable) reelection campaign TV commercial of 1994, with its "they keep coming" refrain, was partially correct: People were coming. But at the time, many were also still returning to Mexico. The reduction of that return flow seems to have grown directly out of U.S. policy, a policy that Wilson helped shape.

And thereby hangs another tale. A year or two before the Wilson reelection campaign of 1994, the chief of the U.S. Border Patrol in the San Diego district had ordered the erection of a fence from the Pacific Ocean to the San Ysidro port of entry, some five miles inland. That led to illegals making nighttime "banzai runs" around the east end of the fence, near San Ysidro—sometimes in groups of as many as fifty—in attempts to avoid or escape the outmanned agents trying to stop them, then onto I-5, dodging confused drivers in the southbound lanes.[133] The Border Patrol, using infrared photography, shot some of those scenes and edited them into a video called *Border under Siege*, which was used as the centerpiece of its campaign to increase its manpower and funding.

The Border Patrol's footage, which Wilson's campaign used in its ads, also became a major element, as it was designed to be, in further intensifying enforcement at the border, much of it modeled on Operation Hold the Line in El Paso, which significantly reduced crossings and the accompanying nuisance for El Paso residents, many of them Latinos, who had been plagued with border crossers around their homes (and who supported Operation Hold the Line in polls, 78–17). But in San Diego and elsewhere, instead of deterring the flow, the Border Patrol's effort radically changed the economics and patterns of the flow, driving the crossers—as in San Diego—to more costly and dangerous routes, raising the profits realized by coyotes, stimulating a boom in the smuggling business, and sharply increasing the chances that the illegals would stay longer, if not indefinitely. And of course, it had no effect on visa overstayers, most of whom arrive by plane and who represent a significant portion of illegal residents. "Geographic diffusion, combined with a shift toward permanence," say Massey and his colleagues, "guarantees that the effects of Mexican immigration—positive or negative—are maximized."[134]

Hanson is right that immigration policy is stuck in a no-man's-land that virtually guarantees the worst of both worlds. In part it's caused by the tacit alliance he talks about between business and agricultural interests who want an unlimited supply of cheap labor; in part, by Latino activists, immigrant rights groups, and other liberal organizations. But it also reflects a fatal inconsistency within the nation's globalization trade policy, which liberates the movement of goods and capital across the Mexican border while trying to maintain preglobalization restrictions on the flow of labor, all the while pretending there's no problem.

Massey contends that the European Union avoided that problem when it admitted Spain and Portugal, which were then two of Europe's poorest countries. The worry was that, once admitted, the Iberian nations would flood northern Europe with even more workers than they had before: "But in preparation for their integration into the union, substantial EU funds were invested in Spain and Portugal to improve their social, economic, and material infrastructure. As a result, when unification occurred, further emigration did not occur. On the contrary, both countries experienced a large net return migration from northern Europe, despite the fact that per capita income in Spain is still only half that in Germany."[135]

Europe is now confronting the vexing problem of how—and whether—to eventually bring Turkey into the European Union, a decision that may be more important in Western relations with the Islamic world than any democratization in Iraq. But it has found no comfortable way to reduce the growing ethnic and religious friction with its own Muslim communities: Turks in Germany; Algerians, Moroccans, Iranians, and others in France and Spain; Pakistanis in England. In any case, the European model will get us only so far. Unless investment in Mexico is accompanied by wholesale political and economic reform, it's not likely to succeed. Given Mexico's corruption, unmanageable tax structure, and class rigidities, one democratic Mexican presidential election and one trade agreement won't do it.

The problem, said Robert Pastor, director of North American studies at American University and former Latin American advisor at the National Security Council, is not what NAFTA did but what it omitted. Said Pastor, *"Problems can no longer be contained in any of the three countries* [Canada, the U.S., and Mexico], *and new opportunities benefit all three"* (his italics). That means a much broader approach and outlook, the creation of what he calls a "North American Community," with coordinated cross-border drug control; crime, transportation, immigration, and trade policies; an international development fund; and ultimately, a common currency.[136] But at a time when Congress, with White House backing, was passing bills to force all states to deny driver's licenses to illegal immigrants, and to impose far more stringent identification requirements on license applicants, as Congress did in 2005, realization of a broader approach and outlook like the one outlined by Pastor seems a long way off.

As ever, America's policy paralysis and inconsistencies rest on the nation's historical ambivalence about immigrants. Hayes-Bautista called it the split between the (inclusive) Quaker and the (exclusive) Puritan traditions. In the nineteenth century, we imported Chinese workers to build the western railroads and levees, then tried to run them off. We recruited Hungarians and Poles to do the hard, dangerous work in the steel mills, then decided they were stupid and would contaminate the gene pool. In the first half of the twentieth century, we recruited Mexicans when we were short of labor in the fields, then expelled them when there seemed to be too many—as we might have done with the Okies, if we'd only had a place to which to deport them. During World War II and the years after, the United States brought in hundreds of thousands of braceros, who laid the foundations—created the know-how and social capital—for the immigrant networks that persist to this day. "There is no such thing as a guest worker program," said Philip Martin, a migration expert at UC Davis. "We wanted workers and got people."[137]

We are not even sure if the problem is immigration or assimilation. Clearly the less there is of the first, the easier the second will be, but in the way that the country is trying to control immigration it's throttling the assimilation we say we want. In 2001 President Bush caused a near revolt in some wings of his own party when he seemed to promise Vicente Fox some form of regularization of the status of illegal Mexican aliens. In 2004, after the post–September 11 hiatus, and shortly after the House overwhelmingly rejected a proposal by California congressman Dana Rohrabacher that would have required U.S. hospitals to report all illegal aliens seeking treatment to immigration authorities, Bush brought it up again.[138] In Congress, meanwhile, the Senate Judiciary Committee approved the bipartisan Dream Act that would allow the children of illegal aliens who've been here at least five years and who've graduated from high school to obtain conditional permanent residency in the United States. But in the House, a similar bill was bottled up in the Judiciary Committee, whose chairman in 2004, James Sensenbrenner of Wisconsin, along with Intelligence Committee chairman Duncan Hunter of California, was busily working to write amendments into an intelligence reform bill prohibiting the states from issuing driver's licenses to the undocumented.[139] The following year Sensenbrenner succeeded, this time by putting the restrictions into an unrelated military appropriations bill.

As all this was going on, California, one of the states that had imposed such a prohibition in 1994 (but had never really thought of it before), only to briefly repeal it in 2003 and then repeal the repeal, continued to treat illegal immigrant students who attended California high schools as legal residents. It granted them in-state tuition (but not financial aid) at the state's colleges and universities, while citizens and legal U.S. residents coming from Oregon or Nevada had to pay much higher out-of-state tuition. (But then again, California's undocumented alien students can't legally drive to the campuses that treat them like residents.) Texas actively recruits Mexican students for its public colleges and universities and grants in-state tuition and financial aid to low-income students from Mexico.

But for the future, the most important element in this picture of ambivalence and paralysis may be the fact that the policy—or nonpolicy—already reflects the growth of Latino political power both in the voting booth and in government and thus, paradoxically, of assimilation itself. Some 9 million Latinos voted in the 2004 presidential election, up 40 percent from 2000. The total was still only 7.5 percent of the electorate, but in an election that was won by 3 million votes, plenty enough to pay attention to. Despite Rohrabacher and Sensenbrenner, the Republican Party, which embraced severe restrictions on public benefits even for legal aliens in the years immediately following Wilson's election and the passage of California's Proposition 187 in 1994, rather quickly changed course in the face of the Hispanic backlash that followed it.

By 1996, when Bob Dole ran against Bill Clinton, Wilson was a pariah in his own party. In the 2000 presidential primary, Senator Jim Brulte, the most influential California Republican, was among those who pushed hard to make Bush the GOP candidate. Bush had won an unprecedented 40 percent of the Hispanic vote in his reelection campaign as governor of Texas in 1998, and unlike Wilson, he had cultivated good relations with Mexico. In September 1999, a few months before the first primaries, Bush unveiled the idea for his No Child Left Behind education program and its associated slogan about "the soft bigotry of low expectations" before the Latin Business Association of Los Angeles, which loved it. Bush, who would win 41 percent of the Hispanic vote in 2004, was the un-Wilson. The big winners, of course, have been the Latino voters themselves. But as Brulte later said, if Proposition 187, the measure denying schooling and virtually all other services to undocumented immigrants and their children, were on the ballot now, "it would pass by an even larger margin than it did in 1994."[140]

2

DYSFUNCTION, DISINVESTMENT, DISENCHANTMENT

In the generation after World War II, California, always well endowed in its climate and natural beauty, became an exemplar not only for its universities and its huge investment in schools, parks, roads, and water systems but also for the modern, professional government that the state established to oversee that investment. Its progressive social policies—the open housing and other civil rights laws and perhaps the most liberal abortion law of its time (signed by Ronald Reagan in 1967)—were enacted under both Republican and Democratic governors, among them Earl Warren, Goodwin Knight, Pat Brown, and Reagan himself, and by legislators of both parties.[1] Now, forty years on, they seem almost quaint. At the time they were powerful innovations. Later, after things had descended into ugly and spiteful partisanship, some of those legislators, by then long retired, would get together and reminisce fondly about the good old days when they could comfortably work together, even when they disagreed.

The California boom began in earnest during the war, and in some measure even before, with the arrival of millions of men and women—GIs shipping out to the Far East or training at Fort Ord or Pendleton or Mather or a dozen other bases; workers at the state's burgeoning aircraft assembly plants, shipyards, steelworks, and other defense industries;

as well as the hundreds of thousands of Mexican braceros who'd been re-cruited to work in the fields. Many of those people remained in Califor-nia or, joined by hundreds of thousands of other Americans, returned after the war. They arrived at a rate of fifteen hundred a day from every state in the nation, turning acre after acre of citrus groves and barren hill-sides into exotically named developments of modest little houses priced at a few hundred down, eighty dollars a month, for two or three bed-rooms. The ebullient Pat Brown, who had been elected governor in 1958, called it "the greatest migration in the history of the world."[2] The California of the 1950s and 1960s welcomed and was preparing for its new immigrants. Is the California of the first decade of the new millen-nium as well prepared?

California had drawn immigrants for decades before the war. It drew them through the classic virgin-land mythology that portrayed the West as the land of opportunity, through the gold rush (the first time, as es-sayist Richard Rodriguez says, that the whole world met), through the fliers and offers of cheap land and the arcadian "California Calls You" scenes circulated by railroads and real estate developers, through the broadsides promising paradise that were designed to draw cheap farm labor from the Dust Bowl to the San Joaquin Valley, and even through the classic Sunkist labels on orange crates and the Sun Maid labels on raisin boxes. California was opportunity, it was fresh fruit and sunshine, it was the place of romantic rancheros, colorful Mexican fiestas, and, for a little spice, sinister Chinese opium dens. It was the American dream en-larged. And, of course, there was Hollywood, which spread the golden vi-sion of California to every part of the world during the dark days of the Depression and the war.

California was the ultimate America, where you came to remake yourself. In the generation after the war, the vision was reinforced and concretized with the new immediacy of the good life. The emerging high-tech industries and the neat gadgets they produced, plus the swim-ming pools, the beaches, the palm trees, the car culture, the new eman-cipated lifestyles: those were the things the country had dreamed about, and in the postwar years they brought the young families seeking to match both the state's natural resources and their own aspirations with the highest quality of public services imaginable. California would take the perfection that nature had bestowed and improve on it.

By 1962, when California's population, at a little over 16 million people, passed New York's, making California the largest state in the union, it generated the most effusive outburst of national media attention that any state—and perhaps any nation—ever received in a short period of time: California, not just as the promise but also as the embodiment of the good life. "California," wrote George B. Leonard, a senior editor at *Look*, then a major national magazine, "is a window into the future."

> The powerful, almost incomprehensible new forces that are reshaping the lives of men everywhere are at their strongest here; the traditional patterns and institutions, community and class (which hold back change) are at their weakest. California presents the promise and challenge contained at the very heart of the original American dream: here probably more than at any other place or time, the shackles of the past are broken. In helping to create the society of the future, a man is limited only by the strength of his ambition, the dimension of his concern and the depths of his courage to face the dangers of his own creation.[3]

Leonard may have been among the most effusive—he would soon become a prominent member of Esalen, one of California's burgeoning counterculture institutions that celebrated freedom "to discover ancient wisdom in the motion of the body, poetry in the pulsing of the blood"— but he was hardly the only one. In the mid-1960s, they all came to produce TV specials or devote entire issues of magazines to the wonder and awe of the California phenomenon: NBC, *Life*, *Time*, *Saturday Review*, *Newsweek*, *Ladies' Home Journal* ("The California Woman: What Happens When Old Rules Are Left Behind?"). Not surprisingly, there was plenty on the new lifestyles ("The Way Out Way of Life," as one of the *Look* pieces put it); the cults; the health fads; the sun bathing, nude and otherwise; the new California teenager, emblem of the promised life, as

Newsweek put it, "one hand on the wheel and the other around a girl or a beer can, as if the freeway, and all it leads to, were designed for him."[4]

The stories on the fads, the sometimes weird lifestyles, and the rest of the California craziness touched on a kook-and-nut theme that had been attached to perceptions of California for the better part of a century. There had been the episode of the immensely successful evangelist Aimee Semple McPherson, who in 1926 vanished from a California beach and miraculously reappeared, fully dressed, out of the desert two months later. There was the highly profitable cult-scam "The Mighty I Am" of Guy and Edna Ballard, dubbed by author Carey McWilliams as "a witch's cauldron of the inconceivable, the incredible and the fantastic . . . a hideous phantasm." There was Dr. Francis Townsend and his Depression-era Townsend Old Age Revolving Pensions Plan movement, headquartered in Long Beach, then called the "geriatric capital" of the nation, plus a lot of other wacky made-in-California phenomena.[5] The Townsend Plan called for the government to pay two hundred dollars a month to every person over sixty who promised not to work and to spend it within a month, thereby making the United States, in the words of its promoters, "the ideal spot on earth in which to live."[6] It's because of the climate, Assembly Speaker Jesse "Big Daddy" Unruh famously said in the 1960s, "that we grow so many fruits and nuts."[7]

But beyond the nuttiness, there was a great deal that was serious and lasting. There was the full-time legislature, complete with a small staff of professional experts in the major fields that government dealt with, that Unruh himself engineered and persuaded the voters to agree to in 1965–66. More important, to accommodate its explosive and demanding population, the state built thousands of miles of new roads and freeways; put up schools at a rate of two or three a week; professionalized its teacher force by requiring each new teacher to have a liberal arts education and not just be a nuts-and-bolts education major; and created new public universities at a stunning rate.

Along with the federal government, California built major new flood control and water delivery systems—dams, levees, canals—to mitigate the periodic inundations in the north and deliver water to the dry, booming south. It bought and developed thousands of acres of new parklands, nurtured public institutions that were unmatched anywhere on earth, and never thought that it had to make tough fiscal choices. "We'll build the water project," said Pat Brown, who served as governor until 1967 and who presided over, and often exemplified, much of this public optimism. "And we'll build new universities and new state colleges and new community colleges, and elementary schools, too. We've got plenty of money and we've got to do it." What governor has said such a thing since? Pat Brown, his daughter Kathleen said many years later, believed "in the absolute destiny of California to grow."[8] In the mid-1960s, the state ranked among the top ten in the nation in the amount it spent per pupil in its public schools; its per capita investment in its infrastructure was among the highest in the nation.

But perhaps the greatest symbol of the era was higher education: the nine new state college campuses that the state opened between 1957 and 1966; the new University of California campuses at Irvine, San Diego, and Santa Cruz; the three new UC medical schools; and the great expansion of other UC facilities. There were the Nobel laureates that the university, then led by Clark Kerr, was drawing to Berkeley, UCLA, and its other campuses, and the great laboratories and other research facilities that helped attract the academic stars and the outstanding students who began to give department after department top ratings from the nation's learned societies.

Beginning as the chancellor at Berkeley in the 1950s, Kerr *stockpiled* academic stars against the time when he predicted—correctly—that the rising tide of enrollment would justify having them. In 1964, for the first time ever, the American Council on Education rated Berkeley over Harvard as "the best balanced distinguished university on earth." By the end of his tenure in 1967, UC had become the great "multiversity" that Kerr both celebrated and was sometimes awed by, or even fearful of, a place of enormous academic power that was not just serving students or knowledge but also driving economic development of the highest order. Stanford and Berkeley were the root soil from which Silicon Valley grew. The universities, said Kerr, were "bait to be dangled in front of industry, with drawing power greater than low taxes or cheap labor."[9]

In 1960, Kerr, trying to keep the state colleges from encroaching on UC's franchise to grant doctoral degrees, also persuaded the legislature to create a model Master Plan for Higher Education that divvied up the turf and promised to accommodate every student who could benefit from a college or university in an institution appropriate to his or her abilities and interests at little or no cost. Kerr called it a treaty, a process, and a vision. At the top of the pyramid was the University of California, soon to be certified as the world-class graduate and research institution it's become, which chose its undergraduates from the top 12.5 percent of high school graduates as measured in test scores and grade point average. Then, for the top third of graduates, came the California State University, an institution devoted primarily to quality teaching, and then the two-year community colleges for anyone who cared to enroll. The plan also assumed that large numbers of community college students who successfully completed required freshman and sophomore courses would transfer to one of the other two segments as juniors. None of those systems would charge tuition, a word California still doesn't use; students would be required to pay only moderate "fees" for noninstructional services. In industry, in education, in government, in lifestyles, California looked like the future.

II

More than forty years on, the optimism of the 1950s and 1960s seems a sentimental echo, barely remembered, of a long-lost past. Early in 2005, as one indicator, the nonpartisan Government Performance Project gave California's government a C minus rating, tying the Golden State with Alabama as the state with the poorest performance in the nation in public management, infrastructure, and other major governing characteristics.[10] But that assessment was hardly unique or, given the larger picture, even particularly noteworthy. By the 1990s, California had slipped below the national average and, in most major categories, far below average in virtually every measure of governance and public services: in the condition of its roads and highways and other public infrastructure, in the services and accessibility of its libraries, in its spending on elementary and secondary education, and in the achievement of students in its public schools, whose scores on national tests were among the lowest in the country.

Worse, the state's ability to govern itself was tied in knots by a twenty-five-year succession of ballot initiatives: by tax and spending limitations combined with complex mandatory spending formulas for schools, putting roughly 40 percent of the state budget beyond the discretion of legislature, which in turn caused the legislature to seize local property tax money, leading to cuts in local services and, ultimately, another ballot measure pushed by cities and counties to prevent future legislative raids on their money; by mandatory spending measures sponsored by conservation groups for parkland and other projects; by rigid "three strikes" sentencing laws that drove up prison populations and, in tandem with huge pay and benefits increases for prison guards, doubled the slice consumed by the corrections budgets; by tight legislative term limits; by a statewide ban on racial preferences in public employment and education; by broad restrictions on bilingual education in the schools; and by supermajority requirements for virtually all state and local tax increases, except for property taxes, where all increases were prohibited by the tight limits imposed in 1978.

How could a state that had locked itself into such constraints, but whose citizens nonetheless continued to demand high levels of public services, cope with the new California and the new world that had grown around it? Equally important, to what extent had the rise of that new California driven the decline in the public's willingness to tax itself and to trust a government whose representatives, despite the low voting turnout of the new Californians, seemed to many old Californians to be too representative of new Californians' demands and interests? By the beginning of 2005, the legislature and two governors, trying to reconcile pressure for continued high levels of services with a generation of tax limits, five years of tax cuts, and the economic blows inflicted by the recession of 2001–2003, had run up huge deficits that they papered over with creative financing and a record $15 billion-plus in loans.

The optimism and expectations generated in the 1950s had always been too great to last—how did one improve on perfection?—and by the late 1960s they were already beginning to fray. California had long had its dark side in its nativism, racism, and violence: the enslavement and destruction of the Indians by Spanish missionaries, among others, that began long before the gold rush; the virulent discrimination against the Chinese in San Francisco in the last decades of the nineteenth century and the first half of the twentieth; the Alien Land Act that prohibited Japanese immigrants from owning property. There was, in addition, the brutality set off by the hop pickers' strike in Wheatland in 1913; the battering that the Okies got from the farmers and deputies in California's San Joaquin Valley in the 1930s; the ugly Depression-era longshoremen's strikes on the San Francisco waterfront; the widespread support for the removal and internment of Japanese Americans; the Los Angeles Zoot Suit Riots in World War II; and, from the beginning, the push-pull-love-hate relationship with Mexicans.

The darkness and exploitation, moreover, had long echoed through the California myth: in the novels of Frank Norris, John Steinbeck, and Nathanael West; in the classic California noir mysteries of Raymond Chandler and Dashiell Hammett; in the novels and essays of Joan Didion (and later in the apocalyptic visions of Mike Davis and in films like *Blade Runner*); and in countless songs, from Woody Guthrie's "Do-Re-Mi" to Ry Cooder's broken-promise land.[11] It should have been no surprise, therefore, when the dark side began to show itself again. In a culture with California's powerful streak of utopianism, it was almost inevitable that anything short of perfection would launch struggles to find and expel the demons—real and imagined—in the garden.

The demons had begun emerging even during the good times: pollution, overcrowding, foreign immigrants, the voter backlash against the Rumford Fair Housing Act of 1964, which outlawed racial discrimination in rental housing. There were the student uprisings that began at Berkeley in December 1964 and the deadly Watts riot of August 1965, in which thirty-four were killed, more than a thousand were wounded, four thousand arrested, and hundreds of shops torched or looted over an area of more than forty square miles.[12] These things were not supposed to happen in California, where blacks lived not in crowded tenements as they did in Newark or Detroit but in detached little houses. California thought itself immune to such urban stresses. And what of those students in Berkeley's Sproul Plaza? The state had given them a first-class educational opportunity at almost no cost, and they were trying to shut the place down.

Brown, who, along with his predecessor, Goodwin Knight, had presided over the great burst of investment of the postwar era, had stumbled in 1960, when he vacillated over the execution of the convicted rapist Caryl Chessman. Now Brown, along with Kerr, who had long been undermined by University of California regent Ed Pauley, who wanted to run the place himself, took the rap for not cracking down harder on the scruffy, longhaired Berkeley demonstrators. When Ronald Reagan ran against Brown in 1966, much of Reagan's campaign centered on the university as a place dominated by "a minority of malcontents, beatniks, and filthy-speech advocates" whose sex and drug parties were "so vile I cannot describe them to you." For the students, he said, it was a choice of "observe the rules or get out."[13] Brown also had the misfortune of being out of the country when Watts erupted in 1965—he was in Greece on vacation at the time—leaving his lieutenant governor, Glenn Anderson, to deal with it. Anderson was slow to call out the National Guard, which was hardly Brown's fault, but which nonetheless reinforced Brown's image as a ditherer. Unruh called Brown a "tower of Jell-O."

Together, the Berkeley Free Speech Movement and the Watts riot cast the clouds over the California idyll that doomed Pat Brown's political career. For Joan Didion, seeing the smoke from Watts was a reminder of Nathanael West's great scene, in *Day of the Locust* (actually a description of a painting within the novel), of Los Angeles burning. "What struck the imagination most indelibly," she wrote, "were the fires. For days one could drive the Harbor Freeway and see the city on fire, just as we had always known it would be in the end."[14] (In the coming decade, there would be more violence: the mayhem in 1969 at the Altamont Rock Festival east of San Francisco, billed as "Woodstock West," where the Hell's Angels, many of them high on drugs, who—incredibly—had been hired by the promoters to provide security, beat up concertgoers, and where four people were killed; the two-night Manson Family killing orgy in Los Angeles that took the lives of actress Sharon Tate and five others, also in 1969; the mass murder and suicide of hundreds of members of the People's Temple, a San Francisco cult, in the jungles of Guyana in 1978; and the bloody riots Los Angeles in 1992 that followed the acquittal of the cops who had beaten up black motorist Rodney King.)

Despite Ronald Reagan's reputation as a conservative and his role, barely two weeks after he became governor, in the firing of Kerr, Reagan's administration from 1967 to 1975 was as much a continuation of the Pat Brown era as a break with it.[15] In 1967, his first year in office, Reagan supported and signed the largest tax increase in California's history, and, as noted above, agreed (six years before *Roe v. Wade*) to the state's Therapeutic Abortion Act, a pioneer liberalization of California's abortion law: it allowed termination of pregnancies in cases of rape, incest, or when a doctor determined that carrying to term could impair the physical or mental health of the mother, or when there was a serious chance that the baby would be born deformed. (Although Reagan later said he'd changed his mind after signing the law, he probably never thought that much about it either way.) In 1971, he also agreed to a major welfare reform bill that, while reducing eligibility for aid, also raised benefits by pinning them to a cost-of-living formula that guaranteed at least nominal annual increases to those on the rolls. He signed clean air laws, expanded the state's park system, and let state spending more than double, from $4.6 billion to $10.2 billion, and state taxes per $1,000 of personal income increase from $66.40 to $76.20.[16]

The big explosion that, more than anything else, marked the end of the golden era was the passage of Proposition 13 in June 1978 and the tax revolt—state, national, and, in its influence on Margaret Thatcher's England, international—that it set in motion. There had been periodic attempts for more than a decade to pass caps on taxes or spending or both. In 1973 Reagan had sponsored Proposition 1, a tax-reduction ballot measure that was so long and complicated—even Reagan, it seemed, didn't fully understand it—that it was comfortably defeated, 54–46.[17] But with the sharp run-up in California real estate prices in the 1970s and the concomitant spike in property taxes, the pressure began to reach intolerable levels.

As in most other states, individual California property values in the pre–Proposition 13 era were assessed every two or three years by county officials on the basis of the general market for that type of property in that neighborhood. Tax *rates* were set by the many jurisdictions—city, county, school district, mosquito abatement district, fire district, park district—in which the property was located. So, as the California real estate market heated up to what then seemed to be stratospheric prices—a market driven in part by the same attractiveness that brought those millions of residents in the first place—California homeowners, many of them the families who had bought those little tract houses after the war, found their tax bills soaring to three, four, or five times what they'd been. The legislature and Governor Jerry Brown, who'd succeeded Reagan in 1975, fiddled, toying with various fixes. But with the divisions between urban and rural members and between conservatives and liberals (including Brown himself) pursuing their own agendas, they could never agree on a plan. What made agreement particularly difficult was the California constitutional provision—nearly unique among the states—that required a two-thirds majority to enact any budget and thus gave any political minority veto power on all appropriations and, thus, on the funds the state needed to mitigate property taxes. Later Brown confessed that he should have paid more attention, but that would have required "more time than I had attention span to deal with."[18]

Meanwhile, Howard Jarvis and his partner, Paul Gann, the authors of the initiative that would become Proposition 13, were collecting what finally amounted to the million-plus signatures that they eventually delivered to put it on the ballot. Jarvis, the dominant partner in the campaign, was a pugnacious conservative who'd run against California's moderate Republican senator, Tom Kuchel, in the 1962 GOP primary—Kuchel, he said, was really a Democrat in disguise. Jarvis had also run for the State Board of Equalization in 1970 and against Tom Bradley for mayor of Los Angeles in 1977. Each time he finished third. He didn't really expect to win, he said. He was just "using my campaign as a platform for tax reduction."

Alone or in partnership with others, Jarvis had also run a number of tax limitation measures. One almost made the ballot in 1976—it fell short, by some ten thousand signatures, of the roughly five hundred thousand that were then needed for a constitutional amendment. It was then that he hooked up with Gann, a former Sacramento realtor who had been running People's Advocate, a tax limitation organization that he'd established there. The Jarvis-Gann initiative was a model of brevity—it was less than four hundred words long—a terse document of simplicity and apparent clarity. It rolled all assessments back to their 1975 levels and, with the exception of a maximum annual increase of 2 percent for inflation, prohibited reassessment until the property was sold or transferred. It capped the total tax rate at 1 percent and, because there was no other realistic way to do it, assigned to the legislature the task of distributing what remained of the tax to the various local jurisdictions that had set their own rates before. All told, Proposition 13 rolled back local tax revenues by nearly 60 percent and, in effect, gave control of the property tax to the state. It thus handed Sacramento enormous new authority over local government, eviscerated the locals' ability to control their own fiscal destinies, and inadvertently gave city councils, county boards of supervisors, and countless other governing bodies wide latitude to avoid corresponding accountability for problems in their domains.

On June 6, 1978, Proposition 13 passed by an overwhelming margin, 65–35. The polls had shown the voters to be closely divided until a few weeks before the election. But in May, Los Angeles assessor Alexander Pope, under pressure to release assessments early—normally they didn't go out until tax bills were mailed in October—prematurely announced new valuations that, in fact, confirmed Jarvis's dire predictions that many property owners would see their taxes double or even triple. (Pope said the tax on his own home, which had been $1,224, would have gone up to $3,130.)[19] Pope's announcement generated a frenzy of stories—on television, on radio talk shows, and in the papers—of homeowners, many of them retirees on fixed incomes, many in tears before the cameras, who said they wouldn't be able to afford their taxes and feared they'd lose their homes. From the beginning the Jarvis-Gann organization had received the lion's share of its funding—much of it in donations of $25 or less—from such people: Jarvis himself was seventy-four at the time, Gann sixty-six. With the publicity of the final weeks of the campaign, a state that only fifteen years before had thought of itself as a place of bright, optimistic young families had morphed into a society of elderly homeowners who couldn't afford their property taxes.

III

It has long been a California cliché that the passage of Proposition 13 initiated a new era, but it's largely correct. Despite a $5 billion state surplus, which the legislature used to bail out local governments in the years after its passage, the cut in local property tax revenues rolled through California like a statewide earthquake. Within days of its passage, all summer school classes were eliminated. In the succeeding months, schools cut the jobs of thousands of counselors, librarians, and nurses; reduced or canceled art and music programs; cut most high school schedules from seven periods to six; enlarged class sizes (to this day, California is second among the states in the size of its classes); and began a generation of what has been politely called "deferred maintenance" of not only schools but all public facilities.

California's per-pupil school spending, which had been fourth or fifth in the country during the 1960s, had begun to decline relative to other states even before the passage of Proposition 13, thanks in large part to the legislature's misconceived response to a pair of state supreme court decisions, *Serrano v. Priest* (1971, 1977), declaring that the state's huge gap in per-pupil funding between property-wealthy districts and poor districts violated the constitution's guarantees of equal protection. Even when a poor district like Baldwin Park, east of Los Angeles, taxed itself at prohibitively high rates, it couldn't generate a fraction of the school revenues that Beverly Hills could raise with ease. "Affluent districts," the court said, "can have their cake and eat it too. They can provide a high quality of education for their children while paying lower taxes. . . . Poor districts, by contrast, have no cake at all."[20] In its effort to comply, the legislature enacted Assembly Bill 65 to "level up" funding for low-wealth districts with additional state money while capping the ability of affluent communities to raise their own school revenues. But in capping the ability of affluent districts to raise and spend additional tax revenues, the law's real effect was quite the opposite.

Proposition 13, by giving the state control over local property taxes, accomplished the equalization of school funding almost overnight. But instead of "leveling up" relative to other states, *Serrano* and Proposition 13 effectively leveled the funding *down*. Where California hovered around the national average in the mid-1970s—a period when the state still had plans to raise spending—the passage of Jarvis-Gann, in slashing overall tax revenues and sharply circumscribing government's authority to raise revenues, accelerated the decline. California school spending reached near-bottom among the states in the recession of the early 1990s and never fully recovered, even during the boom of the late 1990s.[21] In 2003–04, the most recent year for which comparative estimates are available, California spent $7,722 per pupil, as against a national average of $8,156, and ranked far below the nation's major industrial states in expenditures. (In 2005–06, Governor Schwarzenegger raised school spending, though not by nearly enough to significantly change the picture.) In percentage of personal income devoted to K–12 schools, it ranked fortieth in the nation. And since California is a high-cost state with powerful teachers' unions, teachers' salaries continued to increase. In 2003–04, they were the highest in the nation in absolute dollar terms (at an average of $56,000) and showed no sign of declining.[22]

That meant, of course, that everything else—counselors, libraries, textbooks, building maintenance, and equipment—got even less money.[23] In 2003–04, California ranked dead last in number of students per guidance counselor (at a ratio of over one thousand to one, compared to a national average of under five hundred to one) and dead last in number of students per librarian (at a scandalous ratio of forty-eight hundred to one, compared to a national average of under nine hundred to one).[24] Moreover, despite a statewide class-size reduction program in the first four grades in the mid-1990s, even California's average class size remained the second largest in the nation. Worse, many California schools, particularly those serving poor and minority children, had severe shortages of experienced teachers or even certificated teachers of any kind.

That problem was exacerbated, particularly in high-poverty schools, by the Class Size Reduction Program that Governor Wilson forced through the legislature and into all schools in grades K–3 beginning in 1997–98. There had been no trial and little real study of the effectiveness of the kind of class-size reduction California was adopting. The one solid study, based on research in Tennessee, showed that limiting class size to thirteen to seventeen students seemed to improve achievement for disadvantaged students; there was no research support for the program Wilson was proposing. But because Wilson had found himself with a sudden spurt in revenue, much of which had to be spent on schools and community colleges as required by an initiative passed in 1988, and because he had had a long and ugly fight with the teachers' union, he was determined not to put the additional money on the bargaining table. And since the California Teachers Association had run ads against him complaining about California's large class sizes, he now attached all the new money to effecting the reduction of primary-grade classes to no more than twenty students. That meant that thousands of new teachers, many of them lacking credentials or any other obvious qualification, had to be recruited almost overnight. It also meant that districts had to cannibalize gyms, cafeterias, libraries, even storerooms to find enough classroom space. Thus was policy made in the new California under the old California rules.[25]

But the spike in unqualified teachers, significant as it was, is now just another footnote to the list of chronic school ailments in the state. Affidavits filed by scores of students and teachers in *Williams v. State of California*, a lawsuit brought in 2000 by the American Civil Liberties Union and other civil rights groups, and surveys conducted on their behalf, showed that, in many schools, students were (and are) taught by an indefinite procession of substitutes or by teachers who had never studied the subject they were trying to teach; that students lacked books to take home and sometimes had no texts for classroom use either; and that they attended classes in leaky, vermin-infested buildings. In some cases schools were so overcrowded that hundreds of thousands of students—in Los Angeles particularly—were assigned to a convoluted, fragmented schedule called Concept 6, under which they could attend school only 163 days a year of the 180 days that state law theoretically called for. It meant that many couldn't play sports unless they came to school during their vacation breaks, couldn't take summer jobs, and often had to take college admissions tests and other crucial exams after weeks of being away from school—and sometimes before they had a chance to study the subject. Some complained that, after having begun a course without books, a teacher allowed them to take an open-book test, only to discover that the book didn't cover the material they were being tested on.[26]

Governor Davis spent some $20 million on high-priced corporate lawyers, at $325 an hour, to fight the suit, essentially by denying that the state bore responsibility for substandard schools and by trying to challenge the reliability of the students themselves and badgering them in lengthy legal depositions. In the summer of 2004, Governor Schwarzenegger settled the case by agreeing to appropriate up to $800 million over four years to rehabilitate the worst schools, to provide more textbooks, to mandate periodic inspections of school facilities, and to carry out other improvements. But the agreed-upon fixes, even if fully carried out, were unlikely to lead to major changes. There were only the vaguest promises in the settlement to attract and keep better qualified and committed teachers in the classrooms that most needed them, or to give them the help and conditions they needed. As to Concept 6, the state promised to phase it out by 2012.[27] Even the $800 million wasn't new money; it was just money that would have gone to other school programs.

Because there was no reliable way to compare student achievement among the various states before the National Assessment of Educational Progress began to provide state breakdowns in the early 1990s, there will never be a way to prove whether the state's chronic underfunding of education was responsible for its near-bottom achievement record in mathematics and reading. Even in the heady days of the 1960s, California's sunshine, beaches, and go-go opportunities may have been greater determinants of academic achievement, or lack thereof, than the rich resources many schools then provided. But there was no contesting the conclusion of Heather Rose, Jon Sonstelie, and their colleagues at the Public Policy Institute of California, who pointed to the large gap between California's high academic standards and the "modest means" the state provided to achieve them.[28]

Nor was it possible to ignore the scores. In fourth-grade math in 2003, 25 percent of California students were rated as proficient or higher by the National Assessment of Educational Progress, compared to a national average of 32 percent, 41 percent in North Carolina, and 33 percent in New York and Texas. The scores were similar for eighth-grade math. In reading, 21 percent of California fourth graders were ranked as proficient or higher, compared to a national average of 30 percent, 32 percent in New York and North Carolina, and 27 percent in Texas (and 40 percent in Massachusetts). Again, the eighth-grade scores were similar. On the Scholastic Assessment Test I (SAT), which many seniors take for college admission, but which is much less reliable for state-by-state comparisons, California was at the national average in math and somewhat below average in reading. Overall, said a major foundation-funded study by the Rand Corporation published early in 2005, "California's public school system lags behind most of the nation on almost every objective measurement of student achievement, funding, teacher qualifications and school facilities."[29]

The schools weren't alone in the hits they took from the property tax cuts or the general budget restrictions, state and local, that followed from them. In the years after 1978, a wide range of services was curtailed or eliminated altogether. Even though case loads at probation, children's protective services, and welfare agencies were increasing, counties were turning back state and federal money because they didn't have the local matching funds. In some counties, case loads tripled or quadrupled; in others, they changed not at all as the local systems simply triaged the cases away. Park and public swimming pool admission fees increased, often to the point where families of modest means could no longer afford them, and sometimes pools and parks were closed altogether. Park maintenance, street tree pruning, and other urban services were reduced or eliminated.

Budgets became chronically stressed for counties, which are charged with most of the dirty work that the public wants done but doesn't want to think about, much less pay for: mental health care, drug- and alcohol-abuse treatment, welfare, health care for indigents, facilities for the developmentally disabled, jails, shelters for the homeless, and children's and adult protective services. Budgets were probably never more stressed than during the state fiscal crisis that began in 2002, which set off another round of cuts and resulted in the shutting of emergency rooms and trauma centers, the closing of outpatient clinics, curtailment of some

Medi-Cal dental services, reduction in access to facilities, and elimination of nursing positions for low-income family crisis services, among others.[30] The state's eligibility rules for Medi-Cal (Medicaid) services were among the nation's most inclusive, but California's per capita expenditures were the lowest in the country—just a little over half the national average—and, because of distortions in federal funding formulas, its per capita federal reimbursements were also among the lowest. All this put, and continues to put, additional stress on the state's medical system, public and private.[31]

In many communities, public libraries sharply curtailed their hours and cut book purchases to the bone. A major survey in 2001 reported that California ranked forty-ninth in the country in the number of librarians per 25,000 people, forty-sixth in the number of library books per capita, and forty-first in book circulation.[32] In 2004, after a series of budget and service cuts, the city of Salinas (population 150,000) announced it would shut down the John Steinbeck Library, its main library, and the two remaining branch libraries because it had no money to run them. Last-minute donations temporarily postponed the closing—but just barely. The John Steinbeck Library was to be open just eight hours a week. If the library system is finally shut down for good, Salinas would be the largest city in the country without one.[33]

Despite the state's prison-building boom, the years after 1978 also saw county jails becoming more and more overcrowded and police services more strained. As happened with teachers, the high cost of living and union power drove pay and benefits for California's public safety officers—cops, firefighters, prison guards—to the point where they're among the most generous in the country, which, in an era of straitened budgets, meant austerity everywhere else. In Los Angeles County in the 1990s, a new $373 million "state of the art" jail with four thousand beds stood empty for more than a year because there was no money to staff it. More recently, in October 2004, Los Angeles sheriff Lee Baca, trying to secure passage of a sales tax increase for law enforcement, announced that budget problems had forced the early release of more than sixty-three thousand prisoners from the county's jails, many of whom, he said, had served as little as 10 percent of their sentences. Among them were people convicted of spousal abuse, robbery, battery, assault with a deadly weapon, drunk driving, and car theft.[34] The sales tax measure got 64 percent of the votes, but under California's stringent post–Proposition 13 requirements, it needed a two-thirds margin.

More dramatic, perhaps, particularly for Wall Street, was the spectacular bankruptcy of suburban Orange County, just south of Los Angeles, which, in an effort to generate more revenues in the post–Proposition 13 era, had relied on high-risk, creative-financing investments. In 1994, the investment bubble burst with the collapse of the $20.6-billion Orange County Investment Pool, two-thirds of it borrowed, that County Treasurer Bob Citron had created. It was the largest municipal bankruptcy in U.S. history. The full story of the failure of Citron's pool, which was loaded with derivatives, "inverse floaters," and other complex financial instruments, and which damaged many of the two hundred little cities, school districts, and other public entities that had joined it, makes a great story of folly, chutzpah, and something-for-nothing greed all by itself.[35] But the effects were devastating. Because Orange County's conservative voters refused to approve even a modest tax increase to dig themselves out of the emergency, three thousand county jobs were eliminated; major public buildings, including the county administration building, were mortgaged or sold; income earmarked for redevelopment, flood control, and other special funds was raided to pay off creditors; and virtually all county services were sharply reduced. The county called its recovery scheme a "Robin Hood" plan.[36]

Maybe the most obvious hit was to California's once-exemplary highway system. In 2004, highway expert David Hartgen ranked California dead last among the states in urban interstate congestion, forty-eighth on the condition of those roads, and forty-third on the condition of its rural interstates. Another study, based on Federal Highway Administration data, conducted by TRIP, the industry-supported organization called The

Road Information Program, listed six California urban areas among the ten in the nation with the "highest share of major roads and highways with pavements providing an unacceptable ride quality." The four places with the roughest roads—Los Angeles, San Jose, San Francisco–Oakland, and San Diego—were all in California. They were also among the nation's most hopelessly congested. Two-thirds of Los Angeles's road miles were rated poor.[37] California, as a number of commissions have pointed out, had been coasting on the capital investment of the 1950s and 1960s and had, in effect, been disinvesting by letting that infrastructure deteriorate ever since. In 1960 California spent nearly $1.50 per person for infrastructure. In the 1980s and 1990s, it spent roughly $0.25. California's backlog on infrastructure—the schools and other public buildings, roads, and water and sewer systems that needed to be built, repaired, or modernized—was conservatively priced by the California Business Roundtable in the late 1990s at $90 billion, by a state commission in 2002 at $100 billion, and by others at considerably more.[38]

When they could, local governments got voter approval for sales tax increases, as San Bernardino did, to fund transit and road projects. But even local government leaders like Norm King, the executive director of the San Bernardino (County) Associated Governments, who ran the county's sales tax campaign, acknowledge that, since the sales taxes are not specifically levied on vehicles, particularly the noxious interstate diesel rigs that cause the most road damage, they do nothing to reduce road use and pollution or increase carpooling and, thus, are no better than stopgaps. It's been many years since the state's now-outdated fuel taxes covered the damage that those trucks cause. By failing to increase fuel taxes (professedly to protect low-income motorists), King said, "we subsidize everybody to subsidize the poor." Even in environmentally conscious California, fuel tax increases are politically radioactive.[39]

Despite major new bond issues and, ultimately, a ballot measure lowering the margin required to pass school bonds from 67 to 55 percent, school construction was so far behind that it would take at least a decade and perhaps more to catch up—even if funding continued to flow. By

1998, over one-third of the state's students—some 2 million in all—were in portable classrooms: some schoolyards, completely occupied by "relocatables," looked more like migrant labor camps than academic institutions. In 2002–03 in Los Angeles, which, despite its booming school population, hadn't opened a new general high school since 1970 and very few schools of any kind, and where the school construction process was convoluted and often mismanaged, some 328,000 students, nearly half the city's enrollment, were on multitrack schedules.[40]

If the effect of California's declining commitment to its schools was profound, the erosion—a word Kerr himself would later use—of the grand scheme of the state's Master Plan for Higher Education was more subtle but often as deep. Republican governors George Deukmejian and Pete Wilson had always tried to treat the University of California, the state's premier system and one with a lot of influential alumni, with special regard. Yet in many respects, particularly cost, the cumulative impact of the state's economic cycles and their boom-bust effect on higher education budgets was to leave all three segments of the state's higher education system—the University of California; the California State University; and the huge community college system, with its 1.6 million students—subject to greater political and fiscal buffeting and uncertainty than they had been thirty years before.

It was probably beyond the bounds of financial possibility, or maybe even equitable public policy, to maintain the low fees—in some cases no fees—that the Master Plan of 1960 had promised. By how much should working-class taxpayers subsidize the university education of affluent students—future lawyers, doctors, accountants—who, the day after they graduated, would be making twice or three times as much as the taxpayers who had supported them? But what happened in California higher education was never planned or even formally discussed. Nor was there any advance notice. In the recession of the early 1990s, the state's tax-limited budget became so tight that literally thousands of college and university classes were eliminated almost overnight. At the same time, fees were raised sharply, without sufficient financial aid to offset costs for the thousands who couldn't afford them. Some two hundred thousand students, the majority of them community college students, were driven out of the system.

The University of California, which had a well-funded pension system, offered early retirement to all faculty members and administrators of a certain age and seniority, without regard to their value to the university. Among the two thousand who accepted were some of the university's stars, including a few of the same people that Kerr had lured to the university in the heady days of the 1960s, among them Nobel laureates Gerard Debreu (economics) and Donald Glaser (physics), sociologist Neil Smelser, cybernetician Lotfi Zadeh, and policy analyst Martin Trow. At Berkeley, the physics department lost 40 percent of its faculty; the history department 30 percent; the music department four of its five distinguished musicologists. Some of these people stayed on to do research funded by outside grants or to teach part-time; others, like Professor James Guthrie, a nationally recognized education policy expert, went elsewhere, in effect doubling their incomes. The disclosure, even as classes were being cut and students were standing in the aisles in overcrowded lecture halls, that the university regents had guaranteed UC's retiring president, David Gardner, a $1 million "golden parachute" as part of his pension package didn't make the situation any more palatable.[41]

The system survived the recession; the fee increases imposed during the early 1990s would be partially (but never completely) rolled back during the boom of the late 1990s (then again increased well above their previous highs), and enrollment again started back up. But California did not start building a single new UC campus after the Kerr boom—and only a few new campuses for the much larger California State University—until it broke ground for its new facility at Merced in the first years of the twenty-first century. By then, as Patrick Callan, who headed the National Center for Public Policy and Higher Education, pointed out, the public subsidy had gone out of undergraduate education at UC; although the university never acknowledged it, virtually all of it was being paid for by student fees. Kerr, vigorously working on his memoirs into his late eighties—he died in 2003—was particularly concerned about the gradual reduction in transfer programs from the community colleges to the universities. He was also troubled that "efforts to achieve better use of resources, including year-round operations, have remained in almost total neglect."[42]

Equally significant, in 1995, just as the recession of the early 1990s was ending (and as the state's minority population was rapidly rising), Governor Wilson strong-armed the UC regents into ending affirmative action in admissions and faculty recruiting, and the university was deeply shaken again. As a state legislator, as mayor of San Diego, and as a U.S. senator, Wilson had been a moderate Republican who strongly supported affirmative action programs. But after he won reelection as governor in 1994 by exploiting the issue of illegal immigration and backing the highly divisive Proposition 187, which sought to end all public services, including public schooling, for illegal immigrants and their children—and now driven by growing presidential ambitions—he seized on what he perceived as the growing public backlash against racial preferences.

UC was an easy target. The university, in its efforts to keep its minority enrollment up, had in fact been giving highly preferential treatment to African Americans and Latinos, both in undergraduate admissions and in admission to its professional schools—far more so in terms of test scores and grades than it acknowledged. That led to questions and then to growing pressure from the parents of high-scoring students who'd been rejected, and from the UC regents, led by Ward Connerly, the black Sacramento businessman who would soon expand his campaign to abolish affirmative action at UC into a national movement to eliminate all racial and gender preferences in public employment, contracting, and education.

UC president Jack Peltason, while contending that the racial preferences were marginal, argued that if affirmative action were ended, UC would lose half its black students and a fourth of its Latinos. Peltason, a highly respected political science professor and former UC Irvine chancellor, who'd been chosen to stabilize things after the Gardner pension

uproar, thus found himself in the middle of a nasty battle he never expected.[43] To explain the apparent contradiction about affirmative action,
UC asserted, perhaps with some justification, that if minority students
couldn't get into their first-choice campuses—meaning Berkeley or
UCLA—they'd go elsewhere, which of course undermined its argument
that without affirmative action California's minority students would be
deprived of a good education.

But the divided regents' vote at a tempestuous meeting in July 1995
came without any real consultation with faculty and against the plain
wishes of the university's administration, including most campus chancellors, thereby stirring up more turmoil. In theory, the university was
constitutionally independent and had a high degree of faculty governance in setting academic policies, including admissions. If this wasn't
heavy-handed political intrusion into those prerogatives, what was?
Richard Atkinson, the former chancellor of UC San Diego, who had just
been named president to succeed Peltason, came close to being fired
when he unilaterally announced a year's delay in implementing the new
rule because, he said, there wasn't time to change the admissions process.
In response, Wilson and Connerly swiftly forced Atkinson to apologize
and modify the timetable. Within a year, Berkeley chancellor Chang-Lin
Tien, a strong believer in affirmative action and an outspoken critic of
the regents' decision—he was also a prodigious fund-raiser for the university—had quit. Gray Davis, then the lieutenant governor, blamed it
on the "shabby" treatment Tien got from the board.[44]

The new policy drove minority admissions down even before it was
formally implemented. The state's well-qualified blacks and Latinos, who
had other places to go—some had attractive offers from Harvard or
Princeton—declared they no longer felt welcome and declined to come
or refused to apply at all. In effect, the regents' decision reduced UC's options in competing with other high-prestige institutions, particularly the
Ivy League, which had no such restrictions. At a time when a rapidly
growing percentage of the new California high school graduates were
Latinos and, of course, Asians, and when the state's future labor force

would almost certainly be dominated by minorities, the regents' decision also threatened to cloud both the state's economic prospects and the university's legitimacy as a public institution.

In response—and without ever acknowledging any link with the affirmative action rule, indeed denying it—Atkinson led UC to a radical revision of its admission procedures. Where the university had long used a numerical formula based almost entirely on grades and applicants' scores on the familiar SAT I, once labeled an "aptitude test," it quietly reduced its emphasis on the SAT I and put more weight on the subject-matter-based SAT IIs, once called "achievement tests." Atkinson and UC also forced the College Board, which controls the SAT, to revise the test itself. Under growing pressure from the legislature's Latino caucus, moreover, Atkinson persuaded the regents to quickly adopt "comprehensive review," used by most of the nation's high-prestige private institutions, under which an applicant's entire record—community service, enriching experiences, diverse background, special skills in art or music or sports, and handicaps overcome—were combined with the conventional academic measures. Copying Texas's "10 percent plan," UC also instituted a policy whereby it would take the top 4 percent of the graduates of any California high school, thereby bringing in students from schools that had never been represented at UC before and in effect doing away with all other academic requirements, provided only that the applicant had completed the requisite menu of UC-required courses in the major fields. Both policies effectively de-emphasized the tests on which most minority students scored below whites and Asians.

At UCLA's law school, admissions officers abandoned their practice of weighting the grades of applicants according to what had been judged to be the academic stringency of the individual's undergraduate school. Henceforth, an A from Southwest Kansas State was judged to be the same as an A from Harvard. In 2001, it also added a special admissions track for students interested in "critical race studies," which skeptics saw as a backdoor preference for minorities.[45] Berkeley law professor John Yoo (who subsequently became better known for his authorship of one of a group of controversial U.S. Justice Department memos that seemed to permit the harsh treatment of prisoners in Iraq) later commented that, while he had always opposed affirmative action, he had belatedly realized that it was a way of maintaining campus diversity while "limiting the damage" to academic standards.[46]

None of the UC admissions reforms, however, brought the numbers to where they had been. In 1995, the year of the regents' vote, Latinos constituted 15.6 percent of the university-wide freshman class. In 2005, they constituted 16.8 percent, even though the state's Hispanic population and the percentage of high school graduates who were Latinos had increased much more sharply. The comparable figures for blacks were 4.2 percent in 1995 and 3.2 percent in 2005. The numbers were even worse for UC's most selective campuses and its professional schools. At Berkeley, the percentage of Latino freshmen declined from 16.9 in 1995 to 11.7 percent eight years later; blacks slipped from 6.6 percent to 4.2 percent.[47]

By 2003, ironically, there was also a new conservative backlash against UC admission practices, articulated most particularly in a set of memos by Regents Chairman John Moores charging that, under its new policies, Berkeley was admitting hundreds of underqualified students, among them 359 who had embarrassingly low SAT I scores (of between 600 and 1,000 on a scale ranging from 400 to 1,600), while more than 3,000 with scores above 1,400 were shut out. The university quickly replied that in fact those students, many of whom were black or Latino, had been almost as successful in their first year as all others, and that Moores's data purporting to show that they had dropped out or failed in high numbers were false.[48] Nonetheless, comprehensive review would inevitably make it harder to justify admissions decisions in a highly competitive system. With a simple numerical formula, there was objective evidence that choices were internally evenhanded, however biased they might be in concept. A less formulaic approach always depended on trust in the integrity of the admissions officers who selected the applicants. Even when race did not appear on the application, surnames, addresses, and biographies would inevitably provide that information. At the same time, the decline in minority admissions seemed to show that nobody had a heavy thumb on the scale.

In 2003, when Moores issued his complaint, the state faced another round of deficits and California's colleges and universities were again under the budgetary gun, which of course added resonance to the complaint about admissions bias. In the 2003–04 budget, Governor Davis's last, university funding was cut by 17 percent—UC's outreach programs were slashed in half—and fees increased by an average of 30 percent, partially offsetting the state funding cuts. At the community colleges, fees went up from $11 to $18 per unit, an increase of roughly $210 a year (they would go up another $8 per unit the following year), leaving fees still lower than in most other states. But the figure was high enough, in combination with the elimination of courses and course sections, to deny access to 175,000 students, according to the National Center for Public Policy and Higher Education.[49]

California's nonpartisan Legislative Analyst contended that many community college districts in the huge system were overestimating projected enrollment, but there was no dispute about the National Center's findings that California, the state that thirty years before had been cited by international agencies as a model in higher education, now ranked twenty-fifth in the nation in the percentage of its ninth graders who got either a bachelor's degree within six years or an associate's degree from a community college within three years of graduating from high school. Of every hundred ninth graders, according to the National Center, seventy finished high school; nineteen got some sort of college diploma.[50] And since the great majority of first-generation students—those whose parents never went to college, meaning Latinos and blacks particularly—went to the community colleges, the program cuts and fee increases hit the new Californians particularly hard.

The clincher, however, was the deficit-driven closed-door deal that Governor Schwarzenegger made with the universities. It called for additional cuts in university budgets for 2004–05, another round of fee increases, and, most dramatically, for the universities to redirect some qualified students to the community colleges. As a result some fifty-eight hundred UC and thirty-eight hundred CSU applicants belatedly received letters telling them that, although they qualified for admission, they'd have to complete the first two years at a junior college. At the end of July, confronting the predictable, and justified, uproar from students, parents, and legislators—and in light of what was in effect a formal acknowledgement that, for the first time in forty-plus years, the promise of the Master Plan would be broken—the governor agreed to provide additional funds.

By then, however—this was no more than a month before classes began—some had agreed to take the junior college option; others had made plans to enroll at other universities. The university expected that no more than sixteen hundred of the deferred fifty-eight hundred applicants would now enroll. And the fee boosts, including a three-year 40 percent boost in graduate student fees at UC, and a 35 percent increase at CSU, would remain in place. A few months later, the regents, after release of a complex statistical study indicating that the university had in fact been accepting students from the top 14.4 percent of high school graduates, not just the top 12.5 percent called for by the Master Plan, raised the minimum grade point average required for admission.[51] Critics pointed out that the difference between the two numbers was in fact within the margin of error—inevitably the regents' action would also lower the admissions chances for minority students—but the decision also suggested that the budget stresses and Moores's complaint had had their effect. It was not the most encouraging message to send to the state's students.

Schwarzenegger would increase funding for higher education in the 2005–06 budget, but fees would also continue to go up, lending additional support to Callan's argument that, both in their funding and in their admissions processes, the universities, in keeping growing numbers of the poor out, were increasingly class-stratified. If the state didn't soon make a long-term commitment to its universities, said Murray Haberman, executive director of the California Postsecondary Education Commission (which was itself on the budgetary chopping block), UC in particular would find it ever more difficult to recruit and keep distinguished faculty, attract the best students, maintain itself as the gold standard in higher education, and keep the university intact as the engine for the state's economy that Kerr had made it forty years before. "We can no longer go on band-aiding," UC President Robert Dynes told the regents in September 2005. Faculty salaries were lagging, class sizes were creeping up, and funding for financial aid was strapped. "We're going to face some stark decisions [regarding] the quality, the accessibility of the university. Something has to break." Some of that may have been crying wolf, but compared to Clark Kerr's optimism about the university forty years earlier, it was nonetheless remarkable.[52]

IV

The favorite target of blame for the deficits of the first half of the first decade of the twenty-first century that so squeezed California's services was overspending by Governor Davis and the Democratic legislature, who had taken the surpluses left them by the capital-gains-and-stock-dividend-driven boom of the late 1990s and, as the belief went, turned them into huge deficits. All of that, of course, paralleled the similar surplus-to-deficits course of the federal budget in the first years of George W. Bush's first term, a comparison that, for obvious reasons, neither party wished to make. And there surely were similarities, particularly in the effect of the recession on both. In 2000–01, the state collected $17.6 billion in taxes from capital gains and stock options; three years later, it was getting just $6.2 billion, an $11 billion decline (in a total general fund budget of about $77 billion).

California's budgets of the late 1990s and early 2000s, reflecting the great spike in revenues and making no allowance for the likelihood that sooner or later the bubble would burst, had grown at a dramatic pace, from $57.8 billion in 1998–99, Wilson's last budget year, to $77.7 billion in 2002–03, a period during which, as Steven Sheffrin, a tax expert at the University of California, Davis, euphemistically put it, "the governor and legislature took advantage of what they deemed to be a new expansive fiscal environment by creating new programs and increasing allocations to ongoing programs."[53]

Davis was the first governor in a decade to put more money into K–14 education than the state constitution required. He broadened eligibility for Medi-Cal, California's Medicaid program, and he reluctantly agreed to a broadly supported bipartisan bill making Cal Grants, the state scholarship program, into a quasi entitlement for low-income students who had the required grades. Given California's history and needs, those were hardly extravagant expenditures. But there was also the usual list of horribles: hefty pay and benefits increases under both Wilson and Davis for the state's prison guards; the usual pork to induce certain legislators to vote for the budget; and, perhaps most dramatically, spiking pension and health benefit costs for retired public employees.

Still, the familiar charge that the state was heavy with bureaucrats was false. California state and local government ranked forty-fourth in the nation (in 2001) in public employees per ten thousand people, well below the national average.[54] And as Sheffrin also pointed out, when it came to the big dollars, a large chunk of the state's spending increases went for increased caseload and inflation in health care, an item where everyone's costs were going sky high. Of the total rise in Medi-Cal spending, more than $3 billion of the increase was due to inflation and caseload. Only 25 percent was driven by expanded program eligibility. The state's Legislative Analyst's numbers were even higher: $11 billion of the $19.9 billion four-year increase in the budget, she reported, was attributable to population and caseload increases and inflation. The story was similar for K–12 schools, where roughly $3.3 billion of the $4.6 in new spending was attributable to increased enrollment and inflation, the rest to Davis's increases.

According to Sheffrin's analysis, of the $19.9 billion spending increase over the four years prior to 2003, $8.9 billion was due to increased caseload and inflation; $3.4 billion to new or expanded programs; the rest, $7.6 billion, to federal mandates and other increases, most of which were, in fact "tax relief," meaning they replaced the money lost to local government because of tax cuts approved by the state government. The biggest of those cuts were the two sharp reductions—one under Wilson, one under Davis, totaling nearly $4 billion a year—in the state's VLF (vehicle license fee), the car tax that Davis allowed to rise (after cutting it earlier) and that would become such a large issue in the recall. The VLF, originally meant to replace the crazy quilt of local personal property taxes on cars when it was first enacted in the 1930s, all went to local governments, as it had for decades. But since the state had committed itself to making up any revenue lost through reductions in the fee, the car-tax-cut backfill showed up on the state's books as increased spending.[55]

The VLF wasn't the only tax to be cut in the boom years. In 2003–04, according to the California Budget Project, the tax cuts enacted since 1991–92 had reduced annual revenue by nearly $9 billion. Because of tax rate reductions and the enactment of various depreciation allowances and other corporate tax loopholes, the share of corporate income paid in taxes in California had fallen by some 46 percent since 1981, to its lowest level since 1960. (In the same period, the personal income tax increased as a share of General Fund revenues, from 35 percent to nearly 50 percent.) In the forty-plus years since the 1960s, sales tax collections as a percentage of personal income had also declined (to $40 per $1,000 from $53 per $1,000), in large measure because a growing share of the economy was based on services—lawyers, accountants, auto repair—which were not subject to the sales tax and, increasingly, on Internet and catalog sales, which usually also escaped taxation. Those declines would be compounded by a drop in the state's share of the federal estate tax that the Bush administration and Congress were phasing out.

By 2004–05, the cost to the state of the federal estate tax cut alone—a cost that was barely noticed by politicians who could become obsessed by almost any five-figure case of Medi-Cal fraud—was over $1 billion a year. In the heady years before the passage of Proposition 13, California had been a high-tax state. In 1968 (which happened to be the year Schwarzenegger arrived as an immigrant and which he cited in his campaign as the golden age to which he would restore California), it was second in the nation in state and local tax collection as a percentage of personal income; in 1977, the year before Proposition 13 passed it was fourth; in 1979, the year after, it was twenty-fifth. In 2004, according to the conservative Tax Foundation, it ranked twenty-sixth in the nation in state and local tax burden as a percentage of personal income, lower than the national average.[56]

Behind those numbers lurked a more ominous item, ominous not so much for its effect on fiscal crises past and present—though it certainly had its effect—as for the future. For the better part of the generation since the tax-cutting era began, cash-strapped state and local agencies had been converting short-term employee union demands for higher wages into long-term commitments for more lavish pensions and retiree health benefits. That was particularly true for police officers and firefighters, many of whom have contracts allowing them to retire in their fifties at 90 percent pay. Those commitments were now coming due—and coming due just when returns on investment in pension funds were flattening out and in an era when the cost of health care had risen far beyond the expectations of the public executives who originally made the deals. In 2004, in Orange County, the huge suburban blob below Los Angeles that had gone broke a decade earlier, and which was devoting almost 40 percent of its public safety payroll to pensions, officials estimated that the county's pension reserve was $1 billion short.[57]

In the same year, in San Diego, a city of 1.3 million people that once had had a reputation as being among the best managed in the country, a $1.7 billion pension fund shortfall that city officials had swept under the rug was threatening to drag it into bankruptcy. What it had done, year after year, was use pension fund earnings for other city purposes, including, ironically, paying health insurance premiums for teachers and firefighters. Worse, in 2002, even as it reduced payments to its pension fund, the city also approved a plan that would allow workers to defer their retirement and collect hefty bonuses when they did. At the same time, it was misreporting its financial condition.

To try to get things under control, the city closed swimming pools, deferred street maintenance, cut more library hours, froze virtually all spending on new equipment—and borrowed. By 2009, according to some estimates, one-fourth of its revenues might be sucked up by the pension deficit. It was "Enron by the Sea"—two council members were on trial, six pension board members were facing felony conflict-of-interest charges, and several others, including the mayor, resigned. Nor were pension and retiree health systems in other places, including Los Angeles, in much better shape.[58] From one end of the state to the other, local and state officials, including the governor, were either issuing or hoping to issue bonds to cover their pension obligations at a rate surpassing all previous records, money that, with interest, was expected to take many more billions out of state and local programs in the years ahead. California was hardly alone in its unfunded pension and health care obligations, but it was almost certainly the national champion.

V

If Proposition 13 had a massive effect on government, it had an equally hefty impact in countless other areas. Overnight, it generated tax windfalls for the state's utilities, oil companies, railroads, and other major corporations.[59] And while the measure was in large part driven by the inflation in real estate values, its passage drove them even higher. What a homeowner didn't have to send to the tax collector she could send to the bank in monthly payments on her mortgage—often it was the same check—which, in turn, was a windfall for the banks. In a study on the early effect of Proposition 13, Kenneth T. Rosen of the Center for Real Estate and Urban Economics at Berkeley concluded that "each dollar decrease in relative property taxes appeared to increase relative property values by about seven dollars."[60]

Because Jarvis-Gann rolled property tax assessments back to 1975 levels, not to be changed until the property was transferred, it also caused widening gaps between taxes on identical and sometimes adjacent properties, soon dubbed the state's "welcome, stranger" policy. In the 1980s, there were endless stories about similar homes where the new owner of one was, on the basis of the new, inflated home price, paying three or four times as much in property tax as the owner next door who'd been there since 1978 or before. One of those new owners, Stephanie Nordlinger, sued, charging that she was being denied equal protection. She'd bought her home in Baldwin Hills in 1988 and was paying $1,700 a year, precisely 1 percent of the purchase price, while her neighbors in virtually identical homes were paying $300 to $400 and, of course, getting precisely the same services. In 2003, when he was listed as an economic advisor to gubernatorial candidate Arnold Schwarzenegger, billionaire investor Warren Buffett, launching a mistimed attack on Proposition 13 and its unfairness (Schwarzenegger, hardly wanting to touch the third rail of California politics, quickly told him to shut up), disclosed that, while he was paying about $14,000 a year in taxes on his Nebraska home, he was paying a meager $2,264 on his $4 million Laguna Beach home. That happened to be precisely what Nordlinger (whose taxes had increased by the modest two percent annually that the law allowed) was then paying on her modest house.[61]

Nordlinger ultimately lost in the U.S. Supreme Court, which acknowledged that the differences in taxes were "staggering" and agreed that owners of some Beverly Hills mansions were paying less than people in much more modest houses. Nonetheless, said Justice Harry Blackmun in the Court's eight-to-one decision upholding the law, the state was within its rights. It has "a legitimate interest in neighborhood preservation, continuity," and thus can structure its tax system to discourage rapid turnover; it can also "conclude that a new owner at the time of acquiring his property does not have the same . . . interest warranting protection against high taxes as does an existing owner" who's already there. "In short, the State may decide that it is worse to have owned and lost, than never to have owned at all."[62]

In his lone dissent, Justice John Paul Stevens, relying on a West Virginia case that had been decided on what appeared to be very similar issues just three years earlier, emphatically rejected all that. "Similarly situated neighbors have an equal right to share the benefits of local government," he said. Precisely as it would be unconstitutional to provide one neighbor better police or fire protection than the other, "it is just as plainly unconstitutional to require one to pay five times as much in property taxes as the other for the same governmental services."[63] A few years earlier, Macy's, which had been involved in a leveraged buyout—thus a transfer in legal ownership, which triggered a reassessment and higher property tax bills—had also sued, charging that Proposition 13 violated both the Commerce Clause of the U.S. Constitution and the Constitution's equal protection guarantees. Quite plainly, it was—and remains—a handicap to fair competition: the new store across the street from the old store would inevitably be paying higher taxes. But as the case moved toward the Supreme Court and started to generate attention, Macy's got so many threats of a consumer boycott, in part organized by the Howard Jarvis Taxpayers Association, in part by other groups, and so many shredded or cancelled credit cards, that it abandoned the suit. For the first time, said Joel Fox, who became the head of the Howard Jarvis Taxpayers Association on Jarvis's death in 1986, the system provided reliability for the taxpayer, not the tax collector.[64]

For a great many people who had bought those small homes in the 1950s and 1960s—for an average price of ten to fifteen thousand dollars—it was a lifesaver. In places like northwest Glendale and the Hollywood Hills, or in San Jose or Los Gatos or other Silicon Valley neighborhoods in the go-go 1990s—where investors had bought up many of those little twelve-hundred-square-foot houses (once derided in Malvina Reynolds's 1962 hit song as the "little boxes made of ticky-tacky") for four hundred thousand dollars, razed them, and replaced them with four-thousand-square-foot $1 million-plus McMansions—the remaining neighbors would long ago have been taxed out of their homes. Even people who'd vehemently opposed Proposition 13—retired teachers, social workers, nurses—recognized this.[65] At the same time, the system, by driving up prices and taxes on newly purchased homes, made it harder for new entrants into the market—most of them blacks, Latinos, Filipinos, and other limited-income new Californians—to buy decent housing at all. They certainly were paying far higher taxes on the same kind of homes than older (and thus generally whiter) residents.

The same dynamics also undercut the incentive to develop commercial properties for their highest and best uses. Under a conventional assessment system, as Lenny Goldberg, a lobbyist for labor and other liberal groups and then head of the California Tax Reform Association, pointed out, the lot next to the successful new business would be assessed on the basis of what the successful business indicated the lot was potentially worth. But with assessments frozen, there was no great incentive to convert inefficient commercial property into higher-value-producing land, no damper on speculation. And since local governments, their hands tied on most tax increases, had created a whole universe of fees, assessments, and exactions on new development, every new entrepreneur also bore extra burdens before he or she had produced the first widget. At the same time, the neighboring businesses, whose property values go up when the business next door succeeds, and which see the value of their businesses go up as a result, pay nothing for the windfall.

New investment is taxed; the attendant increase in land values is not. Additionally, Proposition 13 encouraged leasing, which also escaped reassessment, meaning that "rising incomes from the property are never captured." Proposition 13, Goldberg said, sent all the wrong signals. The result was large inequities, not only between residential properties, which had sustained a massively increased share of the property tax burden, and commercial property, but also among commercial parcels. In Los Angeles the share of the burden borne by single-family homes rose from 40 percent to 55 percent, while the share borne by commercial real estate declined from 47 percent to 33 percent.[66]

Perhaps the most important signal, however, was also the most subtle, and that was the replacement of the state's optimism and communitarian ethic with a market ethic that shifted an increasing share of the cost of public services from the community as a whole to those who, it was believed, were its most immediate beneficiaries. "If we can meter it," said John Decker, a longtime state fiscal analyst, "we'll charge for it."[67]

It was hard to quarrel with some of the new fees at the universities or with stiffer greens fees at municipal golf courses: Why should struggling taxpayers subsidize weekend duffers or future corporate lawyers? But what of admission fees for parks and playgrounds? What about schools? By transferring an increasing share of the cost of building the roads, schools, parks, and other facilities required by new housing developments—from the general community, which usually footed a large chunk of the bill, to the fees and other charges imposed on the developers and thus either directly or indirectly on the buyers of new homes—the system created sharp divisions and animosities. And since some of those fees, which represent significant boosts in the property tax bill, go to the cash-strapped general community (presumably to mitigate the impact of the newcomers), the possibility for resentment is virtually unbounded. "Nowhere," wrote planning expert William Fulton,

> is this atomization occurring more quickly than in the fast-growing Inland Empire [of Riverside and San Bernardino counties east of Los Angeles]. There, financially strapped school districts are obtaining new construction funds through growth taxes imposed on homeowners in "Mello-Roos" taxing districts. These homeowners are often led to believe that the Mello-Roos taxes, which can cause a homeowner's property tax bill to double, will allow the school district to build schools in their neighborhood. Instead, the money is thrown into a big pot devoted to expanding classroom capacity districtwide. The result is the Mello-Roos kids are frequently bused long distances to attend schools with kids who live in older tracts and don't pay Mello-Roos taxes. Enraged parents complain that their kids should not have to mingle with those who come from lower tax-

paying groups. . . . They paid their money. So where's their school?
This is not the kind of attitude that fosters community identification,
especially in a just-constructed tract.[68]

Conversely, if a new school is built in the new neighborhood, how
many kids can the district ship in from other parts of town before it vio-
lates (in the minds of the local residents) the implicit deal about who benefits? Who does the new park belong to, or the school? Meanwhile, the
new market ethos also led to a new practice by school districts seeking
the necessary two-thirds voter approval for local parcel taxes: exempting
all homes owned by anyone sixty-five or over from the obligation to
share in the burden. Those taxes were themselves regressive, since they
imposed the same burden on any home, hovel, or mansion, regardless of
value, but they were virtually the only taxes that could be imposed under
the restrictions of Proposition 13. In 2004, five of California's six local
parcel tax proposals included such exemptions.[69]

Predictably, the new market ethic also reinforced the boom in the use
of private neighborhood patrols, particularly in affluent places like Malibu, Piedmont, and Pacific Palisades (where lawn signs, like those of
Westec Security, warn about "Armed Response"), as well as the rapid
spread of gated communities, another contemporary phenomenon, some
with their own private security force, where the homeowners' association
serves as a "pseudo government." "Forting up" is hardly unique to California, but, according to Edward J. Blakely, former dean of the School of
Urban Planning and Development of the University of Southern California, the state, where more than a million people live in gated communities, has been a trendsetter.[70]

In a 1990 survey of home shoppers in Southern California, Blakely
said, "54 percent wanted a home in a gated, walled development; the
question had not even been asked a handful of years earlier." Some gated
developments are diverse; some are even composed of working-class
families trying to protect themselves against urban nuisances. But the in-

come required to buy into most virtually assures a high degree of segregation by economic status and, often, age. Some, like Canyon Lake, seventy-five miles southeast of Los Angeles—it has its own golf course, tennis courts, 380-acre lake, and equestrian center—have become incorporated walled cities, what Blakely calls "a typical suburb that happens to have a gate around it." In the gated East Bay community of Blackhawk, where the average price of a home was $1.4 million in 2004, residents "do not say they are loath to vote for a tax or bond issue that will benefit the county of which they are part, but all are quick to defend their right not to." The gate, said one resident, "gives you an option, and you don't have to feel guilty about it either way." Blakely called them "angry voters" who described themselves as "tired of the way government has managed the issues[,] . . . how the money is spent, and [the rate at which] the courts release criminals." Robert Reich, who was to become Bill Clinton's secretary of labor, called it "the secession of the successful."[71]

The market ethic also fueled the drive in many communities for a more direct form of secession. Particularly in places with shopping malls or other lucrative sales-tax payers, residents organized to either incorporate (meaning secede from the county) or secede from the cities to which they historically belonged and, of course, take the big tax generator with them. In the decade after the passage of Proposition 13, there was a wave of secession and incorporation drives, the loudest of them the extended (and so-far unsuccessful) campaign in the San Fernando Valley, an amorphous sprawl of post office addresses northwest of Los Angeles with little common identity, to break off from the City of Los Angeles. Despite some attendant levity about what it might be called—maybe Mini Van Nuys—it was deadly serious. It probably contributed to the defeat of Mayor Jim Hahn, who opposed secession, and continues to have a significant effect on Los Angeles politics. City hall, valley leaders complained, was too distant, both geographically and in its attention to their concerns.

But a lot of those efforts succeeded. In the 1970s, seventeen cities were incorporated in California. That figure doubled in the 1980s and promised to grow even faster, until the legislature enacted a law in the early 1990s requiring the departing entity to leave the parent more or less unharmed revenue-wise. Few of those new cities offered a full complement of services. Some contracted to get police services from the county sheriff and continued to get fire protection from a separate fire district, water from a municipal utility district or private water company, and school services (of course) from the local school district. Some of those districts were also subject to secession movements from some dissatisfied part of their own communities. What the new cities did have was planning and zoning authority, meaning the power to control traffic and development, to block the high-rise office buildings whose developers were often too cozy with the old downtown political establishment, and, wherever possible, to keep out both the poor and the low-income housing that brought them.

In the meantime, the fiscalization battles between cities, and between cities and counties over new shopping malls and auto malls, continued. Cities and redevelopment agencies, which became major weapons in the battle, granted every sort of subsidy to bring the new big-box store, the auto mall, and other lucrative sales-tax paying retailers within its jurisdiction. Where new residents were getting hit with taxes for the schools and streets they needed, cash-strapped local officials desperately looking for new revenues were providing the new malls with subsidized infrastructure, and sometimes freeway off-ramps, too, even as homeowners were paying hefty fees. In a few cases, the new developments even paid for lavish libraries and other community facilities that they might not have had otherwise. But it's of course a zero-sum game. Whatever one city or one county gains, another loses. As Fulton points out, another mall in Ventura doesn't mean more business for the state; it doesn't spur the growth of industry; it creates no net new jobs. It just means less for the city next door. "So while our mayor gets hammered for not doling out enough goodies to lure the retailers, the other two mayors get hammered for literally giving away the store."[72]

VI

While the Jarvis-Gann initiative has been the biggest single force in the erosion of California services and the corresponding dysfunctionalization of California government, it also spawned a string of other tax and spending limitations that compounded the impact. Among them: Gann's own Proposition 4, in 1979, which he called "the Spirit of 13," and which sharply restricted increases in state and local spending (and which Jarvis, in an unguarded moment before an open mike, called "shit"); initiatives allowing residential property owners to transfer their homes to their children or grandchildren without reassessment, thus creating a privileged class of people who could inherit legal entitlements and pass them on to their children; the abolition of state inheritance taxes and indexing of state income taxes; and the imposition of strict limitations on local fees and assessments.[73]

Collectively, they triggered further initiatives to remedy or correct the unanticipated effects of prior measures. When Governor Deukmejian, declaring that the state had hit its Proposition 4 "Gann spending limit" in 1987, refunded about $1 billion to the taxpayers, it was the schools, which always got the largest share of state appropriations, that were hit the hardest. In short order, Bill Honig, the independently elected state superintendent of public instruction, and the California Teachers Association qualified for the ballot what they regarded as a corrective measure, Proposition 98, to prevent that from ever happening again. Their initiative, narrowly approved by voters on the November 1988 ballot, required the state to spend at least 40 percent of its general fund on K–12 schools and to increase school funding each year by at least the cost of living and the growth in enrollment from the previous year's base. In emergencies, the legislature could temporarily suspend its requirements, but it would have to restore the lost funding in better times.

In the decade following its passage, governors were so fearful of raising the Proposition 98 base, however, and thus locking themselves into mandatory increases in succeeding years, that it served more as a spending ceiling than a floor. (It was not until the flush times in 2000–01 that a governor—Davis—added money to the base.) In 1987–88, the year before the passage of Proposition 98, according to education lobbyist John Mockler, one of the state's most knowledgeable school finance consultants (and, as the author of the initiative, one of the few who thoroughly understood it), the schools got $3,621 per year per child; a decade later, they got $3,476 in inflation-adjusted dollars. Not unexpectedly, Proposition 98 also generated widespread concern, if not anger, among competing claimants to state resources, the University of California in particular, that had no such protection.[74]

The passage of other ballot-box budgeting initiatives in the succeeding fifteen years imposed yet additional costs on the state: Proposition 70, a $795 million bond approved in 1988 for the acquisition, development, or restoration of a long and detailed list of parks, wildlife refuges, and other lands, and a $2 billion transportation bond in 1990 for an equally detailed list of projects, both sponsored by the California Planning and Conservation League. Each increased the pressure on unprotected programs, higher education in particular.

But easily the largest of the new voter-initiated costs was Proposition 184, California's uncompromising three-strikes sentencing law, passed in 1994 in the wake of the killing of teenager Polly Klaas by a recently paroled felon. Proposition 184, which was actually redundant since the legislature had already enacted the same bill, required judges to double an offender's normal sentence on conviction of a second felony and to impose a term of twenty-five years to life for any third felony, even if it was nonviolent. In combination with the hundreds of other laws passed in the tough-on-crime years of the 1980s and 1990s, it drove the state's prison population from below 25,000 at the end of the 1960s to 164,000 thirty-five years later, nearly doubling the percentage of the state budget spent on corrections from 4 percent to just under 8 percent (in 2004–05) and ballooning the rolls and benefits of the California Correctional Peace Officers Association. (In the same period, spending on higher education declined from 14 percent to 11.4 percent of the state's budget.)[75]

Collectively, the tough-on-crime bills also sparked the biggest boom in prison construction ever undertaken in this country or, probably, anywhere since the death of Stalin. Twenty new prisons opened between 1984 and 1997, joining the dozen older ones, and several more were on the way. The new ones, most of them designed for 2,000 to 3,000 prisoners, are now also seriously overcrowded, many operating at more than double their design capacity. Most are located in California's Central Valley, where the economy is most depressed, the land cheapest and most plentiful, and the local boosters happy to get a new slammer. From north to south—Susanville, Ione, Vacaville, Tracy, Chowchilla, Avenal, Corcoran, Coalinga, Wasco, Delano, Chino, Blythe, Calipatria—the interior of California is a prison archipelago. Kings County, an agricultural region near Fresno that prides itself on the variety of its products—it produces some of almost everything on your pizza, from the cheese to the tomatoes, or, if you prefer, the beef in your hamburger and the onions that go on it—also has another distinction that the local Chamber of Commerce won't tell you. It's the largest county in the nation in which more than 10 percent of the population is in prison. Of the county's 130,000 official "residents" in 2000, more than 13 percent—some 18,000—were in one of its three correctional facilities. Nearly all came from somewhere else.[76]

As it turned out, the promise of new prison-generated jobs for local people was often a chimera. In places like Delano, once the headquarters of the United Farm Workers, most of the jobs at North Kern State Prison went to outsiders. The screws don't want to live in dusty Delano: they prefer Bakersfield, thirty minutes down Highway 99, or even Visalia, an hour north. Their business goes elsewhere. Prisoners in fact do generate some indirect benefits: because of the quirks of the census, convicts are counted as residents of the counties where they're incarcerated—not where they came from—and thus increase county Medicaid, foster care, and other federal social service funding, though that's hardly something the Chamber of Commerce puts in its brochures. But as Carol Whiteside, the former (Republican) mayor of Modesto and now president of the Great Valley Center, a private regional planning and boot-strapping organization, pointed out, a big prison in a small town, rather than attracting modern enterprises bringing decent jobs, may actually drive them away. Prisons, especially scandal-plagued prisons, are an embarrassment. They're hardly a come-on for high-tech investors or the skilled workers those communities need. Prison or no prison, said a school board member, "Delano is a ghost town." Still, in 2005, after an extended political fight, the state was preparing to open Delano II.[77]

VII

There had been two waves of ballot measures in California before Proposition 13: one during the Progressive era immediately after the initiative, referendum, and recall were written into the constitution, another during the Depression. The most famous measure was Proposition 25 in 1938, the economically unfeasible and patently whacky "Ham and Eggs" proposal—it vaguely resembled the Townsend Plan—which would have required the state to pay every unemployed person over fifty years of age thirty dollars every Thursday. After disclosure that its principal sponsors were, if not "corrupt racketeers" as some of its opponents charged, at least not above some dubious ethical conduct, it was defeated, though not by much. The final tally showed that it lost by some 250,000 votes out of nearly 3 million cast, and some historians now credit it with "reviving the Democratic Party in California."[78]

Culbert Olson, who appeared on the same ballot, was narrowly elected governor, thereby becoming the first Democrat to win the office since 1894. (After he lost to Republican Earl Warren in 1942, not another Democrat would be elected until Pat Brown won in 1958.) In addition, two major ballot measures passed in the 1970s. One was the Coastal Zone Preservation Act (Proposition 20), on the 1972 ballot, which established the state's Coastal Commission and limited development in coastal areas. The other was the Political Reform Initiative (Proposition 9) in 1974, which got nearly 70 percent of the votes; it instituted specific rules for reporting campaign contributions and spending, created the state's Fair Political Practices Commission, and sought to curb lobbyist influence on California politicians.

But it was Proposition 13, more than any other event, that taught voters they could take matters into their own hands. It spurred the commercialization of the initiative process beyond anything that had preceded it—fattening the paid signature-gathering firms, pollsters, direct mail companies, lawyers, and media experts, soon known as "the initiative industrial complex"—and set in motion a rising tide of ballot measures that continues unabated. That tide has shifted the center of gravity of California's policy making from representative government—the legislature, governor, and elected local officials—to direct democracy, creating, in effect, a fourth branch of government.

The California Progressives had instituted the initiative, referendum, and recall in 1911 (along with a long list of other government reforms) as the people's weapon against big money and special-interest influence in government. The fight, Hiram Johnson had said in his gubernatorial election campaign in 1910, was "between the great moral masses [and] the corrupt but powerful few." If the people "have the right, the ability and the intelligence to elect, they have as well the right, ability and intelligence to reject or recall."[79]

But after 1978, the people's weapon turned into a highly organized multi-million-dollar enterprise funded by the same kinds of interest groups that Johnson had railed against: insurance companies, railroads, banks, auto manufacturers, car dealers, oil refiners, utilities, drug companies, Silicon Valley millionaires, realtors' associations, and trial lawyers, plus a few others—Indian casinos, labor unions, churches, and deep-pockets animal-rights activists like Doris Day—that Johnson probably never dreamed of. Indeed it was accessible to almost anyone with a couple million dollars. And, of course, it included the politicians themselves: Attorney General John Van De Camp, Lieutenant Governor Leo McCarthy, Governor Wilson, and, after he won in the recall, Schwarzenegger himself. By 1990, when the Southern Pacific Railroad, the "Octopus" of yore, kicked in a half million dollars to the campaign for Proposition 116, a $2 billion transportation bond initiative written by Gerald Meral, head of the California Planning and Conservation League, it was clear that the bad guys that the initiative process was supposed to check had become some of the biggest players in the game.

Environmentalism, dating back to the California Coastal Act, had always done fairly well on the California ballot. But beginning in the late 1990s, voters also passed a series of other liberal measures. Among them: Propositions 215 (1996) and 36 (2000) reforming the state's drug laws, both funded by three liberal deep-pockets: financier George Soros; John Sperling, founder of the for-profit University of Phoenix; and Cleveland insurance billionaire Peter Lewis. Proposition 215 gave patients who had a physician's recommendation the right to personal use of marijuana and to possession of a limited amount of the substance. Proposition 36 mandated treatment rather than prison terms for those convicted of possession, use, or transportation of heroin, cocaine, and other controlled substances for personal use. Proposition 215 passed with 55 percent of the vote, Proposition 36 with 61 percent.[80]

Like Proposition 13, the California drug reform initiatives were also at the front of a national wave. Since 1996, Soros and his partners have funded most of the successful medical marijuana initiatives in Alaska, Arizona, Colorado, Maine, Montana, Nevada, Oregon, and Washington, as well as successful lobbying efforts for legalizing needle exchanges, elimination of provisions making the police the beneficiaries of asset forfeiture, and requiring treatment rather than prison for drug offenses. Their real target was Congress, which so far has failed to budge on the issue. Yet even after a major adverse U.S. Supreme Court ruling that the Constitution's Commerce Clause gave Congress the power to regulate or ban even small quantities of marijuana grown for personal use, and that state medical marijuana laws were no protection against federal seizure or prosecution of medical marijuana users, medical marijuana laws continue to have a considerable impact in the states that have them.[81]

In 1996, the same year that California voters approved the medical marijuana law, they also voted (61–39) for a labor-funded initiative to increase the state's minimum wage. Two years later they approved Proposition 10, an initiative funded largely by actor Rob Reiner ("Meathead" on the old TV show *All in the Family*) raising the state's tobacco taxes to fund—at an additional $750 million a year—a range of state and local early childhood development programs. (Two years later they overwhelmingly rejected an initiative funded by tobacco interests to repeal Proposition 10.) The Reiner measure may also have helped spark Schwarzenegger's Proposition 49, designed to take $445 million out of the state's general fund to expand before- and after-school programs in any year when state revenues increased. Like many other pieces of ballot box budgeting, Proposition 49 promised the voters, who approved it with a 57 percent majority in November 2002, something nice for nothing. Schwarzenegger had long been involved in philanthropic activities, particularly in his work for the Special Olympics. But Proposition 49, run in collaboration with the California Teachers Association, burnished Schwarzenegger's image as a man concerned about children and helped set the stage, as it surely was intended, for some future venture into electoral politics. As it happened, the chance would come just eight months later.

The four ballot-box budgeting proposals that confronted voters in November 2004—all concerned with health care—were firmly in that tradition. Three of them passed: Proposition 63, the tax surcharge on millionaires for mental health programs; Proposition 61, authorizing a $750 million bond for children's hospital facilities; and Proposition 71, a $3 billion stem cell research bond. The fourth was Proposition 67, which would have raised some phone taxes to help bail out an emergency care system that was rapidly failing. In the decade after 1994, some sixty-four hospital emergency rooms had closed and there was every likelihood that more would close. But Proposition 67 was buried under an $8 million avalanche of negative advertising, nearly all from telephone companies, including $5 million from SBC alone. It lost by an overwhelming 72–28.[82] Californians, once again, seemed to be demonstrating that, when a nice thing was offered at what appeared to be no cost—or if the only obvious cost was borne by millionaires or smokers—they were happy to vote for it. If it was something they had to pay for, they weren't so sure.

Yet even if one discounts the string of tax cuts and spending limit measures set in motion by Proposition 13, the preponderant emphasis in the escalating twenty-five-year run of plebiscites that's dominated California politics since 1978 has been conservative and sometimes reactionary:

- California's strict term limits law in 1990, which not only limited assembly members to three two-year terms and state senators to two four-year terms—with a lifetime ban thereafter—but also sharply cut staffing in the legislature, thereby curtailing the ability of the highly respected Legislative Analyst's Office to analyze fiscal bills and budgets.

- Proposition 187 in 1994 seeking to deny illegal aliens and their children the right to public education and other social services, much of which was subsequently declared unconstitutional by a federal court, and Proposition 184, the three-strikes sentencing initiative discussed above, passed on the same ballot. Wilson had long complained, often correctly, that illegal immigration and the federal government's failure to control it was costing the state and local governments hundreds of millions of dollars, for which they got no federal reimbursement—complaints that were muted in the last years of the administration of the first President Bush and then became vociferous after Bill Clinton replaced him in the White House. Wilson used immigration as he used the three-strikes initiative: it was a wedge issue seeking to divide blue-collar Democrats from ethnic minorities, in the one case, and a telling political point, in the other, to prove that Kathleen Brown, his opponent in his 1994 reelection campaign, was soft on crime. Like her father, former governor Pat Brown, and her brother, former governor Jerry Brown, she opposed capital punishment and was thus automatically suspect on the crime issue.

Kathleen Brown, who had led by large margins in the polls six months before the election, tried hard to contend that, notwithstanding her personal views on the death penalty, she would enforce the laws as written.[83] But in the face of Wilson's uncompromising anticrime stand and the anti-immigrant theme—including those TV commercials showing shadowy figures running across a freeway and the announcer's ominous refrain, "They keep coming"—her lead evaporated. Wilson beat her by a hefty 14 points. The charge that Proposition 187 was racist or anti-immigrant, Wilson later said, "was a bum rap." He insisted that it was the people who lumped illegal and legal immigrants together (meaning those on the left) who were the real racists. In its attempt to get the feds to do something about illegal immigration, Proposition 187 was "the loudest protest against the central government since the Boston Tea Party."[84] But it was a perfect illustration of how a political candidate could ride the initiative process to electoral victory.

• In November of 2004, voters came within a hair of passing a ballot measure amending the three-strikes law to require that, in order to sentence a multiple offender to twenty-five years to life, the third felony had to be a violent crime, not a burglary or conviction for shoplifting, as sometimes happened under the law they passed a decade before. The initiative, funded largely by the parent of a man who had been sentenced for a nonviolent third strike, had been ahead in the polls until the final days of the campaign. But then Schwarzenegger jumped into the No campaign, and Pete Wilson raised a sizeable last-minute contribution for it, largely to pay for ads warning that, if the revision passed, thousands of violent felons would be released, and the measure went down.

• UC regent Ward Connerly's Proposition 209 (1996), also backed by Wilson and funded by the Republican Party, which, echoing the decision of the University of California regents the year before, outlawed race and gender preferences in public education, hiring, and contracting. Wilson, hoping to run in the GOP presidential primaries, tried to use both immigration and affirmative action in his campaign. (Wilson even went to the Statue of Liberty to declare that he was not opposed to legal immigration, just illegal immigration.) The Connerly measure, the California Civil Rights Initiative, had first been conceived as an ordinary statute by two California academics, Glynn Custred, a sociology professor at Hayward State University, and Thomas Wood, chair of the traditionalist California Association of Scholars, who had become exasperated by what they regarded as blatant favoritism for blacks and Latinos at the University of California. It was, not surprisingly, flatly rejected by the legislature, and then it lingered for lack of funding until Connerly persuaded Wilson to back it.

• Proposition 227, sponsored by Silicon Valley millionaire Ron Unz in 1998, which sharply curbed bilingual education in the state's schools. It probably did much less to raise the academic achievement of children who came to school speaking only limited English than Unz later claimed. To the extent that academic improvement was achieved among those children, it was probably due primarily to more stringent state and federal testing requirements and accountability programs that pegged school success to achievement by all major ethnic and economic subgroups. But while it didn't end battles over the divisive issue, it did give immigrant parents the power to reject the dead-end bilingual programs into which many schools had segregated them.

• Proposition 22, the Limit on Marriage Initiative passed in March 2000, declaring that only a marriage between a man and woman is recognized in California. The measure, sponsored by a conservative state senator named Pete Knight, was funded by an $8 million war chest assembled by Catholic, Mormon, and various fundamentalist church groups, among them the Helping Hands Ministries of Tallulah Falls, Georgia, which gave four hundred thousand dollars; the U.S. Catholic Conference, which gave fifty thousand dollars; and more than eight hundred individuals who contributed a thousand dollars or more. The effort also received some nine thousand smaller donations, many of them generated by an official letter from Mormon leaders, who described the measure as "inspired and coming from the Lord" and urged church members "to do all you can by donating your means and time to assure a successful vote."[85] It passed by a 61 percent majority. The day after the election, Gordon Hinckley, president of the Mormon Church, acknowledged that, while the church didn't engage directly in politics, "we do become involved if there is a moral issue or something that comes on the legislative calendar which directly affects the church. We tell our people who are citizens of this land and other lands that they as individuals have a civic responsibility to exercise the franchise that is theirs, so they become very active. . . . We were actively involved there. We were part of a coalition that very actively worked on that matter. We are not anti-gay. We are pro-family."[86]

Four years later, in November 2004, voters in eleven states approved similar bans on gay marriage, prompted in considerable part by decisions of the Massachusetts Supreme Judicial Court legalizing gay marriage and by San Francisco Mayor Gavin Newsom's widely publicized gay marriage ceremonies at city hall. Some four thousand couples were married in San Francisco before the California Supreme Court stopped the weddings and invalidated them as a violation of Proposition 22.

In the postmortem analysis of the "family values" vote component in Senator John Kerry's defeat in the 2004 presidential election, Senator

Dianne Feinstein, among many others, declared that Newsom was at least in part responsible. It was, she said, "too much, too fast, too soon."[87] In Ohio, which turned out to be the crucial state, and where gay marriage was on the ballot, and where a million more voters turned out than in 2000 and 750,000 more than in the state's previous record year, Kerry lost by 135,000 votes. The "values" factor in the election, discredited by later surveys, nonetheless became a prime part of the argument, echoing Fred Barnes at the *Weekly Standard* and "Lexington" at *The Economist*, who said that California was hopelessly out of touch and to the left of the nation. What almost no one recalled was that California's ban on gay marriage had been passed by 61 percent of the voters four years before most of the red states ever thought about it.

Contemporary defenders of the initiative have always contended that, while money certainly plays a role, it's rarely decisive. Daniel Lowenstein, who was the first chair of California's Fair Political Practices Commission, later made a strong case that, although money could beat a ballot measure, it was rarely enough to carry one. As long as opponents could create enough confusion and uncertainty, the electorate would vote no.[88] It took a lot of money to get a measure on the ballot—without paid petition circulators, gathering a half million or more valid signatures in the 150 days the law permitted was nearly impossible—and a hefty budget almost always guaranteed success in qualifying a measure. But money alone wasn't enough to pass it.

Yet even the acknowledged fact that it now took big money to get a measure on the ballot—and that almost anyone with enough money could succeed in qualifying almost any initiative—ran counter to the original intention of the initiative, which was supposed to have two major hurdles: qualifying a proposal and then passing it. But money had long rendered the first hurdle negligible for monied interests. It's only "the people" for whom it remains not simply a barrier but a nearly insurmountable one.[89]

Even the part of the argument about the limited power of money to *pass* an initiative is increasingly dubious. In 1998, Indian gaming interests spent $65 million on a ballot measure, Proposition 5, vastly expanding the scope of gambling—slot machines, banked card games, lotteries—in Indian casinos. Opponents, chiefly Nevada gambling interests, spent $25 million to beat it. After an intensive campaign that relied heavily on TV images and mailers appealing to voters' consciences about past treatment of the Indians—a hugely expensive campaign designed to prove that its well-heeled sponsors were poor Indians—the measure passed with 62 percent of the vote. It would be hard to describe this fight as anything but a battle between large economic interests.

Tellingly, moreover, the whole issue of Indian casinos might never have arisen had Kimball Petition Management, a firm of signature collectors and initiative consultants, not test-marketed the measure that created the California lottery, then persuaded the wonderfully named Scientific Games, a manufacturer of lottery tickets in Atlanta, to pony up virtually all of the $2.3 million necessary to qualify it and fund the 1984 campaign—a campaign based in large part on how much money the schools would get out of it.[90] (The schools' share of lottery proceeds—roughly one-third of all ticket sales revenues—now amounts to less than 2 percent of total school funding.) Because federal law requires any state with legal gambling to permit the same games on reservations, it was the lottery and its subsequent expansion to casino-like games that opened the door to Indian casinos.

Increasingly, big money—with its power to dominate television and the mailings (and in the face of virtually no TV news coverage)—tends to beat little money regardless of which side it's on. In 2000, the Silicon Valley venture capitalists and other proponents of Proposition 39, which lowered the margin required to pass local school bonds from 67 percent to 55 percent, outspent their opponents at the enfeebled Howard Jarvis Taxpayers Association by roughly nine to one—$27 million to $3 million. By almost any gauge, the initiative, which passed with 53 percent of the votes, made the bond-approval process more democratic and rational. But the campaign to pass it, with its overwhelming money advantage, also seemed to persuade voters, as it was clearly meant to do, that Proposition 39 was really about assuring more fiscal accountability in the disbursement of bond funds, not about making it easier to approve bonds. Nobody except the taxpayer groups complained, because, in the view of most of the state's leadership, the good guys won.

More recently, in 2004, corporate and business groups put some $14 million into passing Proposition 64 ("to stop shakedown lawsuits"), an initiative designed to limit the right of individuals to sue businesses for unfair competitive practices and for violations of environmental, public health, and consumer protection laws. The lawsuits, they said, were costing California jobs and mostly enriching lawyers. Opponents, mostly lawyers, raised $2 million in their losing effort to beat it. In the same election, the state Chamber of Commerce, fast food restaurant chains, and retailers like Wal-Mart put some $12 million into a ballot measure, Proposition 72, to overturn the law passed and signed by Gray Davis a year earlier that would have required employers of fifty people or more to provide some health insurance or pay into a state fund that would offer it. (Because it was a referendum, a no vote against the health coverage law was, in effect, a yes vote for the Chamber of Commerce and the other sponsors of the measure.) The measure was voted down by a narrow 49 to 51 vote, meaning that, as with Proposition 64, its well-funded business sponsors won.

VIII

Since the late 1990s, the escalating number of initiatives and referenda on state and local ballots has sparked an accumulation of reports and studies about direct democracy and an increasingly intense debate about the initiative process among politicians, journalists, and academics. There are institutes devoted to the accumulation of data on "I and R," and almost constant symposia, journal articles, university courses, and books.[91]

Is it the failure, the unresponsiveness, maybe even the corruption, of the legislatures that's prompted the wave of ballot measures not only in California but also in the two dozen other states, most of them in the West, that have the initiative option in their constitutions? If these things are to blame, what is it about the legislatures in almost every initiative state that's made them unreliable or distrusted enough to require the wave of term limits initiatives (as well other reforms) that has swept the nation since the early 1990s? Or does the cause lie somewhere else— in the broader decline of trust in government and other establishment institutions? Or is the cause, more broadly, as *Washington Post* columnist David Broder believes, the widening gap between the E-pace of a society accustomed to click-of-a-mouse responsiveness and the inherently slow and deliberative processes of traditional government?[92]

And, most important, is the initiative a healthy process for America— even one at the national level, as people like former U.S. senator Mike Gravel have proposed (through a campaign called Philadelphia II, which says that citizens can simply empower themselves without a constitutional amendment)—or is it sinking rational policy-making and accountable government in a swamp of hyperdemocracy?[93] When voters face a dozen state ballot measures, plus maybe a dozen local ones, as they sometimes do in California—plus votes for the U.S. Senate, a representative in the House, governor, lieutenant governor, attorney general, treasurer, controller, secretary of state, insurance commissioner, state senator, assembly member, county supervisor, city council, school board, community college board, municipal utility district board, regional transportation district board, a few judgeships, plus perhaps three or four others depending on date and locality, can they really make informed choices on even a fraction of them, no matter how diligent they are?

If there is any original sin in this story, it's California's constitutional requirement, cited earlier, that budgets and other fiscal bills be approved by a two-thirds majority in each house. That provision, added to the constitution as part of a Depression-era deal creating a sales tax in 1933, makes California one of just three states—the others are Arkansas and Rhode Island—to require a supermajority this large.[94] Proposition 13 had also enacted a two-thirds requirement for the legislature to increase any taxes. But taxes can be lowered by a simple majority, which, over the years, has created a sort of ratchet effect.

In the spring of 2004, a group of public employee and other labor unions, backed by the League of Women Voters, the state Parent-Teacher Associations and other organizations, tried to secure the passage of an initiative, Proposition 56, which would have lowered the margin needed to pass a budget in the legislature or to raise taxes, to 55 percent, the same out-of-the-hat number that the voters had previously okayed for the passage of local school bonds. The backers spent about $13 million, the opponents $8 million, much of it from the tobacco, liquor, and oil companies, presumably among the likeliest targets of any tax hike, but the proposal was overwhelmed by a margin of nearly two to one. The voters simply didn't trust the legislature with their money. Some of the supporters of the initiative later came to believe that if they'd limited the initiative just to lowering the vote margin on budgets, without the taxing provision, it might have had a chance.

Defenders of the system contend that it's an effective way of keeping profligate legislatures from running up the bills, though it's equally true that political minorities—Republicans for most of the past generation—have used their veto to impose their will on the majority, as they often did in their successful strategy during the 1980s to prohibit Medi-Cal funding for abortions. From 1978 until 1989, when the state supreme court finally pounded the last gavel in these cases, state trial and appellate courts regularly struck those bans down as violations of the state constitution's privacy protections, which are tighter than those under the U.S. Constitution.[95] But until recently, individual members still leveraged their votes to extort pork projects for their districts, thereby increasing rather than constraining spending. "Rather than holding down spending," said a Citizens Budget Commission created by the nonpartisan Center on Governmental Studies, "the two-thirds vote requirement places the power to control or block the budget into the hands of a small minority in either house of the legislature, thereby promoting gridlock and enhancing special interest group influence."[96]

What's certain is that the two-thirds requirement has repeatedly delayed budgets and further clouded accountability. When one party has majorities in the legislature and state house, they and the governor usually get blamed for the delay and the resulting hardships to state workers and contractors who don't get paid, even if it's the other party that throws up the roadblocks. It's also certain that, while state taxes would almost certainly have been higher—though perhaps also fairer—the two-thirds requirement contributed mightily to the budget crises, rolling deficits, and general fiscal irresponsibility that chronically plague California.

Still, the debate over what, or who, started the orgy of initiatives may, more than anything else, be a chicken-and-egg dispute. By definition, each ballot measure either mandates some policy, some budget expenditure, or some new set of laws, or it prohibits something. Thus each measure restricts the powers and choices of elected government, state and local, to respond to future (and often unexpected) situations, which in turn makes elected leaders less able—and often less willing—to respond. Is political inertia, in fact, a lack of responsiveness or—in this age of overnight polls and focus groups—is it the product of excessive fear of voter revolts? In tying their hands and in shifting the power to control and allocate what had previously been local revenues to the state, as it does in California, the initiative process also confounds the ability of voters to understand how government works. Almost inevitably, the fog, complexity, and confusion of the resulting "system" also make it far easier for special interest lobbies, which have the requisite expertise and money—corporations, business associations, unions, lawyers—to exercise their influence in the legislature and governor's office.

The almost inevitable result of the constraints on elected government is more government dysfunction and voter frustration and yet more calls for ballot-box remedies, which in turn start a new cycle: the spending restrictions of Proposition 4 (1979), described above, producing Proposition 98 (1988), mandating a minimum allocation of state general funds

to schools and community colleges, which in tough times led the legislature to grab some of the property tax that had gone to cities and counties to meet its Proposition 98 obligation (most of which was never restored, even when the economy improved), which led directly to the
ballot measure Proposition 1A (2004) to keep the state from snatching
any additional money from the locals. "We're one recession away from
catastrophe," said David Janssen, the chief executive of Los Angeles
County. "This is the world's sixth-largest economy. How can we have a
political structure that's so dysfunctional?"[97]

The legislators' budget problems are further compounded by the
string of big-dollar initiatives—the tough-on-crime laws mandating long
prison terms, the park bonds, the unfunded preschool programs like
Schwarzenegger's Proposition 49. As with the bonds for stem cell research or children's hospitals, many are driven by appealing causes, perhaps even inspired ideas. By their very nature, however, they're ad hoc
decisions, with little regard for their long-term impact on budgets and
other, equally desirable programs. The stem cell and children's hospital
bonds passed in 2004 alone add $7.5 billion to the state's long-term debt.
Is it better to fund stem cell research or provide health insurance to more
children or restore counselors and enrichment programs to elementary
schools? What the initiatives like the measure raising the surtax on millionaires for mental health programs, probably a worthier and more appropriate program for the state than stem cell research, confirmed was
that even people on the left were giving up on conventional governmental processes and committing themselves to the sort of ad hoc programs
that would almost certainly shrink the state's ability to support the other
social programs they deeply cared about. That was all true, said Darrell
Steinberg, the liberal assembly member and budget committee chairman, who was the chief sponsor of the mental health initiative. But mental health had been starved ever since Ronald Reagan had started shutting down the state's mental hospitals in the early 1970s without
providing the funding for community mental health programs that he
promised would replace them. What choice was there?[98]

The conventional legislative process, for all the logrolling that sometimes accompanies it, is usually subject to a whole range of institutional checks that the initiative is not—committee hearings, expert witnesses, public debate, two-house agreement, executive veto, as well as the intrinsic legislative impulse to compromise and accommodate as many sides and interests as possible. None of that occurs in direct legislation, which is a winner-take-all process that, by its very nature, is rarely respectful of political minorities. Draft initiatives are often tested in focus groups or in private polls, but the final text is subject only to what its sponsors believe can achieve the support of the majority that votes on it. Beyond that, sponsors seek to maximize their causes. And, almost by definition, minorities, other than those with huge bankrolls, don't get to play at all.

Compounding the effects of the majoritarianism of the California system is the process itself. California is one of some two dozen states that have some form of the initiative, most but not all in the West and most written into state constitutions during the Progressive era between 1890 and 1920. But uniquely among them, it is the only state that does not permit some form of legislative repeal or amendment of statutory initiatives, either directly after passage or after a specified period of years. Thus unless the measure itself contains a sunset clause or provides for its own amendment by the legislature, anything enacted by initiative can be changed or eliminated only by another vote of the people. It's set in stone.[99] Even when a measure is sloppily drafted or produces unintended consequences, as many do, the system doesn't allow any legislative review or any other amendment unless someone ponies up the money to put it on the ballot again.

For their part, voters must rely largely on ballot arguments, the wording of the measure itself, occasional endorsements by public figures or groups, and thirty-second TV commercials. Scholars like Arthur Lupia, now a professor of political science at the University of Michigan, argue that voters get clear enough signals when they know who backs and who opposes a measure, and that, as others have argued, they rarely regret the votes they've cast. But they nonetheless do it on far less information and with far less regard for long-range and side effects.[100] They have no technical experts at their disposal, rarely have the time to read the fine print of the measure—which sometimes runs to many thousands of words of legal language—that lies behind the advertising slogans for and against particular measures. In 1988, five dueling ballot measures designed to deal with an auto insurance crisis, some sponsored by insurance companies, some by trial lawyers, one by consumer groups, filled more than two hundred pages of fine print in the ballot pamphlet, much of it referencing highly technical provisions in the state's insurance code. Altogether, the deep-pockets combatants spent some $100 million in that campaign, roughly the same amount that George H. W. Bush spent that same year in his presidential campaign.[101]

Nor, of course, do voters have to record their votes, as politicians do, much less confront those who believe they've been damaged by those votes. Moreover, voters can't be run out of office if they make serious errors, are not accountable to their fellow citizens for the consequences and required to consider the trade-offs or to be attentive to minority rights or the public weal. There have been waves of complaints that the courts meddle in initiative issues too much, particularly in their occasional decisions striking down measures that they deem to be in violation of the constitution's provision that all initiatives be limited to a single subject. But the lack of any institutional mechanism requiring real deliberation or study in the initiative process has led some scholars—the late Julian Eule of UCLA Law School most prominent among them—to argue that, in the absence of other checks, the courts should apply *stricter* scrutiny in reviewing the constitutionality of initiatives than they do to conventional legislation.[102] In the initiative process, the majority rules absolutely.

IX

With the possible exception of tax limits, however, the greatest constraint voters imposed on representative government was term limits, approved in California in 1990. The state's term limits law, Proposition 140, was one of more than twenty enacted in the various states in the early 1990s, but in restricting assembly members to six years, and state senators to eight, in a lifetime, and in cutting legislative staff, it was not only one of the strictest term limits laws in the nation but also a rollback of the modern, professionalized legislature that Speaker Jesse Unruh had hoped to create a generation before. The measure was passed with ballot promises that it would run off career politicians and again create a citizen legislature of dedicated public servants who would spend a few years in Sacramento and then return to the plow or maybe the country lawyer's office. (A decade and a half later, there were still grumpy voters who said that, whatever the drawbacks, just getting rid of Willie Brown, the black and unabashedly powerful longtime Speaker of the assembly, made term limits worthwhile.) It would also, said the sponsors in their ballot argument, "remove the grip that vested interests have over the legislature [and] end the Sacramento web of special favors and patronage."

Inevitably, the term limits law hastened turnover in the legislature, ending the careers of people like Ralph Dills—he had been in politics since 1934, when he was a member of Upton Sinclair's EPIC (End Poverty In California) campaign, and in public office since 1938, both as legislator and municipal court judge—and closing down what one critic called "the geriatric ward of California."[103] (Dills was termed out in 1998 at the age of eighty-eight, sixty years after he was first elected.) The law brought new faces, greatly increasing the proportion of women and Latinos, but it did not end careerism, much less dismantle the "web of special favors and patronage" that its backers promised. If anything, by making politicians even more anxious about their postlegislative careers, it might have enlarged that web. Many of the new members had come from local offices—they'd been city council members or county supervisors—but they showed no more interest in returning to private life once their terms expired than their predecessors had. On the contrary, after one term, and sometimes less, many were already casting around for the next opening— a seat in the state senate for assembly members, a seat in Congress, a run for some higher state office, a job on a state commission, or even a move to the assembly for senators who were not termed out in the lower house.

Some members just switched seats, among them Republican Bill Leonard of San Bernardino County, one of the original "Proposition 13 babies," conservatives who'd been swept into office on the tide of the tax revolt. Leonard served in the assembly (before term limits) from 1978 to 1988. He was then elected to the state senate, where he served until he was termed out in 1996. He was then elected to the assembly seat vacated by the termed-out Jim Brulte of Rancho Cucamonga, who, in turn, ran for and won Leonard's senate seat. Brulte eventually became the very effective leader of the GOP caucus in the senate, a post he held until he was finally termed out at the end of 2004. (After Leonard was termed out in the assembly in 2004, he was elected to the State Board of Equalization, where he won't be termed out until 2012.) In effect the state capitol became a kind of plush Greyhound bus terminal, where some people were just arriving, some were just getting ready to leave, but no one stayed around very long. The assembly, said Bruce Cain, director of the Institute of Governmental Studies at Berkeley, "has become the training wheels for the Senate."[104]

Even with all the seat switching, term limits have taken their toll on experience, institutional memory, loyalty, long-term perspectives, and the incentive to compromise. In the term limits era, freshmen (almost necessarily) become committee chairs and second-termers become Speaker of the Assembly or Senate President Pro Tem. In 2004 Fabian Nunez became Speaker as a freshman. Because Nunez came from a safely Democratic Los Angeles district, the only contested election he ever won was the Democratic primary, in which fewer than 20,000 people voted: on that basis, Nunez, a former labor organizer and school district lobbyist who looks even younger than his thirty-seven years, became a major legislative leader in a state of 35 million people. The Democrats' hope was that he would be able to serve in the post for four years, rather than the two that most of his Proposition 140–era predecessors had been allowed. He might thus have a chance to gain some experience in the job and, they hoped, bring some continuity before his term ended.

Some of the legislature's lack of experience might have been eased by the presence of experienced staff, but that too was undermined by the provision in the term limits initiative mandating a 40 percent cut in legislative personnel, presumably in the hope that it would comb out a lot of the capitol's political hacks. But it was mostly the hacks who stayed—they were crucial to the political careers of the members. It was the policy staff, the fiscal experts, the people who knew the complexities of school finance or riparian rights or insurance law who were cut or, in some cases, moved to other agencies where they didn't fall under the staffing limits. The nonpartisan and very crucial Legislative Analyst's Office lost half its staff after Proposition 140 passed, which meant it could no longer send its fiscal experts to important legislative hearings and markups of bills; staffing for the Senate Office of Research was cut by 33 percent. More pervasively, the turnover of legislators also produced a greater turnover of members' staffs, senior people left, and the overall capacity and competence of the professionals went down.

The most systematic study of the effects of term limits, published by PPIC, the Public Policy Institute of California, in 2004, found "that instead of cutting the size of personal staffs, which often provide partisan political advice for members, the Legislature subverted the will of Proposition 140's backers by eliminating many nonpartisan aides. Along with many voluntary retirements, this outcome led to an immense loss in policy expertise."[105] The authors of the PPIC study, Bruce Cain and Thad Kousser, may have been generous about the "will" of Proposition 140's backers—it's not clear the backers' intent was ever so surgical—but the conclusion was nonetheless correct. With the passage of Proposition 140, as well as successive attempts to reform campaign finance, the legislature has become ever more like one of those primitive animals with small brains and oversized reproductive organs.

The PPIC report also confirmed other things that legislative veterans had complained about: the draining effect of term limits on the legislature's powers against the executive branch and the oversight it exercises over it; the erosion of fiscal accountability because of the lack of effective gatekeeping by committees; the legislature's growing reliance on lobbyists and special interest groups for information, something that was hardly unknown before but has increased significantly; the growing focus of members on specific projects and their indifference to overall budget issues and long-term consequences that they know they won't have to deal with or be accountable for.

"The governor," said the report, "has gained power over the Legislature in budget negotiations[,] and . . . legislative oversight of executive agencies has declined." The study couldn't ascribe the legislature's increasing partisanship to term limits. A number of veteran politicians, among them former Republican assemblyman Bill Bagley and the very conservative and notoriously unflamboyant former governor (and legislator) George Deukmejian, also blamed the decline in moderation and collegiality on the political reform initiative of 1974 that banned the convivial bipartisan dinners, poker parties, and, on occasion, the other entertainment that lobbyists used to provide in Sacramento's downtown watering spots and in their suites at the old Senator Hotel across L Street from the capitol. ("If you can't eat their food, drink their booze, screw their women and then vote against them," former Speaker Unruh famously declared, "then you don't belong here.") As Bagley would say, you could disagree on policy, but you could hardly launch personal attacks on people you'd been playing cards with the night before.[106]

The short tenure of members certainly made it harder to make long-range deals with people who probably wouldn't be there when it came time to ask for the return favor. Overall, the PPIC study warned, "term limits may usher in a new era of executive dominance in California politics."[107] In 2004, Governor Schwarzenegger liked to accuse the legislature of fiddling with trivial bills, something every legislature does, but as its perspective and discretion were increasingly constrained, both the opportunities and the incentives for foresight and long-term planning—much less any broad, visionary departures—were constrained with them.

The state's misbegotten and ultimately disastrous electricity deregulation scheme, passed in 1996 with hardly any debate by legislators who had virtually no idea what was in it, said Senator Debra Bowen, was "an advertisement for why term limits were a bad idea."[108]

At the end of 2004, the fourteen-year clock that began ticking with the term limits initiative in 1990 ran out on the last of the old veterans. Among them: John Vasconcellos, the kvetchy New Age champion of "authenticity" in politics and sponsor of several much-lampooned self-esteem bills (one of which was signed by Deukmejian, California's most conservative governor since World War II), but also an inveterate battler for higher education and a shrewd master of the budget process, who had been in the legislature since 1966. Another was Republican Jim Brulte, who started his political career as a member of the staff of Senator "Sleepy" Sam Hayakawa, then worked his way through various political jobs until he was elected to the assembly in 1990, and, in 1996, to the senate, where he managed to be conservative and pragmatic at the same time. A third was the irascible John Burton, who had served in the assembly for a decade, then six terms in Congress, before returning to the legislature for another sixteen years, where he became a passionate defender of the poor and the sick—maybe the last who did it with such devotion and persistence. At the end, Vasconcellos observed that he arrived in Sacramento under Reagan and retired under Schwarzenegger—"actor to actor, dust to dust."[109] A great many other people of skill and deep experience, men and women of both parties, had been driven out by term limits before them. But as the last, they were the symbols of an era of legislative possibility that might never come again.

One doesn't have to look far to understand why the polls all show that voters have more confidence in the initiative than they do in the conventional institutions of representative government, state or local. It's instantaneous, requires less attention, provides at least the illusion of control, and, perhaps most of all, trumps a legislature that represents people rather than voters. California's legislative districts are the largest in the nation—each state senator represents some 900,000 people, more than each member of Congress. Each assembly member has 450,000 people in his or her district, far too many to allow any real acquaintance between representative and constituents, particularly in huge cities like Los Angeles, San Diego, or San Jose, where the media, TV particularly, scarcely attend to the local representatives except in days of scandal. "The districts are too large," said Robert Hertzberg, a former Speaker of the assembly, "and the media are completely irrelevant."[110]

As required by the constitution, districts are divided by population, not by the number of people who actually vote. Thus districts with large numbers of immigrants, minorities, or low-income residents have far fewer voters than white, affluent districts, which in turn means that the legislature disproportionately represents low-income minority voters who tend, on the whole, to be heavily Democratic and liberal. And since economic and social stratification, reinforced by legislative gerrymanders, have produced electoral districts that are either safely Republican or Democratic, elections are won in party primaries, which are largely dominated not by independent voters or moderates but by the faithful. That's increasingly led to the election of Democrats who are to the left of their districts, and of the state, and of Republicans who are to the right—which of course is one of the reasons compromise and moderation is in increasingly short supply both in Sacramento and elsewhere, including Washington.

California, as demonstrated by recent elections, has tended to be Democratic—Bill Clinton carried the state twice, Al Gore carried it in 2000, and John Kerry in 2004, in the latter case with a margin of about 11 percent. But probably none of those votes were for a candidate whose politics were as far off center as the politics of many members of his party in the legislature—just as the vote for the socially moderate Schwarzenegger in the 2003 recall was far closer to the center than the positions of his fellow Republicans in California's legislative and congressional seats. Thus the initiative, which voters use to trump the legislature—to pass conservative crime bills or tighter welfare restrictions or prohibitions on affirmative action over a body of representatives that routinely killed them.[111]

The obvious response is that, if the legislature represented the voters' will more faithfully, no ballot measures would be necessary. But it doesn't take a long disquisition in political philosophy to understand that each member may reflect the *population* of his district quite accurately. California's voters are still overwhelmingly white, and older, and more affluent than the general population. They have relatively few school-age children, making them less prone to support services they no longer feel they need—which, of course, is the main reason they're often exempted from the obligation to pay school parcel taxes. The general population, and particularly those with school-age children, is increasingly Hispanic or Asian, younger, and less affluent, but because they're poorer and often not citizens, they vote in much smaller numbers.

Collectively, those "minorities" are now a majority of California's population: they are the new California. Which is to say that there is a huge gap between those who disproportionately depend on schools and other public services—people who on average are poorer and browner—and those who vote on statewide issues. The initiative process and the long string of supermajority votes required to raise taxes that have been written into California law, often by way of that same initiative process, appear to be the prime elements used by likely voters in their efforts to protect themselves against that majority of minorities. Indeed, is California's dysfunctional political system itself—the fact that it doesn't work well, and often not at all—a not-unwelcome instrument, however unintended, of the status quo and the effort to hold the new California at bay? With every passing day that system appears ever more detached from, and unresponsive to, the state's economy, population, and global relationships.

3

ACTION HERO

If Ted Costa were a character in a play, he'd be referred to as Fifth Business, a minor element in the drama, but the one who's essential in getting the action started.[1] The drama in this case, of course, was the recall of California governor Gray Davis in 2003 and the election of actor-bodybuilder Arnold Schwarzenegger to replace him. Costa, though never a household name, was the man who launched it.

The sixty-two-year-old Costa, who ran a political organization called People's Advocate from a modest office in a suburban Sacramento strip mall, was a longtime political activist and tax-fighter who had worked for the late Paul Gann, the coauthor, with Howard Jarvis, of California's Proposition 13. Gann was also the author of Proposition 4, the Gann spending limit, passed the following year, which sought to cap the growth in state and local expenditures. Costa wasn't around in the late 1970s, when those initiatives were passed, but in working for Gann in the 1980s, and, after an ugly set of legal battles following Gann's death, in taking over his organization, he wears the antitax populist mantle as well as anyone. His organization helped take twelve voter initiatives to the California ballot. Although generally soft-spoken and personally unassuming—he lived with his wife, a veterinarian, on a suburban spread with a donkey, a peacock, doves, pheasants, and chickens—he was also, in the words of a Sacramento political consultant, "California's pre-eminent shit kicker."[2]

In 1990, Costa launched a short-lived attempt to privatize Sacramento's publicly owned electric utility. In 1992, he ran an initiative to impose term limits on California's congressional delegation, which the voters passed but which the U.S. Supreme Court declared unconstitutional. In 1999, he launched a ballot measure combining a change in the state's reapportionment system with cuts in legislative pay. That proposal pleased the state's congressional Republicans, who wanted the process to be run by someone other than the Democratic governor and legislature who then controlled Sacramento, but it angered Republicans in the legislature who didn't like the prospect of having their pay reduced. Fortunately for the latter, the state supreme court kicked that measure off the ballot as a violation of the state constitution's single-subject rule before the intraparty bloodletting could really begin.[3] Costa, who sat on the board of a suburban water district, had also run for county supervisor, for the state assembly, and for the State Board of Equalization, an elected tax board, and lost each time. As much as anyone, he was the direct link to the antigovernment revolt that erupted in California in 1978 and that crested with the recall of Governor Gray Davis and the election of actor Arnold Schwarzenegger just twenty-five years later. Given his record, it was hardly surprising that he was the one who launched the recall.

Nor had he wasted any time doing so. On November 17, 2002, barely two weeks after Davis was narrowly reelected to his second four-year term, Costa was talking with friends about some sort of ballot measure. The precipitating event, he said, was Davis's postelection disclosure that the state was facing a $28 billion budget deficit. In the following month, the estimate would go even higher—a fact that, except for the exact figure, should have been plain to most people well before the election, and that Davis's opponent in the 2002 race, businessman Bill Simon, had repeatedly tried to make an issue of.[4] Their first thought, said Costa's colleague Mark Abernathy, was another state spending limit, but one tighter than the one that Gann himself had driven through the initiative process in 1979, and which was, in greatly modified (and weaker) form, still on the books. But the talk quickly turned to the idea of a recall, something that at the time seemed an improbable idea, one that neither Costa nor Abernathy knew much about.

To qualify a recall required signatures equivalent to 12 percent of the total vote for governor in the last regular election, a lot less than most other states required, though still a formidable number. But because the turnout in 2002 had been so low, that threshold was not out of reach. Nonetheless, a recall was still unprecedented. In the ninety-plus years since 1911, when the California Progressives wrote the initiative, referendum, and recall into the state constitution, there had been lots of local recalls, especially of school board members, and dozens of attempts at recalling governors: almost every governor had been the target of a recall drive. But no recall of a statewide official had ever made it to the ballot, let alone succeeded. Indeed, in the nation as a whole, only one governor had ever been recalled, and that was the governor of North Dakota, Lynn J. Frazier, in 1921.[5] (The next year Frazier was elected to the U.S. Senate, where he served until 1940.)

Yet within a couple of days, Costa and his colleagues decided that the recall was feasible and that, in Abernathy's words, it "would be tailor-made for somebody like Schwarzenegger. He doesn't have to go through the primary and all that very partisan battle. He could go out to the general public and utilize the attributes that he has. So we definitely thought Schwarzenegger would be the kind of candidate, possibly the candidate . . . who could win in this case. . . . I remember saying to Ted, 'This is a thing of beauty, a thing of beauty.' " By December 18, they'd decided to go ahead. In their formal notice to the governor, they charged him with "gross mismanagement of state finances by overspending the people's money."[6]

They had some reason for their optimism, despite the fact that they had practically no money when they began. Gray Davis had never been widely liked, even within his own party, where many regarded him as a political opportunist. Although he had regularly won elections—as assemblyman, controller, lieutenant governor, governor—he'd done it largely on the strength of his relentless fund-raising and by beating weak opponents against whom he ran highly effective and often negative campaigns. By 2002, even onetime supporters complained that he was inaccessible, and that his "pay-to-play" money demands, exemplified by a set of fund-raising scandals, had begun to verge on extortion.

Like his predecessors, Davis was deeply beholden to the state's prison guards' union and to other powerful interest groups. He'd even been embarrassed by the disclosure that his handlers had "suggested" that the Democratic students at Berkeley who wanted to chat with him at a campus appearance pony up one hundred dollars each for the privilege. By 2002 he had alienated the powerful California Teachers Association and many of his other onetime allies. "Davis hit us up two or three times for a $1 million contribution," said CTA president Wayne Johnson at the time. "He doesn't understand the intensity of dislike for him by California teachers. They loathe him."[7] He'd also alienated Democrats in the legislature with his remark, made shortly after he was first elected in 1998, that it was the legislature's job "to implement my vision."

Davis had been vulnerable ever since his fatal dithering during the California energy crisis in 2000–01, with its spike in rates and its attendant rolling blackouts. Those problems were rooted in a badly flawed restructuring of the state's utility regulatory scheme enacted in 1996 under Davis's Republican predecessor, Pete Wilson, which Davis had nothing to do with. (Wilson himself later recognized that it had "flaws.")[8]

But in 2000 it became Davis's problem. Beginning that summer, in the face of rising demand for energy resulting from the sharp economic recovery and a drought-caused shortage of hydropower in the Northwest, the new scheme began to unravel. Combined with the yearlong failure of FERC, the Federal Energy Regulatory Commission, to cap wholesale rates, the scheme allowed energy marketers, among them Enron, Reliant, Mirant, and others, to manipulate the state's electricity supplies, either by shutting down plants for unneeded repairs or by "roundtripping" power in and out of the state, and thereby jack up the rates, driving spot market prices to obscene rates. During some periods those prices reached levels one hundred times what they'd been the year before. (In response, Vice President Dick Cheney, who headed the administration's Energy Task Force, declared that it was the fault of California's hyper-environmentalism, which had blocked the construction of new power plants.) At the same time, according to Loretta Lynch, who then headed the state's Public Utilities Commission, the Independent System Operator, which was the traffic cop for energy transmission in the state under the new scheme, and which was then dominated by energy industry officials, may itself have facilitated the market manipulation. Lynch said the manipulation ultimately cost Californians $40 billion in current and future bills.[9]

But Davis's failure to push for long-term contracts that would have stabilized wholesale prices contributed to the crisis. Such contracts would have freed the system from the volatile spot market that left it vulnerable to "Fat Boy," "Death Star," "Get Shorty," and the other price manipulation schemes that became notorious after Enron's collapse. Paul Maslin, Davis's pollster, had been warning as early as December of 2000, before the issue had hit the intensity it reached in the late winter and early spring, that the crisis could become a political "perfect storm." At the height of the crisis, Davis told editors at the *Sacramento Bee* that "I don't want to spend my entire life working on utilities." Two years after prices had stabilized, in part because the state managed to dampen demand and accepted long-term contracts, in part because the Federal Energy Regulatory Commission finally restrained wholesale prices, Davis acknowledged that he hadn't really known how to handle it. "I knew nothing about electricity," Davis said later.[10]

But the biggest irritant—the one that ultimately most angered voters—may have been the Davis reelection tactic in 2002 in which he spent nearly $10 million in the *GOP* primary to soften up former mayor Richard Riordan of Los Angeles, a Republican moderate who was given the best chance of beating Davis that November. Davis's attacks on the pro-choice Riordan's past support for antiabortion causes and politicians,

combined with Riordan's own missteps, verbal gaffes, and occasional be-
fuddlement, were so effective that he lost the primary to Simon, an
earnest but hapless conservative.[11] Davis then went on to narrowly beat
Simon (by five points) in a general election that, despite campaign spending totaling some $100 million, a record high, brought out the lowest
percentage of voters in history.

It was an unpleasant and costly victory, and Davis knew it. The heavy-
handed intrusion of a politician of one party into the primary of another
was something that even in the no-holds-barred political culture of this
era was unprecedented and widely regarded, particularly by Republicans,
as the last breach of political civility. Although it was, of course, the voters in the GOP primary who picked Simon, the episode left many people
feeling that they'd been deprived of a real choice and that the election,
as one Republican operative said, "was invalid." By the time the recall was
launched, Davis's approval ratings were the lowest ever recorded.[12] "It's
unbelievable," said Senator Jim Brulte, at the time the Republican leader
in the state senate, "how hated he is." In the month or two after the 2002
election, Davis himself seemed more accessible, even a little more hum-
ble. For the governor, said his press secretary, Steve Maviglio, the narrow victory was "a near-death experience." People who saw him on the
night of his reelection said they'd never seen him more depressed.[13]

The Costa campaign, Davis Recall, nonetheless ran into heavy
weather almost from the start. Did the authors of the recall process ever
intend it as a remedy for alleged fiscal mismanagement, or was it appropriate only when, as Senator Dianne Feinstein, the state's most respected
politician, would say, "serious malfeasance and corruption is found"?[14] A
number of the state's most visible Republicans, among them Gerald
Parsky, who was Bush's man in California, and Dave Cox, then the Republican leader in the assembly, came out against it, as did the California Business Roundtable. In their judgment, the state, with its budget
problems (and the GOP, gearing up for a presidential election in 2004),
had more important matters to attend to.[15] There was, in addition, the
voters' own reluctance to venture into the radical and uncharted territory

that such a move entailed. Was mismanagement of the state's budget or
the manipulation of another party's primary really the kind of conduct
that justified such a remedy?

That, however, didn't deter Costa and his People's Advocate organization from launching their campaign to collect the nine hundred thousand signatures required to get the recall on the ballot—in reality, to
allow for duplicates and unqualified signers, it required at least 1.2 million. But because they didn't have the money to pay the petition circulators—the going rate at the time was about $1.50 for each of those signa-
tures—their chances seemed almost negligible. In signature campaigns,
anyone who had between $1 million and $2 million could get almost anything on the ballot. But while the initiative and recall had been created
as a "people's" remedy for defalcations and misfeasance of corrupt or unresponsive legislators, in the modern era the only people who got to the
table were those who, as Thomas Hiltachk, a Sacramento Republican
campaign lawyer, famously put it, could affirmatively answer the million-
dollar question: "Do you have a million dollars?"[16]

Costa had hoped to rely on the Internet to help circulate his petitions.
Early on, moreover, the recall also began to get strong support from con-
servative talk radio hosts, chief among them Melanie Morgan in San
Francisco and Roger Hedgecock, the defrocked former mayor of San
Diego (he dubbed his show "recall radio" and conducted "drive-by" pe-
tition signing), who helped circulate the petitions through their own
Websites and made it their crusade.[17]

The talkers' support was generated in large measure by a second
group, calling itself Recall Gray Davis, which entered the field in the belief that success could come only to a campaign unconnected to any antitax movement—and could thus appeal to the liberals who, its leaders
believed (probably correctly), hated Davis almost as much as Republicans
did. Sal Russo, another longtime Republican operative, said he'd talked
to Democrats in late January who told him, "Gray Davis is recallable, but
we don't think that it can be done if it's a right-wing Republican taxpayer
group" running the campaign. Russo would never disclose who those

Democrats were. But he was certainly right when he said, "We have tools available to us that we've never had before, and that is the marriage of the Internet with talk radio. . . . We had 45 radio talk show hosts that were taking our material and using it every single day the entire course of the campaign." The talkers were crucial to the recall.[18]

Still, the chances that the two recall campaigns, always a little uneasy with each other, would collect enough signatures seemed slim. The chances were even slimmer that they'd collect them soon enough to force a special election in the fall of 2003, rather than having to hold the recall on the same ballot as the 2004 presidential primary. The delay would have helped Davis, not only because a contested primary for the right to oppose George W. Bush might have drawn many more Democrats than a special vote on the recall but also because the extra time might have muted the anger and allowed Davis to mount a more effective campaign. Costa and Abernathy, seeing the crowds lined up to sign their petitions, were confident, as Abernathy said, that "this is going to be a prairie fire." Still, by early April they'd gotten no more than one hundred thousand of the 1.2 million they needed by July if the thing was going to make it to a fall ballot.

All that changed in early May, when Darrell Issa, a deep-pockets Republican congressman from Southern California, announced he'd fund the recall, which virtually guaranteed success in getting the necessary signatures. Issa, who'd made his fortune in a car-alarm business, and who hoped to become governor himself if the recall succeeded, ultimately pumped nearly $2 million into yet a third organization, Rescue California, that, despite Gray Davis's effort to tie up or drive off most established petition-circulating firms, found the paid signature collectors that the campaign needed. Issa, who had run for the U.S. Senate in the 1998 primary and lost, had, despite his conservatism, always been something of a maverick in his own party, and he got little support from the national party in the recall now.

Despite rumors, mostly circulated by suspicious Democrats, that Karl Rove, George W. Bush's "boy genius" political advisor, was surreptitiously helping to engineer the recall and thus was hoping to repeat the Florida election debacle of 2000 and steal yet another election won by Democrats, Issa's campaign people continued to get the cold shoulder both from the White House and from the state's own Republican leadership. Rove, having been frustrated in his plans to dump Davis, then the only Democratic governor of a major state, and put Riordan into the governor's office in 2002, was, in the view of many California politicians, baffled by California, and he saw the recall effort as a diversion of both money and energy from the Bush reelection campaign. "The White House," said GOP political consultant Dan Schnur, "hoped the whole thing would go away." Cox, the Republican assembly leader, called Dave Gilliard, Issa's campaign manager, and told him, "You're crazy. You're ruining our plans for taking over the assembly by doing this."[19]

Issa badly wanted to get the recall on a special election ballot in the fall, not in March, so he could run for reelection to Congress in the spring primary if his gubernatorial plans failed. Thus it had to qualify before the end of July to make the constitutional deadline. In fact he probably never had a realistic chance of becoming governor himself (though he may have been unaware how vulnerable he was). He was too conservative and, worse, his record was too full of embarrassments—charges about unethical and allegedly felonious business practices; a suspicious fire at one of his enterprises; a conviction on a weapons charge, plus several arrests, though no convictions, for car theft as a young man and as a twenty-seven-year-old army officer; and bad conduct ratings and demotions as a member of an army bomb-disposal squad.[20]

But while Davis's antirecall campaign, which had been slow to get off the ground—early on, nobody on his staff took the recall seriously—worked assiduously to link the recall to Issa's announced intention to run himself (and, of course, to his dubious background), the money uncapped the steam that had been building against the governor ever since the electricity mess two years before.

Taken individually, perhaps none of Davis's problems—the budget deficit, the energy crisis, the meddling in the GOP primary, the strong-

arm fund-raising—might have been enough to generate a successful recall. Even after Issa's money had virtually assured that the measure
would qualify for the fall—ultimately his committee alone spent $3.6
million to bring Davis down—the polls showed ambivalence, if not reluctance, among voters to take such a step. But in combination the problems were lethal. Worse, during the summer of 2003, Davis, desperate to
balance a recession-stressed budget that was deep in the red, was again
confronting the adamant refusal by Republicans in the legislature to
agree to any tax increase. Though a minority, the GOP had an effective
veto because of California's constitutional requirement that all budgets
and tax increases be passed by a two-thirds majority. In the past, governors had been able to peel off a few Republicans to get the necessary two-
thirds vote. This time, threatened with serious retribution by caucus
leaders, and smelling Davis's blood in the water, no one buckled. Davis,
then resorting to one of the few devices left open to him, allowed the
California's vehicle license fee, the so-called car tax, to triple.

Californians had been paying the VLF, a 2 percent annual fee on the
value of each car, for more than a half century without complaint until a
conservative state senator named Tom McClintock, picking up on the
success of an anti-car-tax campaign in Virginia, made it an issue. The tax,
whose proceeds had gone to the cities and counties, had been cut by two-
thirds during the boom years, with the state agreeing to replace the locals' lost revenues from its own resources. But when the legislature approved the cuts it also created a trigger mechanism that would allow the
tax to be restored in bad times. Now, in the face of multi-billion-dollar
budget holes, Davis, who'd tried for every other sort of revenue increase,
and confronting adamant resistance from the Republicans in the legislature to anything that looked like a tax increase, pulled the trigger, the
only resort he had—more red meat for the drive-time radio talkers. In
San Diego, "recall radio" talker Hedgecock managed to wrap the car tax
around his other favorite evil—illegal immigrants, "whose cost to the
state of California is almost exactly the budget deficit." Nobody much

cared that the governor had done what the law, enacted under his Republican predecessor, Pete Wilson, had always contemplated.

II

The recall qualified in July—indeed, overqualified, with the backers claiming that they had more than 2 million signatures, almost twice what they needed—early enough to require a special election, eventually set for October 7, 2003. That election was to consist of two issues: Should the governor be recalled, and if so, which candidate should succeed him? Even voters who cast ballots for the retention of the incumbent were allowed to vote on a successor. The process provided for no primary and runoff, meaning that the candidate with the greatest number of votes won, even if he or she didn't get a majority.[21] With enough candidates in the race, it was theoretically possible for someone to win with only 25 or 30 percent of the votes, or perhaps even less, meaning that a successor could be elected with fewer votes than the incumbent got for retention.

And since the law allowed any adult citizen who could get sixty-five signatures and pony up thirty-five hundred dollars to get on the ballot, it opened the door—indeed, provided the come-on—for the political Oklahoma land rush that followed. All told, 135 candidates entered the race, from *Hustler* publisher Larry Flynt and porn queen Mary Carey to Bill Simon, who had lost to Davis in the general election the previous fall. The list also included Tom McClintock, the conservative California state senator who had come within sixteen thousand votes (of some 7 million cast) of becoming state controller in 2002; Green Party activist Peter Camejo; bail bondsman Leonard Padilla; actor Gary Coleman; columnist Arianna Huffington, once a conservative (and ex-wife of former Republican congressman Michael Huffington, who had run for the U.S. Senate and had also thought about entering the recall), now a born-again liberal; and businessman Peter Ueberroth, the former baseball commissioner, who had run the Los Angeles Olympics Organizing Committee in 1984. Also an Indian chief, a sumo wrestler, a denture manufacturer, a retired cop whose cause was the legalized ownership of pet ferrets ("the ferret candidate"), a used car dealer, a professional golfer, several lawyers (including a "marijuana legalization attorney"), and one man who described himself simply as a "comedian." The possibility that a candidate with a small plurality—and with fewer votes than the recalled governor—could become the next governor raised troubling questions of legitimacy. It would also reinforce the charges that—as in the 2000 presidential election recount fiasco in Florida and in House Majority Leader Tom DeLay's heavy-handed drive to muscle a second congressional redistricting that would favor the GOP through the Texas legislature—Republicans were once again trying to undo the will of the people. It was, Davis said at the time, "an effort by the right wing to overthrow the results of legitimate election . . . and stick taxpayers with a $35-million or $45-million bill (for the cost of the recall)."[22]

Adding still more unpredictability was the string of lawsuits that the uncertainties of the untested recall process generated: One challenged the reliability of the error-plagued punch-card ballots still being used in some counties that the California secretary of state, expecting no election until 2004, had prohibited, and demanded that the vote be deferred until the punch-card system could be replaced. Not to do so, said the American Civil Liberties Union, one of the plaintiffs, meant that some forty thousand votes could be lost or miscounted and those who cast them thereby disenfranchised. (Davis, who also sued unsuccessfully to be on the ballot to succeed himself, was a plaintiff in a similar suit.) Another lawsuit contended that, under the succession provisions of the state's constitution, if the governor were recalled, it should be the lieutenant governor—in this case Democrat Cruz Bustamante—who would succeed him, not the winner of any successor election. Although a panel of the Ninth U.S. Circuit Court of Appeals agreed with the challenge to the voting machines, that decision was soon overturned. The state courts, always reluctant to get into the middle of an intense political fight, soon rejected the other suits.[23]

From the start, the numbers calculation—the strong possibility that a small plurality of votes would be enough to put someone in the governor's chair—drove the political strategy of the respective parties. If the Republicans were represented by more than one strong candidate, they'd probably split the vote. For the Democrats, it was important to keep *any* major figure from running and thus deprive loyal party members of the option of—or perhaps the excuse for—voting against Davis. There was no question that Feinstein would have liked to be governor. She probably saw, and still sees, it as more compatible with her own executive inclinations. In the byzantine speculations of the time, if she were to become governor, she could name her own successor in the Senate—possibly choosing Bustamante, thus inducing him not to run against her for governor in the recall, and then filling his post with yet someone else, creating a whole dynasty. But because Feinstein had herself faced a nasty recall effort when she was mayor of San Francisco—she handily beat it but was still offended by it—she now worked overtime to keep her fellow Democrats out of the lists. Although she had run for governor (against Pete Wilson in 1990) and clearly would have made a strong candidate, she said repeatedly—albeit not quite unequivocally—that she wouldn't run now.

As it became clearer toward election day that Davis was not likely to survive, Feinstein faced heavy pressure from fellow Democrats like San Francisco congresswoman Nancy Pelosi, the House minority leader, to run or to encourage someone else—perhaps Leon Panetta, Bill Clinton's former budget director and chief of staff—to provide a single strong Democratic alternative to the list of Republicans who had announced or were likely to. That list included not only Ueberroth, McClintock, and Simon but also, as then seemed likely, Riordan, the man that Davis, abetted by Riordan's own inept campaign, had helped destroy in the 2002 GOP primary.

To most political insiders, it never made much sense for any Democrat to deliver a mixed message: to vigorously oppose the recall but run as a possible successor. "The only way to beat the recall," said Garry

South, who had been Davis's political strategist until the end of the 2002 election campaign, when he went to work in Senator Joseph Lieberman's short-lived presidential campaign, "is to beat the recall." Anything else was fantasy.[24] Ultimately, the discipline worked, with one significant exception. The big-name Democrats—Panetta, Attorney General Bill Lockyer, Treasurer Phil Angelides, Insurance Commissioner John Garamendi—stayed out. But, spurred by his campaign advisor, Richie Ross, Bustamante, the highest ranking Latino in state office in over a century, jumped in, running on the slogan "No on the Recall—Yes on Bustamante," precisely the kind of mixed message South warned about. "Even if it's a down year for Democrats," said Ross after the election, "the advertising slogan for the New York State Lotto is 'Hey, you never know.' " No other Democrat was going to run, so Bustamante decided "he would take his shot."[25]

The biggest question mark, of course, was Schwarzenegger himself. Would he or wouldn't he? The man whom almost everyone called Arnold and who loved nothing so much as attention, liked to play guessing games. No decision would be made, Schwarzenegger said, until after the release of his film *Terminator 3: Rise of the Machines* in early July. Still, it was no secret that he had lofty political ambitions. In 2002, in collaboration with the California Teachers Association, whose three hundred thousand members made it one of the most powerful organizations in the state, he had funded a successful initiative to carve an additional $455 million out of the state budget for before- and after-school programs. More tellingly, perhaps, a group of political consultants had been working with him—and on him—for the better part of two years. The campaign team was already in place.

But there were still problems. As many people suspected, and as the whole world was to learn, during his career as bodybuilder and Hollywood celebrity, Schwarzenegger had accumulated a hefty record of personal misconduct—the groping, the abusive remarks to inferiors, the blatant sexism on what he, in a public election-eve apology, called "rowdy movie sets"—that might alienate both conservatives and the suburban women who would be crucial to his prospects. Those episodes could provide a field day for the tabloids, print and electronic.[26] Did he really want to put his family through that? In addition, there were the nude body-building photos; the Nazi father; the German accent; the friendship with former Austrian president Kurt Waldheim, who was involved in Nazi atrocities in Bosnia in World War II; and the alleged statement, made in passing on one of his early movie sets but still in circulation, admiring the oratorical skills of his fellow Austrian Adolf Hitler (and of John F. Kennedy). Through his large contributions to the Simon Wiesenthal Center in Los Angeles and his association with its founder, Rabbi Marvin Hier, who vigorously defended him, Schwarzenegger had largely insulated himself against charges of anti-Semitism and tangential admiration for Nazis. But did he really want to open all that up again?[27]

Thus, up to the last day before the August filing deadline, he was playing an Alphonse and Gaston game with his friend Riordan about who should run, and peekaboo with the media. Whoever ran, they agreed, would get the full support of the other. But it was also clear that, if Schwarzenegger were going to run at all, the recall process was far and away his best chance—and probably his only one. As that rarest of breeds in California—a Republican who was in favor of gun control and liberal on abortion, gay rights, and other social issues—as the husband of TV reporter Maria Shriver, the niece of Teddy Kennedy, and as someone personally close to the Kennedy family, his chances of winning a Republican primary were minimal at best. In addition, the two-month campaign mandated by the recall calendar, combined with the advantages of Schwarzenegger's celebrity status, would make it much easier to talk in lofty generalities and avoid the thorny details of the complicated California governmental process. And yet, when he went on the Jay Leno television show to make the much-awaited announcement on the night before the rolls closed, his staff already had press releases in hand declaring that he was not running. "I was the most surprised person in America," said George Gorton, one of Schwarzenegger's chief campaign strategists, when Schwarzenegger said he would indeed run. Apparently even Riordan didn't know. But to anyone who knew about Schwarzenegger's body-building career, and the tricks he had pulled even on his best friends when he competed against them, this kind of feint was hardly unprecedented. "With his body building opponents," said Laurence Leamer, one of his biographers, "he not only had to beat them, he had to destroy them."[28]

By general consensus among political consultants, Schwarzenegger and his advisors, several of whom had worked for former governor Pete Wilson (among them Gorton, who was one of three Wilson consultants who'd helped run Boris Yeltsin's reelection campaign in Russia in 1996), conducted a brilliant campaign, keeping their candidate away from the print press and their questions about his agenda and in front of the cameras.[29] They didn't need time to construct an "eight-point plan" or "ten-point plan" for the campaign; they needed only time, in the words of Davis campaign manager Larry Grisolano, "to construct the insulation around him so that he didn't need the eight-point plan."[30] From the start, the strategy, as one of this advisors said, "was to play to the people, not the press." He didn't need the political press. The cameras and celebrity media were sufficient.

In fact, his campaign hardly needed to do anything. Schwarzenegger's show biz celebrity, the personal fortune that could be tapped for the race, and the widespread dislike of Davis carried the campaign almost without effort. The Terminator liked to compare himself to Hiram Johnson, the California Progressive governor who had been elected on a campaign lambasting the Southern Pacific Railroad and other "special interests," and who had, among other reforms, gotten the initiative, referendum, and recall written into the California constitution in 1911. Schwarzenegger declared that, like Johnson, he'd come to politics to clean out the evildoers in Sacramento. "The special interests in those days ran over people," he said at a campaign rally in Sacramento. "Hiram Johnson stopped them."[31] The refrain was "action, action, action." Little of that required any specifics.

Meanwhile, the normally astute Davis, in an effort to shore up his

Latino base, compounded his own problems by allowing the legislature's Latino caucus to persuade him to sign a bill restoring the right to obtain driver's licenses to illegal aliens that he'd vetoed twice before. Those vetoes had cost him considerable Hispanic support in the 2002 election. In fact, California had never demanded proof of legal residence until the peak of the anti-illegal-immigrant frenzy of the early 1990s, when Governor Wilson signed a bill changing the law to require it. But that bill didn't really become effective until the end of the decade, when computer programs were developed enabling the state's Department of Motor Vehicles to verify the Social Security numbers of those who applied for either new licenses or renewals. Thus, according to Senator Gil Cedillo of Los Angeles, the sponsor of the driver's license bill that Davis finally signed, an estimated million or more illegal aliens who had once driven legally no longer could do so, putting at risk their livelihoods and, in the case of newly arrived illegal aliens who now would not take tests but would drive nonetheless, the safety of other drivers. But since the measure was widely unpopular—some 60 percent of voters opposed it—it almost certainly cost Davis far more votes than it gained him.[32] It also reinforced his image, as if this were needed, as an unprincipled politician who'd do anything to win votes.

More surprising, the tabloids, instead of digging into the allegations of Schwarzenegger's behavior on those "rowdy" sets, put out special sections and glossy inserts glorifying his career. In September, just before the election, American Media, the publisher of the *National Enquirer* and the *Star*, the two leading supermarket tabs, issued a 120-page glossy magazine called "Arnold, the American Dream." Not long after, the *San Jose Mercury News* reported that the previous January, American Media had made a "lucrative business deal with one of Schwarzenegger's earliest business partners." Simultaneously, Joe Weider, the former partner, told reporters that American Media's chief executive officer, David Pecker, had assured Weider that his publications, which had never been diffident about reporting on Arnold's affairs before, would "lay off" Schwarzenegger, a statement quickly denied by an American Media spokesman, then reiterated by Weider. Pecker later explained that he wouldn't "rehash old stuff" but would run anything that was new. But even that, as biographer Leamer observed, "was a promise unlike that made to anyone else in public life." To cap it all off, the *Weekly World News*, another American Media tabloid, ran an "exclusive" about what the *Mercury News* called "a politically savvy space alien throwing his otherworldly support behind Schwarzenegger. Under the screaming headline 'Alien backs Arnold for governor!' the extraterrestrial not only lauds the actor, but vows to help amend the U.S. Constitution so the Austrian-born candidate can someday run for president." The deal would continue to dog him well into his second year as governor, when it was disclosed that, just after he announced he'd run and as the agreement was being negotiated, American Media paid a woman who had worked in Hollywood twenty thousand dollars in a "confidentiality agreement" not to discuss an alleged affair with him. She denied any such affair—they were just good friends and work associates, she later said. The agreement, she thought, was a lead-up to a book about her life.[33]

Conversely, when the *Los Angeles Times* published a piece a few days before the election chronicling the stories, some of them long familiar, of women who had come forward with stories of their mistreatment by Schwarzenegger on sets and in various other Hollywood situations—the breast fondling and buttock grabbing, the offensive sexual remarks—it resulted in a deluge of cancellations, angry calls, and e-mails accusing the paper of holding the story until the last minute in order to help Davis and do the most damage to Schwarzenegger's campaign.[34] Although Schwarzenegger issued an apology, in effect confirming at least some of the charges—it was then that he talked about having been on some "rowdy" sets—it was not the substance of the *Times* story but its timing that became the issue. (Schwarzenegger promised an independent investigation into the groping charges, which was quickly dropped after the election because, in Schwarzenegger's words, "the people have spoken" and therefore it wasn't needed.)[35] Californians were nothing if not tolerant, especially of a celebrity in Hollywood, where most people assumed such things were commonplace.

Even a year after the election, it was already hard to recall the frenzy that Schwarzenegger's entry generated—the TV crews from every corner of the earth in pursuit of one of the great celebrity stories of the decade, the magazine feature writers, the academics probing what all this meant for democracy and popular government. California had for more than a generation been regarded as the prime source of plebiscitary movements. Was this, like Proposition 13 of 1978, which rolled back the state's property taxes by nearly 60 percent and capped both assessments and rates, the start of another uprising against the "system" that would sweep the nation and, as in Margaret Thatcher's election in Great Britain, parts of other nations as well? Would there now be a wave of recalls in the states that allowed them and who-knew-what in the states that didn't?[36] Was it like the revolt against affirmative action in 1995–96, or like Proposition 187, the anti-immigrant initiative, in 1994? Was it like three strikes and other measures mandating life terms on three-time offenders? Was it like Proposition 140 in 1990, which imposed strict term limits on all elected state officials in California and helped launch a national term-limits movement, state and local, that swept much of the country and that, had the courts not declared it unconstitutional at the national level, would have capped congressional terms as well?[37]

III

Notwithstanding Schwarzenegger's show-biz celebrity, for some weeks after the real campaign began, voters seemed hesitant about leaping into the unknown territory of the recall. And while even the early (pre-Schwarzenegger) polls showed voters favoring the recall 51–43 (in the poll by Mark Baldassare for PPIC, the Public Policy Institute of California) or 51–36 (in the *Los Angeles Times* poll), many people, among them Davis pollster Paul Maslin, believed that the recall would tend to behave more or less like other ballot measures, which generally lost support between the early polling and election day as voters learned more about them and as opposition campaigns sowed doubts about them. Maslin recognized that this was different, since it started out with the strong and unwavering support of Republicans and Davis-haters. Still he believed that, if major Democrats stayed out of the successor race, doubts, uncertainty, and confusion would top the hot yes vote.[38]

Schwarzenegger's entry into the race changed everything. It immediately made him the focus of the attention, brought Bustamante in, drove Issa out, and sucked the air from Simon's campaign and from the campaigns of what Simon advisor Wayne Johnson called the other institutional Republicans, meaning mostly McClintock. In fact it rendered moot the earlier calculus showing that, where there were two major candidates from one party, they'd fatally split the vote and hand the victory to the other party. Johnson later recalled that when they surveyed voters they concluded that people were not going to vote for anyone who held all of Schwarzenegger's positions. "And then when we came back and put Arnold's name in, they voted for Arnold. . . . Nothing traditional we could do was going to change that."[39] With subsequent hindsight, it seemed almost like a prefiguring of the results of the 2004 presidential election, where, again, identity politics prevailed over issue politics.

Although Schwarzenegger had articulated a few specifics—rolling back the hated "car tax" and repealing the bill on driver's licenses for illegal immigrants that Davis had signed—most of the campaign rested on broad themes: getting the state's deficit-plagued fiscal house in order; restoring the state's business climate and bringing back the jobs that the state was said to have lost because of its high workers' compensation costs and other "job killer" policies; and reorganizing government, what Schwarzenegger would later describe as his intention to "blow up the boxes," not just rearrange them. He was not going to raise taxes. He was going to end the power of the "special interests" in Sacramento; he was rich enough that he didn't need their money. "I cannot be bought," he often said, both before and after the election. He was going to go to

Sacramento "and clean house."[40] He was going to give California back its future.

That promise was underlined by the candidate's version of his personal story: how he came from his native Austria to California in 1968 to realize his dreams because the state, unlike "socialist" Austria, offered unlimited opportunity. The story would later be expanded and reiterated for the whole nation, this time in red, white, and blue, in Schwarzenegger's speech at the 2004 Republican National Convention, where he conflated accounts of the Soviet occupation of Austria and the Russian tanks he said he saw in the streets with Austria's "socialist" government and then with Hubert Humphrey in the 1968 presidential campaign, who, he said, sounded to him like a socialist. In his GOP convention speech, he claimed it was that experience that made him a Republican.[41]

In fact, as Austrian historians quickly pointed out, he got his history mostly (and probably conveniently) wrong. Since he lived in the British zone, there were no Russian tanks in the streets (though he might have seen some on his occasional trips into the Soviet zone); Austria had coalition governments, whose chancellors were all conservatives.[42] Worse, he got his American history wrong. His arrival in California in 1968 came at the end of twenty years of unprecedented public investment in schools and universities, in roads, bridges, and other transportation infrastructure, in flood control and water delivery systems, in public parks. More pointedly yet, in 1967, the year before Schwarzenegger arrived, Governor Ronald Reagan, the ultimate icon of modern Republicanism, had signed the largest tax increase ever approved in California or any other state.[43] In 1968, California was a high-tax state; in 2003, California was an average tax state.[44]

Nor was there any strong evidence, contrary to the contentions of the Republicans in the race, Tom McClintock particularly, that California had been hemorrhaging jobs to other western states. The state had lost some signature corporate headquarters through mergers and acquisitions, the merger of the Bank of America, once regarded as an intrinsic California institution, with NationsBank of Charlotte, North Carolina, paramount among them. But most of those mergers and acquisitions had nothing to do with California's business climate—they had taken place long before Davis ever arrived in office. On the contrary, in 2003, California edged out New York as the state with the largest number of Fortune 500 company headquarters in the country—a total of 110 of the 500. In any case, California's job losses in the recession that began in 2000–01 were proportionately about equal to national job losses, and lower than those in Colorado, Massachusetts, North Carolina, and other high-tech states.[45]

None of those details seemed to matter, however, either to the public or to the media. That stuff was all too complicated. The political managers, both in California and in Washington, had long taught that the essence was theme and image: Stay on message, and keep it simple. The central theme of Davis's antirecall campaign, which was heavily funded by the firefighters' union (Davis, once a prodigious fund-raiser, had all but suspended his fund-raising activities after his narrow reelection in 2002), was the cost of the election itself: one of the campaign committees called itself Californians Against the Costly Recall of the Governor. (MoveOn, which was born in Berkeley, and which since has become better known for its other causes, also spent nearly five hundred thousand dollars fighting the recall.) But the toughest problem, as Garry South, Davis's longtime advisor put it, was "How do you get 50 percent plus one of the voters to vote for somebody with a 26 percent job approval rating?"[46]

Davis's difficulties were compounded by public warnings from Attorney General Bill Lockyer, a fellow Democrat, that Davis had better not run a "trashy puke campaign" as Lockyer implied Davis had done in some of his previous races. (In a postelection speech at Berkeley, Lockyer also said that, while he'd voted against the recall, he'd voted for Schwarzenegger because he "represented for me what he did for others—hope, change, reform, opportunity, upbeat, problem solving.")[47] The *Los Angeles Times*'s publication of the groping stories on October 2, five days before the election, produced an exceptional short-term anti-

Arnold blip in the polls on the Saturday before the vote—the tracking polls that day had it at 49–49. But then, as South put it, "it bounced back"—in part because Schwarzenegger, while accusing the *Times* of a smear, quickly issued his "rowdy movie sets" apology, and in part because at least some people regarded it as yet another dirty trick by Gray Davis and his friends. By Sunday night, two days before the election, the gap had widened again, to 53–44. Dirty Davis present was a much bigger issue than rowdy Arnold past.

The Schwarzenegger campaign had fumbled a few times in the early days of the short race. When billionaire investor guru Warren Buffett, who, in order to give Schwarzenegger economic gravitas, had been listed as one of the candidate's economic advisors, told the *Wall Street Journal* that California's property taxes were too low and that Proposition 13, the state's seemingly sacrosanct "third rail" property tax initiative ought to be repealed, Schwarzenegger's Republican opponents jumped on the statement as perhaps the ultimate sign that Schwarzenegger didn't understand the issues. But Schwarzenegger quickly distanced himself from his advisor's gaffe. If the seventy-three-year-old Buffett ever mentioned Proposition 13 again, Schwarzenegger said, he'd make him do five hundred push-ups.[48]

As to his status as a novice in government and electoral politics, the word soon got around that most people who knew him said he was a good listener, asked good questions, and, despite his inexperience, was a quick study. And of course, he was a moderate on social issues—and there was Maria. Many were charmed by him. In 1998, Davis had run on experience; this time, the voters, while giving Schwarzenegger low marks on the experience scale, couldn't care less. Davis was the issue. In the only candidates' debate in which he participated, Schwarzenegger, inadvertently aided by Huffington's charge that his attempts to cut her off in the televised free-for-all demonstrated his disrespect for women, showed that he could hold his own. (Schwarzenegger replied that he had a "perfect role" for her in his next Terminator movie, presumably as an icy female villain [Terminatrix?] who'd get zapped in the final reel.) The real debate wasn't about issues, it was about personality, which was Schwarzenegger's strong suit. That's certainly what people like Larry Grisolano, who ran Davis's campaign, believed.[49]

As the two candidates with the most unequivocal positions on state issues, McClintock, the conservative Republican, and Camejo, the Green, seemed to be the viewers' personal favorites in the debate. But candor, of course, was a luxury that, in a state as divided as California, no candidate who seriously hoped to win could ever afford. Three weeks before the debate, Bustamante had led Schwarzenegger 30–25 in the poll to succeed Davis.[50] That evaporated with Bustamante's weak showing before the cameras, disclosures about his heavy reliance on money from Indian casinos, and allegations of campaign money laundering and other improper use of a campaign committee. He may also have been hurt by the backlash against the driver's license bill. More important, the Indian money issue not only damaged the lieutenant governor but also reinforced Schwarzenegger's argument that, while (in the words of one of his political advisors) "the entire California political establishment has been addicted [to their money]," Schwarzenegger was not.[51]

Schwarzenegger won handily—given the circumstances, almost overwhelmingly. While he failed to get a clear majority, he came surprisingly close, getting 49 percent of the roughly 9.4 million votes cast in the 135-candidate race (itself probably some sort of national record), more than the 44.6 percent cast against the recall (and thus at least inferentially for Davis)—and 1.4 million more votes (and a higher percentage) than Davis himself got in his reelection campaign eleven months before. There had been predictions that he'd turn off women, and speculation that his strongest supporters would be young Latino males or white surfers, who were said to be the greatest fans of his movies. But in the end, he won a sizeable plurality among women as well: in the successor race, he outpolled Bustamante 45–35 among women. The recall carried in forty-three of the state's fifty-eight counties. The exceptions were the heavily blue—Democratic—San Fran-

cisco Bay Area, a few other coastal counties, and, by a small fraction, the
county of Los Angeles, where Davis had beaten Dan Lungren, his Republican opponent in the 1998 general election, by a margin of nearly
two to one.[52] According to the *Los Angeles Times*'s exit poll, despite
Davis's signature on the illegal immigrants' driver's license bill he'd
twice vetoed, 45 percent of Latinos voted for the recall, as did 48 percent of the voters who lived in union households. Bustamante, who, de-
fying his party, was the only high-visibility Democrat to run—and who
had also calculated that his best chance was in a race without a primary—got 32 percent of the vote and just 56 percent of the Hispanic
vote. By general agreement, his decision to run effectively ruined his future among Democrats. One consultant called him "the Brutus in our
party."[53]

There wasn't much room for ambiguity in those numbers, and the
message wasn't lost on anyone. What seemed to make the recall particularly stunning was the fact that, eleven months before, Democrats had
swept all the state's major offices: governor, lieutenant governor, attorney general, treasurer, controller, secretary of state, insurance commissioner. Both houses of the legislature were controlled by Democrats. The
state's two U.S. senators, Feinstein and Barbara Boxer, were Democrats.
The state's congressional delegation was heavily Democratic. Bill Clinton had carried the state in the 1992 and 1996 presidential elections and
Gore had taken California by more than a million votes in 2000. (No one
recalled that, barely a decade before, the state had been regarded as generally Republican. Before Clinton, no Democratic presidential candidate
had carried California since Lyndon Johnson in 1964. Davis was the first
Democrat to be elected governor in sixteen years and only the third since
1940. Nor did anyone notice that in 2002 Davis had won only narrowly
and that only one of the five other Democratic winners at the top of the
ticket got more than 50 percent of the votes.) Nonetheless, the results in
1998 and 2002 had led to a wavelet of commentary concluding that California, once the political, social, and cultural bellwether for the nation,
had become a sort of backwater—the "left-out coast" as "Lexington," the

U.S. columnist for the respected British weekly *The Economist*, put it in April 2003, barely six months before Davis was dumped.[54]

"Politically," Lexington wrote, "California has been out of the loop ever since the Clintons moved out of the White House. Californians were never going to warm to George Bush and his southern-fried brand of Republicanism. This is a state . . . where even 54 percent of registered Republicans oppose restrictions on abortion rights. . . . Californians are less inclined than almost anyone else in the country to give the president the benefit of the doubt on anything from tax cuts to homeland security." Three years earlier, in a piece called "Why California Doesn't Matter," in the conservative flagship the *Weekly Standard*, its executive editor, Fred Barnes, had said it even more unequivocally. "By the late 1990s," he wrote, "California was more Democratic, more pro–President Clinton, and more pro-abortion than the rest of America. Its population was more Hispanic and Asian. Its business community was more culturally liberal." Meanwhile, Harold Meyerson, an editor of the liberal *American Prospect*, was celebrating "the leftward evolution of California politics." It was "the next New Deal in tryouts." How had California gone from all that to this?[55]

The widespread conclusion was that the recall wasn't just about Davis, hated as he was, but was, at bottom, a revolt against the system. (That, oddly enough, was almost precisely the opposite of what was said in 1990, when a lot of politicians contended that the term limits initiative wasn't really about the system; it was aimed by its sponsors at Willie Brown, the longtime Speaker—urban, San Francisco-based, African American—of the California Assembly, who was the poster child of the campaign.)[56] In pre-recall polls—and in polls well after—the legislature, meaning the Democrats, got lower approval ratings than even Davis. The people of California, Arianna Huffington had said, "don't really want a recall; they want a revolution." The voters felt no one was listening to them and, as in previous California uprisings, were fed up. With the recall, Costa told a reporter, "the entire political system in California gets the two-by-four across the head."[57] "The rejection of Gov. Gray Davis, and his replacement with a Hollywood action star," said reporter Robert Salladay in the *San Francisco Chronicle,*

> revealed a deeply felt need by a certain class of voters who felt ig-
> nored by the political system and disgusted by it. Call them middle
> class. Call them angry white men. Call them young and disenfran-
> chised. Call them Republicans marginalized from statewide office for
> years.
>
> It would be too simplistic to say that the angry voter went into re-
> volt because of a disgust with special interests. Maybe Schwarzeneg-
> ger's story simply resonated with people. Who has ever seen anyone
> like him? Certainly he is the most unusual candidate in California
> history, far more quirky and fascinating even than former Gov. Jerry
> Brown.
>
> But there also is a segment of voters ignored by Sacramento—and
> they were the ones Schwarzenegger tapped. They are the so-called
> forgotten middle, who don't rely on the government for welfare to
> feed their children or tax breaks for their corporations.[58]

Or in the words of Republican political consultant Dan Schnur, "This anger is directed at the entire political system and everyone in it. The recall was about the car tax. It was about driver's licenses for illegal immigrants. And it was about the energy crisis. But more than anything this recall was about voters who were mad because nobody was listening to them."[59]

And, of course, there were lots of comparisons to the campaign of former Vermont governor Howard Dean, who was then preparing to run for the Democratic presidential nomination and who, on his Website, suggested that what had occurred in California in 2003 could be repeated at the national level in 2004. "What happened on Tuesday was in many ways a manifestation of the force that has powered Howard Dean to the front of the Democratic presidential contest," said *New York Times* reporter Adam Nagourney in a piece headlined "Voter Revolt Could Be Bad for Bush." "From that perspective, the message may be a warning to incumbents, or candidates perceived as too closely tied to the political system." And Dean himself pitched in. "Tonight the voters in California directed their frustration with the country's direction on their incumbent governor," Dean said. "Come next November, the anger might be directed at a different incumbent—in the White House."[60] Was this the beginning of another nationwide revolt against politicians? Conversely, did it signify a new opening for Republicans in California, where their social conservatism—on abortion, gay rights, and gun control—and their failure to reach out to women, immigrants, and minorities, had fatally marginalized them? Could Schwarzenegger, the social moderate, lead them out of the wilderness into the promised land of moderation? "This is a new attitude," said the Reagan biographer and longtime journalist Lou Cannon, "in a state party noted until recently for its ineffectiveness." The recall, he found, "boosted Republican registration and fund raising." Republicans seriously expected to cut into the Democrats' 48–32 majority in the assembly.[61]

In Sacramento, *Bee* columnist Dan Walters had another perspective. California, he observed, seemed to have these uprisings roughly every dozen years, a sort of cyclical housecleaning that came with semigenerational regularity: the election of Ronald Reagan as governor in 1966; Proposition 13 and the tax revolt in 1978; the initiative imposing legislative term limits in 1990; the recall in 2003. But if the recall was a revolt against the system, who created that system? Was it the venal politicians or was it the voters and the political culture that they were themselves part of? Davis was surely right when he insisted, as he often did, that governors got more credit than they'd earned in good times and more blame than they deserved in bad times. The recession made 2002 a bad election year for all incumbent governors.[62] There were lots of other states that ran serious deficits in 2000–2002. In his four-plus years in office, Davis not only had enjoyed the boom, especially in high-tech, and the great spike in capital gains and stock options it had produced for the California treasury in the late 1990s but also had suffered as the bust and fiscal mismanagement turned state surpluses to deficits. In October 1999, *Time* magazine had run a story about Davis headlined "The Most Fearless Governor in America: California Thought It Was Electing a

Timid Inoffensive Governor; Instead Gray Davis Is Knocking Heads, Even Passing HMO Reform."[63] During the boom when the piece ran, Davis's approval rating was over 60 percent.

In fact California's surplus-to-deficit turnaround was proportionately no greater than what happened to the national budget under George W. Bush at the same time. Many other states, having raised spending and cut taxes during the good times, were now confronting hefty deficits (albeit none as great as California's) and were raising taxes. The New York legislature, one of whose houses was controlled by Republicans, even overrode Governor George Pataki's veto to do so.[64]

But in California the political situation was quite the opposite. Because the state constitution had long required a two-thirds legislative majority to pass any budget, or any other revenue measure, and because Proposition 13 mandated a two-thirds majority to increase any state tax, the tightly disciplined Republican minority in the legislature had a veto over any tax increase and all state budgets. Taxes could be cut by majority vote, as indeed they frequently were after the mid-1990s, but they could be raised only by a supermajority.

Davis was never a big-spending liberal. He was, rather, a calculating and cautious—often overcautious—political pragmatist who reluctantly bent to pressures when he felt it necessary and, like other politicians, took credit for doing things he'd only grudgingly agreed to. But during the four years and ten months he served as the state's chief executive, he responded too easily to demands from the teachers' unions (and to the general needs of California's badly underfunded schools), to the state's powerful union of prison guards, and to the general needs of a state that, in the face of both state and local tax limitations, had badly neglected the high levels of services and infrastructure development that it had set for itself in the postwar generation.

Thus, while he tried to allocate as much as he could to onetime infrastructure expenses, thereby hoping to avoid long-term commitments, Davis had allowed state expenditures to ride up with the boom of the late nineties. And like his predecessor Pete Wilson (and like other governors at the time), he'd also approved a broad range of tax cuts. To help balance the budget during the recession of the early 1990s, Wilson had agreed to roughly $6 billion in tax increases; those taxes—taxes on high-income earners, sales taxes, corporate taxes—had long since been allowed to lapse. As discussed earlier, the state had also approved new tax breaks for business and reduced the so-called car tax by two-thirds, which by itself reduced revenues by nearly $4 billion a year. In addition, California's Medi-Cal program and its other state and local health services— like those of every individual and business—were being battered by rates that, by the most reliable estimates, increased by nearly 60 percent between 2000 and 2004. School districts were facing bankruptcy because of their escalating health costs; grocery clerks and hotel workers were on strike over controversies about who should pay the escalating insurance premiums. Of the state's spiking expenditures, probably at least half went to health care.

Once the capital gains and stock options bubble burst and state revenues went down, Davis was trapped between, on the one hand, constitutional spending commitments, the legislative Democratic majority, and the big public employee groups and, on the other, Republicans who refused to vote for any tax increase, but who were also reluctant to vote for spending cuts. The result was two years of budgets that relied heavily on cuts for areas, particularly higher education, that were not protected by constitutional mandates, and a complex mix of deferrals, borrowing (including, among other things, "securitizing" expected tobacco suit settlement revenues), and other devices.[65] But none of those things closed the state's so-called structural deficit, the gap between the curve of expected revenues and projected expenditures.

Davis had started what turned out to be his last year in office hoping to raise tobacco taxes, sales taxes, and perhaps taxes on upper-bracket incomes, but all those plans were blocked by Republicans. In earlier years, he had been able to peel off a few GOP votes for his budgets by granting selected favors—a little pork here and there in members' districts. But 2003 was a different story. At the national level, the conservative

Club for Growth had launched attacks on, and threatened to challenge the reelection of, moderate Republicans like Senators Arlen Specter of Pennsylvania and Olympia Snowe of Maine. Now, GOP senate leader James Brulte warned that he would personally campaign in the GOP primary against any Republican voting for even a dime in new revenues.[66] No one broke ranks.

It may have been this strategy that, as much as anything else, set the stage for the recall. It left Davis with the one option that he'd rejected early in the year: declaring the fiscal emergency that allowed the vehicle license fee to rise to its old level, roughly three times what it was at the beginning of the year. It was the VLF increase that changed the abstractions of what became, by Davis's own subsequent estimate, a $35 billion deficit (itself perhaps an inflated figure to justify the tax increases he wanted) into the hot immediacy, especially for the drive-time radio talkers, of a unilaterally imposed tax increase. When he later signed the driver's license bill, the two car issues, both obvious California things—and guy things—fused in a lethal combination. For Californians, and for California males particularly, the driver's license was perhaps the most universal token of adulthood, perhaps even of citizenship.

Schwarzenegger promised to undo them both, and, once elected, quickly did. Despite the additional hole it put in the state's budget, he reversed the car tax increase on his first day in office, bringing it back to the 0.65 percent rate that it had been in the years before Davis declared the emergency, and negotiated a deal with Cedillo, the author of the driver's license bill—the terms were never quite clear—under which the legislature repealed the law in return for a Schwarzenegger promise that he'd consider (work together on? sign?) such a bill if it took care of what he said were his security concerns. What if a terrorist . . . ?

The Democrats, in fact, had little choice—in part, as Schwarzenegger frequently reminded them, because they were even less popular than Davis had been and would probably have also been collectively recalled if there had been a process for doing so. In addition, ballot measures were already being discussed to repeal the driver's license law and, very likely, to impose other restrictions on illegal aliens as well. Given polls showing strong voter disapproval of giving licenses to illegal aliens, even a vague promise from the new governor was better than the almost-certain ballot measure waiting in the wings that would foreclose any possibility of future legislative action. The law, of course, would never have been signed in the first place had it not been for Davis's desperate effort to save his job in the recall. Cedillo succeeded twice again in getting Democratic majorities in the legislature to pass his bill, each time with some additional provision that Schwarzenegger, again citing terrorist threats, had asked for. Each time Schwarzenegger vetoed it. Had he signed it, said a longtime Republican assemblyman, it would have been "Hasta la vista, baby."[67]

The recall did not generate the governmental chaos that some people had predicted. Nor was it a right-wing revolt. On the same day that they ousted Davis, Californians overwhelmingly rejected an initiative sponsored by Ward Connerly, the Sacramento businessman who had successfully sponsored the initiatives prohibiting affirmative action in public university admissions and public sector employment in California and Washington State, that would have prohibited California public agencies from collecting or publishing any data with ethnic classifications except for information required by law enforcement, by medical research, or where mandated by the federal government.[68] The recall did not destabilize government, though in weakening and distracting Davis the recall campaign skewed the budget negotiations and, as in the matter of Davis's approval of the driver's license law, influenced the fate of bills as the recall campaign progressed.

Nor, despite the enormous amount of media attention that Schwarzenegger drew—and continues to draw—was it the great renewal of democracy that others saw. The recall was a novelty item spiced by the cast of colorful characters who jumped into the race and by the Hollywood glow of its star. The percentage of eligible voters who cast ballots in the recall was slightly higher than the vote in the 1998 gubernatorial election—43.1 percent as against 41.4 percent—but hardly a triumph of public engagement. (The Gore-Bush contest in 2000 brought out about 52 percent of eligible voters; the 2004 presidential election between John Kerry and George W. Bush brought out 60 percent.) Nor, again, was it any great break from the past. If it was a revolt against the system, it was a system largely created by the voters themselves, in which the initiative process—direct democracy—not representative government, is the central force in public policy.

The recall, in effect, was very much part of the system, an extension of the plebiscitary politics that have influenced state government at least since the 1970s and have become dominant in the years since. In the 1960s, nine initiatives made it to the ballot; in the 1970s, twenty-two made it; in the 1980s, forty-five qualified; and in the 1990s, the total was sixty-two, and the pace showed every sign of continuing into the first decade of the new century. They dealt with every conceivable subject— a few, such as those restricting the use of animal traps and the slaughter and sale of horsemeat for human consumption, were marginal in the larger scheme of things, but others covered virtually every major facet of government. In such an environment, the only surprising thing is that it took so long for a recall to qualify.

IV

Not long after Schwarzenegger's victory, Ted Costa, the "people's advocate," who had devoted most of his career to conservative populism and who had started the recall, was busy developing yet more ballot measures, among them two versions of a proposal transferring control of the state's decennial reapportionment process from the legislature to a panel of retired judges (one version of which Schwarzenegger would later endorse and make his own). Another of Costa's proposed measures would have abolished California's full-time legislature in favor of a part-time "citizen legislature" that, with some minor exceptions, would meet for no more than ninety days every two years.[69] By that time, eleven initiatives and one referendum were among the sixteen measures that would qualify for the November 2004 ballot, all to be neatly explained in 250,000 words of fine legal print in two official state ballot pamphlets totaling 184 pages (or, alternatively, in quick-hit mailers and thirty-second TV commercials).

Among them were dueling initiatives on gambling, one sponsored by Indian casinos seeking to further expand California's already huge tribal gambling operations; the other sponsored by California racetracks and card rooms that wanted to get into the casino gambling business on the same terms as the Indians. Although neither of them passed, total spending on those measures would top $53 million. In addition, there were dueling ballot measures on primary elections. One was Proposition 62, sponsored by a bipartisan group of strange bedfellows that included former Davis campaign strategist Garry South, State Controller Steve Westly, former Clinton White House staff director Leon Panetta, all of whom were Democrats, and Republican Richard Riordan, the former Los Angeles mayor whom South helped destroy in the 2002 GOP primary. Its competition was Proposition 60, which came from the legislature itself. The former proposed to create an "open primary" in which voters of any party (or no party) could vote for any candidate of any party. The two highest vote-getters, regardless of party, would then face off in the general election. That meant the race might be between two Democrats in liberal San Francisco or between two Republicans in conservative parts of Orange County or the Central Valley.

The idea was to mitigate the hyperpartisanship generated by electoral districts that had been gerrymandered into safe seats for one party or the other. As it was—and as it would remain—the real races were in the primaries, which, since they drew partisan voters, not independents or members of the other party, generally sent the more extreme and uncompromising candidate to Sacramento. Proposition 62, in opening the process to voters of all parties, was designed to bring more moderates to the legislature and thus reduce the bitter partisanship that marked state politics. (Similar primary systems and districting patterns in other states have fueled increasingly bitter partisanship in congressional politics as well.)

Proposition 60, the opposition poison pill backed by a bipartisan vote in the legislature—it was one of the few issues the two parties could passionately agree about—was approved and put on the ballot with lightning speed to kill its competitor. Unless Proposition 62 passed—and passed with more votes than Proposition 60—the system would remain unchanged. But Proposition 62 eventually failed, despite Schwarzenegger's endorsement. Costa's redistricting reform might mitigate those partisan gerrymanders, but given the state's politically polarized residential patterns, the judges who would oversee the drawing of the lines would have only limited ameliorative powers. The state's political demographics made the creation of a lot of genuinely competitive districts geographically impossible.

To cap the list, the 2004 ballot had the five health-related measures discussed earlier. That was itself a reflection of the wider national health care crisis: the surtax on millionaire incomes to support the state's frayed mental health system; the proposed increase in the surcharge on telephone service to upgrade emergency rooms and crisis centers that were in even worse shape (and some of which were already closing); the $750 million in bonds for children's hospitals; the measure repealing the law signed by Davis during the recall-stressed 2003 session that would have required businesses with more than fifty employees to provide health coverage for all their workers or pay into a state system that would provide it; and the stem cell research bond that would cost the deficit-plagued state $6 billion, counting interest, to repay. Arnold Schwarzenegger, the supposedly tightfisted, economy-minded governor, endorsed the fifth one.[70]

It was this last measure that, not surprisingly, got the lion's share of attention. It was a hot issue in the culture wars and, in the face of the Bush administration's ban on federal funding of most stem cell research, it had the potential for a massive repudiation of the president's policy. It had the endorsement of the American Diabetes Association, the American Lung

Association, the California Medical Association, a long list of Nobel laureates, leading medical researchers, and an array of other scientists. It
also had the blessings of politicians of both parties, much of the Hollywood community, many city councils, and even some Chambers of
Commerce. Its financial backers, led by Palo Alto developer Robert
Klein, whose son suffered from juvenile diabetes, included major Silicon
Valley venture capitalists, executives of biotech firms, and other deep-
pockets, who collectively raised close to $30 million for the campaign.
The opponents—a coalition of fiscal and social conservatives, Catholic
bishops, and liberals fearful that it could lead to corporatized human engineering for those wealthy enough to afford it—had almost no money.[71]

Like Klein, who put more than $2 million into the campaign and who
would become chairman of the commission that controlled the money,
many of the measure's backers had family members suffering from dis-
eases—diabetes, Parkinson's, Alzheimer's, multiple sclerosis, and other
auto-immune afflictions—for which stem cell work might offer remedies
and had longtime commitments to the cause. The campaign had the potential of giving the state a head start in a science, and possibly an industry, that could deliver major benefits, both medical and economic. But
those industries and the venture capitalists behind them, as Robert Stern,
head of the nonpartisan Center for Governmental Studies, argued, were
also in a position to profit from the taxpayers' massive investment,
should it ever pay off, just as the people on the commission were posi-
tioned to help their friends. "We are talking about Stem Cell Valley replacing Silicon Valley," he told a reporter. "If the state is going to jump-
start this research with lots of money, somebody is going to make
money."[72]

The measure provided no assurance that the state would get any com-
mensurate share of the revenues of the potentially lucrative biotech
patents the research might produce—there wasn't even any assurance
that all the funds would go to stem cell work. Thus there were plenty of
grounds for the charge that, however attractive as a social and emotional
issue, it was potentially a huge subsidy to private industry and another

drain on a state budget that was already facing deficits as far ahead as the eye could see—that it was, in short, a flagrant example of special-interest ballot-box budgeting. It nonetheless passed with nearly 60 percent of the vote. A year after the voters allegedly revolted against "the system," the system, with the voters' strong support, remained very much intact.

4

HYBRID DEMOCRACY

For much of his career, Arnold Schwarzenegger had boasted about his skills as a game player who had succeeded as a bodybuilder by psyching out his opponents. He had also fostered a reputation for himself as a shrewd deal maker, both in Hollywood and in his other business ventures. As soon as he took office in November 2003, just forty days after his election, he began to broker deals. He negotiated with Democrats on a monster $15 billion bond to cover the expected budget deficit the state faced, much of it to replace a legally dubious bond that Gray Davis and the legislature had approved the previous year, and part of it to cover the additional $4 billion in revenues that Schwarzenegger himself had lost when he slashed the car tax on his first day in office.

Thereafter he arranged closed-door deals with Democrats on the reform of the costly workers' compensation system; then with the California Teachers Association, which allowed him to cut $2 billion from the $4 billion funding increase that the state's schools would have been constitutionally entitled to; then with the leaders of the University of California and the California State University system to cap enrollment and raise fees; then with the California Correctional Peace Officers Association, the state's muscular prison guards' union; then with five of the major casino-operating Indian tribes (which he later described as the most powerful special interest in the state); and then with local governments, in which they gave up $1.3 billion in each of the succeeding two years (2004–2006) in return for a constitutional guarantee effectively prohibiting the state from raiding their property taxes in the future as it had often done in budget crises in the past.[1] It was certainly, as he loved to say, action, action, action.

"This election was not about replacing one man or one party," the new governor said at his swearing-in ceremony. "It was about changing the entire political climate of our state. Everywhere I went during my campaign, I could feel the public hunger for our elected officials to work together, to work openly, and to work for the greater good."[2] And in the early months of his first year, he succeeded remarkably well, getting the Democrats to, in effect, accept a budget without tax increases (albeit with $15 billion in borrowing), and getting Republicans to agree to something considerably weaker than the absolute spending limits that they had wanted. After decades of extreme partisanship, he said, "Democrats and Republicans are coming together." The only major opposing voice came from Treasurer Phil Angelides, who had plans to run for governor himself but who seemed genuinely offended at the fiscal heresy of borrowing to pay for current operating costs. With his borrowing, Schwarzenegger was doing just what Bush was doing.[3]

For the first six months, it was mostly hearts and flowers. From one day's headlines: "Governor Gains Praise from Both Parties; Schwarzenegger Winning Over Skeptics" (Carla Marinucci in the *San Francisco Chronicle*); "Here's the Real Uniter, Not Divider" (Daniel Weintraub in the *Sacramento Bee*); "Even Gray Davis Has Praise for Schwarzenegger" (Dion Nissenbaum in the *San Jose Mercury News*).[4] Every day there were clusters of people around the governor's door at the capitol, above which he'd had his own name chiseled, hoping to get a glimpse of the man who was almost certainly the best-known American public official after the president himself.

He also got surprisingly good marks from people like Darrell Steinberg, the thoughtful Democrat who chaired the Assembly Budget Committee. Schwarzenegger was accessible, Steinberg said two months after the new governor took office; he listened, he was personable, and he was willing to change his mind when new facts came along. It was heartening how well he was working with the legislature. Steinberg's colleague Assemblywoman Lois Wolk, a Democrat from Davis, said almost the same thing. Arnold, she declared during the early months, was a centrist who played things right down the middle. There also was almost a sense of relief in the capitol that Davis, who was always seen as remote, guarded, and calculating, was gone.

Arnold was willing to take risks, to "engage," as David Janssen, county executive for Los Angeles, put it. Schwarzenegger, said Senator John Vasconcellos, the legislature's apostle of self-esteem, who earlier had threatened to quit if the recall succeeded, was "bright, charming, like Clinton, plus a couple of notches. . . . There's a hunger [among Americans] for authenticity."[5] Schwarzenegger's chief partner in many of those negotiations, particularly on the budget and workers' compensation, was the famously grumpy senate president pro tem, John Burton, the veteran labor liberal from San Francisco. He'd served in Congress, in the state assembly, and now was in his last year in the senate, and he was passionately devoted to improving health care and other social services for poor people. For much of that first year, Burton and Schwarzenegger seemed genuinely to enjoy each other's company, often meeting in the tent the governor had set up in the inner courtyard outside his office on the ground floor of the smoke-free capitol, where he could smoke his cigars and hand them out to his visitors. Burton brought the coffee. "He liked to bullshit me," Burton later recalled. "And I bullshitted him."[6]

But even in the early months, Schwarzenegger was not reluctant to issue threats of retaliation against Democrats who opposed him on things like workers' compensation reform. He warned that he would go into their districts and rouse their constituents, and on a few occasions he tried, though judging from calls and e-mails to legislators, with very limited success. He would go to the ballot again if the legislature resisted, had indeed already collected 1.2 million signatures for a workers' com-

pensation initiative and was ready to go to the voters. And he would seriously consider supporting a constitutional revision reinstituting the
part-time legislature—essentially the same idea that Costa himself was
then hoping to put on the ballot, but one that, in failing to generate much
enthusiasm in the polls, was soon dropped. They had too much time for
silly bills, the governor said, like John Burton's bill prohibiting the sale
of foie gras and the force-feeding of geese to produce it. (When he got
the bill, however, maybe as a favor to his old friend, he signed it. Then,
a few weeks after signing it, he made fun of it again.) And then, when
talks stalled over the deal Schwarzenegger had made with local governments in the final days of budget negotiations, he made his famous "girlie
men" remark.

The honeymoon with the Democrats had started losing its luster well
before the "girlie men" episode. Schwarzenegger had shrewdly finessed
them in his deal with the teachers' union, among the strongest of the
Democrats' constituency groups. In return for a onetime $2 billion re-
duction in the legally required level of the school budget to which they
agreed for an indefinite period—it was essentially an open-ended loan
until state revenues went up—he freed local districts from some constraints in spending, shifting money from categorical programs for things
like bus services to unrestricted aid, meaning that more money could
(and would) go on the bargaining table for employees. But the assumption was that, in the following year, funding would be restored to its constitutionally required level. He also end-played the Democrats in his
closed-room deals with the university presidents and chancellors, who
agreed to short-term enrollment caps and student fee increases in return
for a promise of more generous treatment in the years ahead. (In the face
of Democratic resistance, that deal, which for the first time threatened
to turn away qualified students from both systems, was later modified.)

The deals with the education groups had effectively taken away two
of the Democrats' biggest weapons. If they couldn't use school funding
and university enrollments as leverage for additional revenue, they had
lost two crucial bargaining instruments. But their initial anger, at least

about the universities, was directed as much or more at University of California president Bob Dynes and California State University chancellor Charles Reed for capitulating to the governor. (University officials, speaking on background, responded that the legislature had agreed to certain enrollment caps and fee increases during Davis's final year. How could they now rely on the Democrats?)

The clincher was Schwarzenegger's promise to the local governments, again made in closed-door talks, for a constitutional amendment that, after a two-year hiatus, would forever protect their revenues and thus, in future emergencies, prevent the state from using some of them for the health, social services, and other programs that the Democrats deeply cared about. The locals had a legitimate long-standing complaint. With some marginal exceptions, the passage of Proposition 13 in 1978 had effectively destroyed their authority to increase local property taxes. And because the remaining property tax—which in the pre–Proposition 13 era had been divided among cities, counties, schools, special districts, and other local agencies according to the separate tax rates they set—was now capped and thus had to be allocated among them by legislative action, the state got effective control of the tax. And beginning with the recession of 1991, the legislature began to snatch chunks of it from the cities and counties to balance its own budget and to meet the spending minimum mandated for the schools by Proposition 98, the constitutional initiative passed by the voters in 1988. But as the state continued to take some of the cities' and counties' property taxes even after the recession ended—they later estimated that they'd lost some $40 billion, an average of some $3 billion a year—they became, in effect, a kitty to be raided whenever Sacramento wished. The consequences were, and continue to be, obvious in the underfunding of many local services.

In 2004, after two or three false starts, the League of Cities and the California State Association of Counties, which in the years after the passage of Proposition 13 had become well-organized lobbying groups, qualified their own initiative to stop the state from snatching more money in the future. Schwarzenegger, badly needing to take another $2.6

billion from the locals to balance his budgets in the succeeding two years, got them to "orphan" their initiative in return for his support of a combined ballot measure that would do everything they wanted except in the first two years. But the compromise measure, Proposition 1A on the November 2004 ballot, also locked in the convoluted fiscal relationship and tax structure that had evolved between the state and locals in the years after the passage of Proposition 13. Because that tax structure made sales taxes much more attractive than the severely limited property taxes that Property 13 allowed (and because most housing involved more costs in schooling and other services than it generated in taxes), locals fought fiercely for shopping malls, auto malls, and other retail projects. Those developments generated good sales taxes without burdening the community with more children, or the need for parks, much less the social problems that low-income residents were believed to bring with them. Conversely, local governments tended to give low priority to, or actively resisted, planning for well-balanced mixes of housing—or even for businesses providing good jobs. In the trade it's known as "fiscalization of land use."[7]

For years, Steinberg, at the time the assembly's budget committee chairman, had fought to work bills through the legislature to remedy those distortions, always to be frustrated by the power of the handful of cities that benefited from them. Now, when the governor's deal with the locals threatened to make them permanent, Steinberg and his frustrated fellow Democrats balked.[8] In response, the governor flip-flopped, not once but twice. First he appeared to promise Democrats they would have more flexibility in tight times to protect other government programs, particularly foster care and other welfare and health care services for the indigent. Then when the locals learned of the deal and, supported by Republicans, who were also feeling neglected, issued loud protests—the city manager of Beverly Hills called the legislature "the state's utmost terrorist organization"—Schwarzenegger tacked back again.[9]

The resulting stalemate took Schwarzenegger well beyond his promise that the state would have a budget by June 30, the beginning of the new fiscal year. The deadline had routinely been missed under both Democratic and Republican governors and it rarely had major practical consequences, but it was a simple issue and always seemed to get media attention. For Arnold, then, making the deadline would be another example of the new régime in Sacramento. When he failed, he blamed it on "special interests," as he often did. The "girlie men" remark, which echoed his behavior during his previous careers—making fun of stars like Sylvester Stallone whom he regarded as competitors—alluded to an old *Saturday Night Live* television comedy takeoff satirizing Schwarzenegger's own persona. First made at a shopping mall rally in Ontario, California, in the fast-growing and generally conservative Inland Empire east of Los Angeles, the comment set off a brief tempest of complaints about sexism and homophobia. It was, of course, directed at the Democrats, who were then holding out on a budget issue that Schwarzenegger had already made side agreements on—often with the same kind of special interests that he had accused the Democrats of representing. "If they don't have the guts," the governor said,

> to come up here in front of you and say, "I don't want to represent you, I want to represent those special interests, the unions, the trial lawyers, and I want them to make the millions of dollars"—if they don't have the guts, I call them "girlie men."
>
> Their approval rating is in the 30s. My approval rating is in the 70s. . . . The people know loud and clear they are obstructionists right now. They're stopping the budget. I am representing you, and the people know that they are representing the special interests and not the public's interests.[10]

He liked playing the populist Hiram Johnson role—it became one of his favorites. At an event late in 2004 honoring women where the governor spoke, and where a group of nurses held up a sign protesting his decision to defer a mandate that would have increased hospital nurse staffing from one for every six patients to one for every five, he called them a special interest: "Special interests don't like me because I kick their butt." By the time he made that remark, he had raised more than

$25 million from big business interests for his various ballot campaigns and his travel expenses to the GOP convention, much of it in six- or even seven-figure amounts, from Anheuser-Busch, Blue Cross, Chevron-Texaco, Hewlett-Packard, Rupert Murdoch's Newscorp, Pacific Gas and Electric, SBC, Toyota, and Wal-Mart, as well as from various real estate developers, Silicon Valley venture capitalists, and others—more than Davis, regarded as California's all-time champion fund-raiser, had ever collected in a single year.[11] In the following year, he would raise a lot more.

Nor did anyone around the governor take much notice of the fact that the refrain about special interests ran diametrically counter to the deal making, much of it behind closed doors—and often with the state's most powerful interest groups—that he also prided himself on. Davis and the legislature had been widely—and justly—accused of agreeing to a deal with the prison guards that gave them enormous pay and benefit increases beyond the generous pay and perks (including "fitness pay" for which the individual need pass no fitness test) and the hefty powers they already had. According to Elaine Howle, the independent state auditor, the contract approved in 2002, an election year when the California Correctional Peace Officers Association made large contributions to Davis and key legislators, would cost the state an additional $518 million annually, an increase of 10 percent in the state's already huge $5 billion corrections budget.[12] Over the years, the union had amassed so much power in running California's brutal, scandal-ridden system that the guards often seemed to have more control over the prisons than did the officials to whom they were, in theory, accountable—to the point where Thelton Henderson, a federal judge in San Francisco, threatened to seize the whole system if it wasn't reformed. (In June 2005, he acted. Declaring that the state had been either unable or unwilling to implement remedies, he seized control of the entire prison health system, a $1.1 billion operation that was so chaotic, negligent, and brutal that it was causing more than one unnecessary death a week. The system, Henderson said, was guilty of "outright depravity.") The wardens, as *Sacramento Bee* columnist Daniel Weintraub, generally a sympathetic observer of the Schwarzenegger administration, put it, "were under the thumb of the guards."[13]

Schwarzenegger, eager to prune the state's deficit-ridden budget, had promised to undo at least $300 million of the additional pay and benefits costs in the prison guards' contract signed by Davis. Schwarzenegger now negotiated a new contract that temporarily deferred $108 million of that amount (eventually it would all have to be paid to the guards) while increasing health benefits, giving the union the right to obtain videotapes of prison fights to use in its public relations, virtually guaranteeing that there would be no layoffs, and granting the union still more power within the system.[14] And while a few individual legislators attacked the agreement, they ultimately approved it. The prison guards had a tough job, Burton said afterward, and probably deserved it.[15] Although Schwarzenegger, boasting of his personal wealth, had proclaimed his independence from special interest money—perhaps best exemplified by the Indian casinos and the heavy-spending prison guards—in the end the deal he negotiated was essentially no different from the one Davis had agreed to two years before and, in some respects, worse.

But by far the biggest of Schwarzenegger's first-year deals was that $15 billion deficit bond—essentially a way of stretching out the state's deficit problem for as long as eleven years, depending on economic conditions—that he got the Democrats to agree to, and the accompanying constitutional amendment that he sold to the voters as a promise that the state would never get into the same kind of fiscal hole again. What it did was consolidate all the state's debts into one pot and use new borrowing to cover them. But it did not confront the state's structural problem: the growing gap on every budget graph between the rise in projected spending—much of it constitutionally mandated and a lot more of it necessary simply to maintain even California's mediocre levels of services—and the expected revenues from taxes, the federal government, and a few other sources. The first of the two lines was rising more sharply than the second, meaning that either revenues had to be raised or spending cut, or both.

Governor Pete Wilson, facing a severe deficit during the deep recession of the early 1990s, had agreed to a deal with the legislature's Democrats that, in effect, split the difference between spending reductions and tax increases. That agreement had been followed by what was probably the biggest economic boom in the state's history and, ultimately, not only by the sunsetting of those taxes but by other tax cuts as well. A decade later, California, like the nation, was in a new era in which partisanship and insistence on ideological purity drove things as never before. Schwarzenegger, despite his great popularity and his promises of action, deferred the tough choices just as Davis and the legislature had done the two years before. The governor's budget, said Elizabeth Hill, the state's nonpartisan Legislative Analyst, "misses an important opportunity to make more meaningful inroads toward eliminating the state's long-term structural imbalance—a persistent gap that the state will not be able to simply 'grow its way' out of." All that, she said, has "resulted in a worsening in the state's long-term fiscal outlook."[16]

At his swearing-in on November 17, 2003, Schwarzenegger promised "a new day in California." He had not sought office "to do things the way they've always been done." But like much else in his first year, his first budget, as a growing number of critics began to point out, was not merely similar to the last Davis budgets, but worse. Until he was frustrated by the Republicans in the legislature, Davis, not unlike Wilson, had proposed a fiscally sound combination of about $8 billion in tax increases and matching spending cuts, with relatively few gimmicks and borrowing.[17]

Schwarzenegger had proposed major cuts, particularly in higher education, and he hoped to make more, but was either blocked by the majority Democrats in the legislature or deterred, it was said, by Maria or simply by his desire to please all sides. On a number of proposed cuts, most famously on the plan agreed upon with the universities to send thousands of university-qualified students, including some of California's best and brightest, to the state's community colleges for their first two years, he reversed himself. All those students had received those letters saying, in effect, "Congratulations, you've been admitted to the university, but sorry, you have to start at a community college"—and some had already made alternate plans—when they were informed they could come to some University of California campus or some California State University branch after all. The idea of having a sizeable number of students begin at the community colleges and then transfer to a four-year university had always been a part of the state's Master Plan (albeit never fully realized), but it was never contemplated in this fashion.[18]

The things Schwarzenegger seemed to crave most were power and admiration. (The four most insecure professions in the world, said Bob Mulholland, the sharp-tongued chief strategist for the California Democratic Party, "are bodybuilders, psychiatrists, politicians, and actors, and Arnold is three of them.")[19] He liked to describe himself as an inherently positive person who could achieve anything he set his mind to. Someone in the capitol called him a cheerful narcissist. He also seemed to believe that he had visionary qualities. At the start of his second year in office, he declared that this "is the year when things will change very drastically, because I have a feeling for it, and I always see the thing ahead of time." In his earlier career, he said, "I saw myself as an action star. Never saw myself as, you know, a musical star or something like that. But I saw myself as an action star and then that's exactly what I did. And I saw myself as the governor, and we did it."[20] Throughout his career, he said in another context, "the image has been everything . . . more important than the reality. The most powerful thing is what people believe about me."[21] In politics, however, the two impulses—the drive for power and the need to be admired—often conflict, and in the attempt to please all sides in the capitol's zero-sum budget fights, Schwarzenegger pleased no one. In August, seven months after his unequivocally positive assessment of the governor, Steinberg had second thoughts, as did many of his colleagues. He blamed much of the deterioration in the positive climate on Republicans, who, feeling overlooked, "couldn't stop throwing bombs." The local government issue, Steinberg said, was "their chance to get their pound of flesh." Moreover, he said, while assembly Republicans all signed no-tax pledges, "they refused to vote for any cuts."

But there was no question that the real responsibility had to be the governor's, and that his honeymoon with the legislature was over.[22] Schwarzenegger, Steinberg said, "allowed himself to get whipsawed." But what Schwarzenegger was never willing to negotiate—or risk any of his luster on—was new taxes, as his Republican predecessors had done in similar crises in the past. All the negotiating was within that assumption—tradeoffs between one spending program and another, or between spending and borrowing, but not a cent in additional revenues was offered—and the Democrats accepted it. Nor was there any clarity in Schwarzenegger's first year about exactly where he wanted to go on substantive policy.

He signed a bill allowing over-the-counter sales of sterile syringes in pharmacies, which Davis had opposed, and he settled the *Williams v. State of California* school-funding suit, which Davis had vehemently fought. He also named a group of cabinet officers and senior advisors who spanned the gamut from the very liberal Bonnie Reiss—a Hollywood lawyer with close connections to the Kennedy family and Terry Tamminen, a respected Santa Monica environmentalist—to the very conservative Donna Arduin, his first director of finance, who had been a principal budget-axe-wielder for governors Jeb Bush in Florida and George Pataki in New York. Riordan himself asked for, and got, the job of secretary of education, a powerless position in which, except for one or two public gaffes, the former Los Angeles mayor quickly became invisible (and from which he resigned in 2005). Some—like Sunne McPeak, Schwarzenegger's secretary of business, transportation, and housing; and Kim Belshé, his secretary of health; and three or four other veterans from the Wilson administration—were competent and experienced players in state policy issues. (Schwarzenegger, it was said, talked to Wilson several times each week; he also relied heavily on former Wilson chief of staff Bob White,

who, as a highly paid political consultant, had long been a smiling émi-
nence grise in the capitol.) But it never became clear whether the spread
showed gubernatorial open-mindedness or merely the absence of ideas
on where the governor wanted to go. On taxes and budgets, he was as
conservative as any Republican. The governor was compassionate, said
Assembly Speaker Fabian Nunez late in Schwarzenegger's first year, "but
he's a conflicted person [who] has a hard time keeping his word."[23] A year
later Nunez didn't sound so understanding.

Maybe there was a grander strategy. In the middle of the governor's
first year, California historian Kevin Starr, just then retiring after ten
years as state librarian, said Schwarzenegger was "trying to restore the
self-esteem of the legislature."[24] Similarly, Bill Hauck, the president of
the California Business Roundtable, which had opposed the recall, saw
Schwarzenegger as "a change agent who could go down in the history of
this state."[25] The recall wasn't about Davis personally: It was more than
anything about government. It might even be a test of the question,
Hauck said, of whether one man can change history. Instead of risking
his own immense popularity, was the governor playing it safe on substance in order to restore public confidence in the process so that major
moves could be made later? (In October 2004, a year after his election,
69 percent of California voters said they approved of the way the new
governor was handling his job.)[26]

Many people in Sacramento believed that, with his deficit bonds and
his feel-good promises to higher education and other groups, he was
missing the great opportunity his high visibility and popularity ratings
were giving him to force the choices that the state would eventually have
to make. If Californians really expected the high level of services that
most said they wanted, and that the state had taken for granted in the
ebullient decades after World War II, were they still willing to pay the
taxes to support them, particularly if a lot of those services went to immigrants and their children? At the moment, there was, as Jean Ross, director of the California Budget Project, said, "a fundamental disconnect
between what people want and what they're willing to pay for."[27]

But with Schwarzenegger's unpredictable tacking and, it was said, with the liberal Maria Shriver whispering in his ear, maybe he was laying the groundwork for bigger moves ahead. Schwarzenegger had never joined his party in absolutely slamming the door on all tax increases, though he had certainly leaned pretty far in that direction. Two weeks before the 2004 general election, in endorsing California's $3 billion stem cell research bond initiative, he not only rebuffed his own party and president on a hot ideological issue—the same president he had so strongly endorsed in his red-meat speech at the GOP convention six weeks before and with whom he would campaign in Ohio—but also showed again that his commitment to real fiscal conservatism was perhaps a bit tenuous. Then, just a few days after the November election, he appointed Tom Campbell, a moderate Republican who was then dean of the Haas School of Business at Berkeley, as his director of finance, probably the most influential position in the administration. Campbell, a former Stanford law professor and congressman from Silicon Valley, was a social liberal—he even supported the legalization of marijuana—but a strong fiscal conservative. He described himself as the last of a dying breed of budget hawks, and his appointment immediately started talk that Campbell wouldn't accept the borrowing and gimmicks that the state had depended on.

Maybe the governor was about to set off on yet another new tack. But in his own style, the pattern seemed consistent: sweetness and light when possible, muscle and ad hominem attacks—on special interests or girlie men—when it was not. He always reached out, he said, as he had in Hollywood, and tried to bring all parties into the decision-making process, but he was also "putting the squeeze on the Democrats." By the beginning of his second year, when California treasurer Phil Angelides, Attorney General Bill Lockyer, and state school superintendent Jack O'Connell, all independently elected, all Democrats, criticized him for his budget proposals and for breaking his first-year deal with the school establishment, he called them "the three stooges."[28]

The media credited the governor for his influence in passing or defeating the half dozen ballot measures in 2004 that he'd taken positions on, among them the two Indian gaming measures, which were badly beaten, and the two measures on which he'd strongly supported the business community. One of those, to—in effect—overturn a bill already passed by the legislature that required fast food restaurants and other low-wage employers to provide some health coverage for their workers, might well have been rejected if the governor had not campaigned for it. The other, sharply restricting lawsuits against polluters and companies thought guilty of consumer fraud, backed by a fat war chest from corporate California, would almost certainly have passed in any case. At the same time, the open primary proposal, where his support defied both political parties, lost. And despite his threats to the Democrats—the warnings that he'd go into their districts to campaign against them, even though some of them had voted for his borrowing and his budgets—the Democrats didn't lose one seat in either house, retaining their margin (48–32) in the assembly and their edge in the state senate (25–15).

Since most of those seats were safely gerrymandered for one party or the other, and since some of the Republican challengers were bogged down in personal scandals, effecting any major change was nigh impossible. Thus it wasn't surprising that, once the returns were in, the governor promised to turn his attention to changing the redistricting process pretty much in the way that Costa was planning to do: take it away from the self-serving legislators and hand it to a commission of "nonpolitical" retired judges who would try to maximize the number of competitive seats. But in his first year, the governor had never really risked much for his party. He had done fund-raisers for Republicans but refused to allow the events to be filmed or photographed. He endorsed them, but if they wanted his picture, they'd have to get it somewhere else. (In the end, even one Democrat used his picture.) Just as he had always been protective of his image as a movie star, now he protected it as a politician. What he managed best was his own persona. At the end of his first year, California government—in the initiative process, in public services, in the heavy reliance on borrowing, in the lack of planning—was mostly more of the same.

II

If Schwarzenegger's first year began as an invitation to collaboration and sweet reason, he launched the second with an ultimatum, calling for merit pay for teachers and an end to the old seniority-based pay and promotion system and demanding that the legislature revise the budget process to give its Democratic majority even less control over spending than it already had (and giving the governor still more). He also demanded change in the state's costly pension system, and the reform of the decennial reapportionment process discussed above. If the legislature did not satisfy those demands within a reasonable time, he said, "the people will rise up and reform [things] themselves. And I will join them." Let's make a deal became let's make war.

What that meant was that he would go to the ballot at a special election he would call for the fall of 2005 and shove it down their collective throats. This, he said, reverting to his familiar Hiram Johnson line, was a battle between "the special interests," a phrase he used seven times in his second state of the state speech, and "the people." And, there would be no new taxes. The state (whose taxes as a percentage of personal income were below the national average) had a spending problem, he said, not a revenue problem.[29] His agenda also included a proposal to eliminate some ninety state boards and commissions. Some were mere sinecures for the politically well-connected, some were captives of the professions they were supposed to regulate, but some, like the Quality Education Commission, were bodies that could embarrass the governor if they developed resource standards or other standards that showed how inadequately the state was funding its schools. The magnitude of that inadequacy was brought home again by two reports issued (in one case not coincidentally) during the same week that the governor spoke, one by the

Rand Corporation, the other by the journal *Education Week*, showing California's near-bottom standings both in educational achievement and, even more dismally, in school funding. When measured against California's cost of living, said the Rand study, California ranked forty-fourth in the nation in its per pupil funding.

Many in the media eagerly rubbed their hands at the prospect of what they characterized as an epic confrontation between Schwarzenegger's "bold" agenda and the legislature's Democratic status-quo majority. But the governor's attempts to close another huge budget gap—at the time estimated at $9 billion[30]—made it increasingly unlikely that the schools would soon, or perhaps ever again, get even the minimum funding that state law (in theory) entitled them to, much less start on the path to the adequate and rational resources they needed. Indeed, at the urging of his fiscally conservative finance director, Tom Campbell, the governor's reform proposals sought to make certain that the constitutional school-funding entitlement would be changed to eliminate one of the key escalator clauses that had been built into it. Social services for the poor, including child care for low-income working families, and cost-of-living allowances for welfare recipients and the aged, blind, and disabled, which enjoyed no constitutional protections, were also scheduled for major cuts. When education lobbyists complained that he had reneged on his promises to restore their funding when revenues went up, as they had, the governor replied that he had to protect the vulnerable people in the various social service programs. Later, despite his earlier acknowledgment of the deal, he said he'd never made the promises the education lobby said he'd made. For them to claim otherwise, he said, was "a right-out lie."[31] Hollywood's ethics, said one legislator, made Sacramento's look like the pinnacle of honor. When politicians made deals, they kept their word.

His reform agenda and the threat of a ballot fight made it clear that Schwarzenegger had no intention of playing defense. "I'm an open-minded person," he often said, sounding more than faintly like Professor Henry Higgins. But with no more than a weak echo of the conciliatory "Democrats and Republicans together" theme that began his first year, he went after the legislature and the state's public employees with a vengeance. "I love Barbara Kerr [the president of the California Teachers Association]," Schwarzenegger said about his first-year deal with the union. "She was great to negotiate with."

But with his 2005 push for merit pay and the reform of tenure, he threatened to cut her off at the knees. In light of the deficit, his failure to deliver the promised funding for schools wasn't surprising. But the attack on other cherished teachers' union rights and on the union itself as a special interest—which in many ways it was—was both gratuitous and, as it turned out, impolitic. In the ensuing months, every group that publicly opposed him—police, prison guards, nurses, teachers—was attacked as a special interest. His own deep-pockets contributors included executives of real estate and development corporations, banks, mutual funds, drug companies, auto dealers, energy companies, retailers and media corporations, many of whom contributed six- and even seven-figure amounts—the largest among them coming from A. Jerrold Perenchio, the chief executive officer of Univision, who kicked in $1.5 million, and from Rupert Murdoch's Newscorp. When Schwarzenegger was asked whether those corporations, many of which did business with the state, weren't also special interests, he replied that because he was already rich he couldn't be bought. But because legislators weren't wealthy, they were always vulnerable. The moral seemed to be that only very rich politicians like him were incorruptible. But as the *Los Angeles Times* learned, his big donors also got closely guarded phone numbers that gave them access to his advisors and, in some cases, the governor himself.[32]

Almost from the start, Schwarzenegger's agenda ran into trouble, much of it inflicted by Schwarzenegger himself. In some cases, the items were little more than labels without much policy substance. If they were vetted at all, it was by the cadre of campaign consultants, pollsters, and media experts that had gathered around him, many of them veterans of the Pete Wilson days (and, of course, from the recall campaign), not by people who understood the substantive policy implications. And since the governor wanted it all on a special election ballot, at least in part because he hoped for a mid-decade reapportionment to be completed before the 2006 election, and in part because it simplified his fund-raising, there was little time for deep thought. Thus his reforms were doubly vulnerable to the errors that the initiative process is always prone to.

At first, the governor endorsed the draft of a legislative reapportionment proposal that, like Costa's, would let retired judges draw legislative and congressional districts. It would prevent the legislature, in collaboration with a sympathetic governor, from drawing a flagrantly gerrymandered map in which few districts were competitive, as happened after the 2000 census, and thus addressed a real problem. But the proposal Schwarzenegger initially embraced also included contradictory provisions. One was a formula by which the margin between registered Democrats and registered Republicans would in no district exceed 8 percent. That provision was itself impossible to meet, since most parts of the state were solidly Democratic or Republican. To meet it would have required gerrymandering on a scale eclipsing even the most flagrant previous examples and violating every constitutional requirement that communities of interest be preserved wherever possible. But it was rendered totally unworkable by an adjoining provision that prohibited the judicial reapportionment panel from considering party registration. (Ultimately, the governor abandoned it and supported Costa's measure, which would go on the ballot as Proposition 77.)[33] On merit pay for teachers, Schwarzenegger admitted he had neither a concrete proposal nor a model, and by April he acknowledged that he was taking the whole thing back to the drawing board.

More politically telling, the proposed privatizing of the state's public employee pension system—essentially to convert it from defined benefits to defined contribution plans like the 401(k)—contained language that, according to the summary written by Attorney General Bill Lockyer (who at the time was thinking of running for governor himself) jeopardized the death and disability benefits of police officers and firefighters. The administration contended that Lockyer's summary was a

political dirty trick, but it drove the public safety unions into an opposi-
tional frenzy and provided lavish fodder for the TV ads that soon followed. Meanwhile, the governor's spending limit plan was going through
what seemed like almost weekly recastings. In its original version, it had
a mechanism that required the legislature to cut expenditures at any time
they threatened to run over receipts or, failing that, see them cut automatically across the board. It was now on "automatic pilot . . . accountable to no one," the governor said in his 2005 state of the state address.
That had to end: "Cruise-control spending is out of control spending."
On that point he was partially correct, although his own ballot measure,
passed in 2002, earmarking some $500 million a year for after-school
programs, was also a ballot-initiated piece of autopilot spending.

But his substitution didn't solve the problem—and was, in fact, simply another autopilot system, as was quickly pointed out by Elizabeth
Hill, California's nonpartisan Legislative Analyst, who turned the
metaphor back on him. "While the 2005–06 proposal has several positive attributes," her report said, "it falls well short of fully addressing the
state's ongoing projected fiscal imbalances. Moreover, its budget reform
proposals would put more future state spending on 'cruise control' and
hamper the ability of future policy makers to establish budget priorities."
The proposed solution "increases the problem rather than addressing
it."[34] In Sacramento, the governor's proposal—which was actually the
idea of finance director Tom Campbell—quickly became known as
"robo-saw."

Robo-saw, officially the California Live Within Our Means Act, au-
thored by Hauck and Chamber of Commerce president Allan Zarem-
berg, would also be rewritten, though not simplified. When signatures
were submitted—it would ultimately become Proposition 76—it provided, among many other things, that spending increases in any given
year could be no greater than the average increase in revenues of the
prior three years. It also provided that, in years when the administration
decided that expenditures threatened to outrun revenues and the legislature could not muster a two-thirds majority to make the cuts, the gov-

ernor could cut whatever he wished. In any year, moreover, when the legislature could not muster the two-thirds vote to enact a budget by the June 30 constitutional deadline (or when the governor had vetoed it), the previous year's budget would be continued—including whatever onetime expenditures had been budgeted for the previous year. It also eliminated a key school-funding escalator clause of Proposition 98 that, if approved by voters, would cost the schools about $4 billion a year, reducing per-pupil spending, already well below the national average, by another $600.[35] In toto, Proposition 76 would give the governor still greater power against the legislature, and conservatives still more clout in trimming public programs.

As politics, the Schwarzenegger program was indeed bold; some of the governor's critics regarded it as nothing short of outrageous. It was a frontal attack on the "special interests" and the likely opening salvo of what would shape up as perhaps the mother of all ballot battles, with the governor and his corporate and business funders on one side, the public employee unions, the Democrats, and some Republican congressmen, who liked their safe districts, on the other. If Schwarzenegger won, he would both augment his personal political power and further weaken the already fragile and fragmented legislature, the shaky Democratic Party, and the unions that generally supported it. John Burton, the Democrats' last strong leader, had been termed out. In the senate, the party, still shell-shocked by the recall, was badly split. Worse, two of its major figures, Secretary of State Kevin Shelley, who later resigned, and Senate President pro tem Don Perata, were then under investigation by separate federal grand juries on similar but unconnected allegations—a fact that Schwarzenegger didn't hesitate to cite whenever convenient—leaving the party seemingly unable to do more than fume, snipe, and further embarrass themselves.

What made it seem particularly portentous at the time was the legislature's impotence. In their weakened state, the assembly and senate, theoretically coequal branches of government, had effectively ceded the tax issue to the governor; a few talked about closing the same corporate tax loopholes for which some had once voted, but otherwise no-new-taxes became a nearly unquestionable position. Legislators, said Hauck, the head of the Business Roundtable, were big shots in the little pond of Sacramento but hardly known anywhere else. They really didn't know how to talk to a wider audience. Their allegiance, and often their experience, was limited not just to the districts—many of them radically different from one another—from which they came but also to the partisans of one party or another who effectively elected them.

The possibility of a special election set off an unprecedented off-year rush—by education groups, labor unions, anti-immigrant coalitions, the Christian right, taxpayer organizations, and a variety of others, some of them expecting the governor's support, some aligned with his opponents, some spinning in orbits of their own—to get initiatives on the ballot. A dozen measures were already approved for petition drives; some sixty or seventy more would be cleared for circulation in the weeks following Schwarzenegger's speech.

Among them: parental notification before minors could get abortions, which eventually became Proposition 73; limits on sex education; an initiative requiring individual consent of public employees before their union dues could be used for political campaigns (Proposition 75); Costa's measure reinstituting the part-time legislature; an initiative to raise taxes on commercial property for the support of schools; a "no urban casino act"; a constitutional amendment forever prohibiting driver's licenses, in-state college tuition, and all other public benefits to un-documented aliens; a "car buyer's bill of rights"; and some forty others (some of them differing versions of the same proposal), most of which failed to qualify. For the political media, the political consultants, and the initiative-industrial complex, it set off a feeding frenzy, "the battle for Middle Earth," in the words of consultant Beth Miller Malek.[36] And, since so many were competing in a short period for the same ballot, as time ran out in May the fee paid for signatures collected would rise to five dollars apiece (and in one case six dollars), boom times for what John Marelius, a writer in the *San Diego Union Tribune*, called the army of "nomadic mercenaries" with the clipboards at the folding tables in the shopping malls.[37] Tom Hiltachk's million-dollar question had turned into a $5 million question.

In effect, Schwarzenegger, elected through the recall, took what Elizabeth Garrett, director of the USC-Caltech Center for the Study of Law and Politics, called "hybrid democracy" to a strategic level. This was not simply running individual initiatives to initiate some policy or program or to roll back some tax. Nor was it the traditional post–Proposition 13 style of initiative-campaign politics, where political candidates like Pete Wilson funded or hitchhiked on hot button initiative issues to advance their own election campaigns. Nor again was it a private deep-pockets citizen proposal to force legislative action on some bill, like that of Silicon Valley entrepreneur Reed Hastings, who in 1998 collected petition signatures for an initiative broadening the state's charter school program. In 2005, Schwarzenegger proposed to use the process as an instrument to enact his whole agenda. He had used the threat of the ballot to force compromise on workers' compensation reform in 2004, but no one in modern democracies had ever attempted to use the institution on such a broad front to enhance his own power and the power of his office and thereby permanently change the balance between the executive and legislative branches. What had been designed to check the power of insiders was now his instrument to enhance it.

When Garrett discussed her ideas at a conference of the Association of American Law Schools, one of the attending law professors asked whether what Schwarzenegger was doing was "Caesarism."[38] There was, of course, no definitive answer; maybe a better word would have been Gaullism. While he wanted to be well liked and had shown a willingness to back off when the opposition got too tough, Schwarzenegger sought power almost reflexively—he hardly denied it—and his administration, according to people in his office, sensed the vulnerability of the legislature and the public sector unions. Still, as Garrett said, people had better get used to this new governing system. "Those who wish to understand the law of democracy and the institutions it puts into place and who wish to propose and implement reforms," she said, "must accept the fact of Hybrid Democracy and work within it."[39] (In Virginia, when someone suggested putting a dispute among legislative Republicans about a tax increase on the ballot, Governor Mark Warner, a Democrat, who was trying to mediate, rejected the idea. A referendum, he said "would turn us into California.")[40]

Schwarzenegger hoped to use the ballot bluster to force deals with the majority Democrats and with the public employee groups whose interests were most affected. The ballot, he said at times, was only a last resort. But what soon developed was what Mary Bergan, president of the California Federation of Teachers, called a game of "initiative chicken," in which the unions and consumer groups, organized as the Alliance for a Better California, began to circulate their own measures—measures that, as John Hein, a former political strategist for the California Teachers Association and now a key adviser to the union campaign, explained, were inherently worthwhile, but which, not incidentally, also attacked the interests of some of the governor's biggest financial supporters.[41] One would require pharmaceutical companies to lower the price of prescription medicines for poor and moderate-income Californians. Another would reregulate the California electricity market, again put energy producers under the control of the state's Public Utilities Commission, and generally restore the system that was in place before California's ill-fated restructuring scheme was enacted in 1996. A third would tighten the state's auto lemon laws. A fourth would require commercial property to be assessed at market value, and not on the basis of the original purchase price like residential property, a change that, if enacted, would cost businesses billions in additional property taxes.

Schwarzenegger and his allies had announced that they were going to raise $50 million for his campaign—nearly all of it in five-, six-, and even seven-figure amounts—from major corporations and executives eager to be identified with what one Sacramento staffer called "Brand Arnold." In circulating their own measures, the unions and their allies were, in effect, putting those potential contributors on notice that, if they did support the governor's measures, they'd have to pony up additional millions to beat ballot measures aimed directly at their pocketbooks. That flagrant jockeying bore little resemblance to anything deserving the name direct democracy. It was a battle among economic giants over money.

But if the governor's initiatives and strategy were bold as politics, as a vision for a better state there was nothing bold about any of it. What it would do is enhance executive power and further check the possibility of any major increase in public spending. Early in his first year in office, Schwarzenegger said he intended to again make California the golden state it once was. But despite some respectful references to the state's needs, his second-year proposals embraced an indefinite continuation of the status quo: the below-par services, the eroding infrastructure, and the light-to-moderate tax burden, all of them inconsistent with what a state with California's history, economy, and ambitions seemed to require. And given the huge federal-income tax cuts the state's wealthiest people had received from the Bush administration and Congress since 2001, plus the phase-out of the estate tax, which cost the state $1 billion annually, the burden on the well-to-do had gotten considerably lighter.

The state did have a structural problem: spending was rising faster than revenues. But the governor's declaration that the state had a spending problem, not a revenue problem, depended entirely on where the base was drawn. If it was set in the trough of the 2001–2002 recession, revenues were rising faster as a percentage of personal income; if it was set in more normal times, revenues were not rising much—and by some calculations were lower than they had been thirty years before.[42] The larger conclusion also depended on just what Californians expected of their schools, roads, universities, and other public programs. The biggest reason "spending" was rising faster than revenues was Schwarzenegger's first-day decision to eliminate the car tax, which forced the state to "spend" $4 billion a year to replace the funds local governments had been getting from the tax—it was, in truth, not a spending increase but a tax cut that caused much of the shortfall.

The problems of the state's pension system, with its overgenerous benefits for cops and firefighters and its rising costs, had to be addressed. Such liabilities were not unique to California or to public agencies—collectively the nation's largest state retirement systems had $267 billion in unfunded liabilities.[43] But in California, unfunded liabilities for present and future retirees were in significant part a legacy of the practice by state and local governments, hamstrung by the budgetary constraints imposed by Proposition 13, of diverting a generation of employee-wage pressure into a commitment of long-term pension and health benefits that would become somebody else's problem. As such, the pension issue, while serious and getting worse by the year, was itself part of the larger troubles in California's fiscal and governmental systems. Schwarzenegger said that, in 2004, his first year as governor, the bleeding had to be stopped. In his second year (and presumably after), he would cure the patient.

But neither the state's dysfunctional systems nor its substandard, Mississippified public services were promised any substantive improvement. California, as Steve Levy, director of the Center for the Continuing Study of the California Economy, said, "was living off its past." Government, said Jean Ross, head of the California Budget Project, had too well hidden the effects of tax limitations on public services, and thus Californians had been spared the tough choice between deteriorating services and higher taxes. But if there was any substance in Schwarzenegger's program, and if it set the course for the future, that choice had already been implicitly made. After the governor announced his 2005 program, among the first to promise to raise money and help in the pension reform effort was Grover Norquist, the executive director of Americans for Tax Reform and the nation's most vocal and determined engineer of antilabor and "starve the beast" policies.

Norquist, a close collaborator of Karl Rove, President Bush's chief political advisor, and a center of conservatism in Washington for over a decade, had been threatening political retribution against any Republican governor who so much as nodded toward any tax increase. Two years earlier, as California was staggering under its budget deficit, Norquist had told the *New York Times*'s David Firestone that he wouldn't mind seeing a state go under. "I hope a state goes bankrupt," Norquist said. "I hope a state has real troubles getting its act together, so that the other 49 states can say, 'Let's not do that.' We need a state to be a bad example, so that the others will start to make the serious decisions they need to get out of this mess."[44]

In 2005, Schwarzenegger picked up the Norquist rhetoric. "We don't want to feed the monster," he told the editorial board of the *Sacramento Bee* as he began his second year in office early that year. "We don't want to feed the state—the public sector—and starve the private sector. We want to feed the private sector and starve the public sector."[45] He didn't think "California should be locked in for eternity on anything," but for the foreseeable future, given the state's deficits and his party's absolutism on new taxes, there was little prospect for anything more optimistic. Where was the possibility for the decent roads, the adequate schools, the parks, and the health care that the new California minimally required, let alone the brighter vision of a great state? In the Norquistian view of the world, deficits and the borrowing that generated them were always a welcome step toward diminution of government social programs and further erosion of the welfare state. In his first year, the governor had been accused by liberals of failing to expend political capital to raise revenues or confront the prison guards. Now he seemed prepared to use it to cut spending and shrink the public weal even further.

III

What no one counted on when the governor launched his big reform drive in January 2005 was the destructive power of his own hubris. In the five months that followed, almost everything turned sour on him. The media, which a year earlier had been respectful, if not adulatory, began to tire of his elaborately staged campaign gimmicks: the appearance to discuss the budget deficit where he turned a spigot that spouted "red ink" and then, of course, turned it off; the drive from the capitol to a Sacramento restaurant in a Hummer labeled "Reform 1" to "collect" signatures on a petition for one of his ballot measures; the appearance in a Sacramento suburb where his campaign workers had laid a stretch of tape between two adjacent homes to show the arbitrariness of the state's ger-rymandered legislative district lines (which, it turned out, was not where the real line was). But perhaps his clumsiest ploy was his quick trip to San Jose to fill a pothole to dramatize the fact that he'd authorized restora-tion of a small portion of the state's transportation funds. The pothole, it turned out, had been dug for the occasion by city work crews just a few hours before.[46] Meanwhile the governor's rhetoric—particularly the re-frain about joining the people against the "interests"—was not just wear-ing thin, it was energizing and fueling the campaigns of the other side. In one union ad, a firefighter declared that the governor "is not fighting the special interests. He's fighting us." In a $2.5 million ad campaign sponsored by the teachers' union, the refrain was the governor's failure to live up to budget commitments he'd made the previous year: Teach-ers taught kids to honor their promises, but "the governor has broken his promise to California's kids."

Although the governor's reform agenda fell far short of solving the state's complex fiscal and governmental problems, it addressed some real issues. In the case of the nurses, the issue was hospital staffing ratios, where Schwarzenegger had reversed a Davis administration order low-ering them to one nurse for every five patients as opposed to six. Such across-the-board formulas were at least debatable and, as a subject of state regulation, even more debatable. For the teachers, the issue was the attempt to weaken the autopilot school-funding formula of Proposition 98 and his attack on the seniority system, both of which were probably ripe for thoughtful reform. For the cops and firefighters, the issue was a pension system that had been manipulated through the power of their unions to provide retirement and disability benefits at unheard-of levels of generosity, often for people who were not much older than fifty.

His proposals, which quickly showed haste and lack of policy in-put in their drafting, soon ran into heavy weather. Combined with Schwarzenegger's attacks on the broad spectrum of public employees who opposed them as "special interests" (which, as well-organized and sometimes well-funded lobbies and unions, they certainly were), his new proposals unified teachers, public safety workers, and nurses far more effectively and solidly than the unions could have done on their own. Within weeks of his January speech, the nurses, teachers, police officers, and firefighters, often joined by parents of schoolchildren, were out in force demonstrating outside hotels and the other venues where the governor's campaign held its fund-raisers, flying "Air Arnold" planes with streamers ("Don't Be Big Business's Bully," said one) over his events, and eventually becoming so intense that the man who, a year earlier, had drawn nothing but cameras and cheering crowds had to slip into his fund-raisers through side doors and garage entrances.

The nurses seemed most creative in managing to insert small groups of protestors into those events—from which they were unceremoniously, and very publicly, thrown out. But the essential power of the demonstrations and the ads—and the pictures of nurses being evicted from the fund-raisers Arnold conducted on behalf of "the people" in glitzy hotel ballrooms with well-heeled executives, some of whom paid ninety thousand dollars apiece for the privilege of being photographed with him— was that they featured individuals representing some of the most respected groups in each community. Schwarzenegger, who liked to flaunt his salesman's skills, had told a visitor in January that with $30 million he could pass any initiative. But somehow he didn't seem to understand that even the best pitchman didn't take on such an array in a frontal attack, complete with gratuitous insults about girlie men and kicking the nurses' butt, and walk off unscathed.

By April Schwarzenegger's approval rating had sunk from 60 percent in January 2005, and nearly 70 percent the previous October, to 40 percent; only 28 percent approved of his handling of education; by June, in another poll, it had declined to 37 percent among registered voters, one of the lowest ratings for any governor.[47] On May 2, the *New York Times* made it official with a front-page story observing that "the larger than life governor has been brought down to size." By late June, the Field Poll reported that nearly 60 percent of Californians said the state was on the wrong track. Some 29 percent believed it was on the right track.[48] Then, in what was almost certainly a response to the polls and protests—it was a move that echoed Pete Wilson's tactics a half generation earlier, and was almost certainly contrived by the Wilson people around him— Schwarzenegger jumped into the immigration fight.

First he called for closing the border, by which, he later explained, he meant increasing border enforcement, not actually closing it. (It was his bad English, said the immigrant governor, that led him to misspeak.) Then he endorsed the self-styled Minuteman Project, the posse of volunteers who, much to the consternation of the U.S. Border Patrol, had been running around with guns, radios, and binoculars on the Arizona-Sonora border to spot the illegals coming across and report them to the authorities. What made the Minutemen particularly unappreciated was the fact that they set off the buried sensors designed to alert the Border Patrol to illegal crossers. President Bush called them vigilantes. Schwarzenegger said they were doing "a fantastic job" and that he would welcome them to the California-Baja border if they came there, as they said they intended to.

As it had temporarily boosted Wilson's poll ratings in the 1994 campaign, the leap into the immigration issue, some by way of the same right-wing talk shows that had helped bring down Davis, would no doubt help with voters. But it was also a good indication that even Arnold's consultants thought that, at least for the moment, things had turned sour. It also showed that Maria Shriver's husband wasn't above a little demagoguery. Still, as his approval ratings dropped—and as the immigration ploy failed—he tacked again, showing himself to be more accommodating than his rhetoric had indicated only a few weeks earlier. By early July, as he and the Democrats were in the final negotiations on a compromise budget that again depended on borrowing, deferrals, and fudges, but which was only ten days late, Maria was taking the fourteen-year-old daughter of his "girlie man" nemesis, Speaker Fabian Nunez, to lunch.

In the meantime, however, the "bold" agenda had been changing and shrinking almost by the week. Schwarzenegger deferred his wounded pension-reform proposal, saying he'd try to negotiate a bill in the legislature; his merit pay and teacher-tenure reform plan had shriveled to a negligible initiative that would extend the time required for new teachers to get job security from two years to five; and his much-advertised "blow up the boxes" plan to abolish the dozens of state boards and commissions that he said were unnecessary or wasteful was dropped altogether. What remained were Costa's—now the governor's—reapportionment reform, which narrowly survived a series of preelection court challenges, and Proposition 76, the California Live Within Our Means Act, the constitutional "spending cap." In addition a handful of other measures qualified, among them the energy reregulation measure, designed in considerable part as a bargaining chip to deter large corporations from supporting conservative initiatives, and two dueling drug-price bills, the one sponsored by consumer and union groups, the other by the industry. By June, members of the Pharmaceutical Research and Manufacturers Association had kicked in some $80 million to beat the consumer-friendly initiative sponsored by unions and consumer groups and pass their competing, industry-friendly alternative. Donations from the industry group included nearly $10 million each from Pfizer, Glaxo-SmithKline, and Merck—almost certainly a record for corporate money—plus contributions of roughly $5 million each from Amgen, Eli Lilly, Novartis, and Bristol-Myers Squibb.

More important, there was a frontal attack on public employee unions that would prohibit them from using any member's dues for any political purpose unless that member agreed annually in writing. It was similar to Proposition 226 in 1998, which had had strong backing from Norquist and Indiana insurance millionaire J. Patrick Rooney, but which—after a previous game of initiative chicken had deterred major California businesses from kicking in, and after a costly union campaign had been mounted against it—was narrowly beaten.

The official sponsor of the new measure, which would become Proposition 75 and which was again named "paycheck protection," was Lewis

K. Uhler, president of the National Tax Limitation Committee, a one-time John Birch Society member who had once worked in Ronald Reagan's administration in Sacramento, and who, with economist Milton Friedman, was a major author of Reagan's unsuccessful 1974 tax- and spending-limitation initiative. Uhler's biggest funder was a "Small Business Action Committee," whose contributors—investment bankers, land companies, developers—wouldn't be disclosed until the initiative had qualified. But from the start, it appeared to have Schwarzenegger's support. There was also Proposition 73, the initiative—which was totally unconnected to the governor's agenda—that required any physician who intended to perform an abortion on a minor to notify her parents no less than forty-eight hours beforehand. It also prohibited any adult from in any way coercing a minor into having an abortion—a parent presumably couldn't threaten to throw a daughter out of the house if she had her baby—and required detailed records to be kept, some public, some not, on all abortions performed on minors.

Despite the fact that it had no connection with the governor's agenda, Proposition 73, the parental notification initiative, funded almost entirely by three wealthy conservative Catholics, was likely to draw the lion's share of the public's—and the media's—attention. It could also bring out conservative voters prone to support the Schwarzenegger and Uhler initiatives and thus become another illustration of how the initiative process could turn into a crapshoot that confounded deliberative policy making. But, aside from the prescription drug measures, the Schwarzenegger and Uhler measures would draw the largest share of the estimated $300 million (including as much as $50 million from the teachers' union alone) that would be spent in the impending brutal battle between consumer groups and public sector unions (on the one hand) and the "Brand Arnold" conservatives who saw those unions as the lifeblood of the Democratic Party and the bane of good government. California had become the Madison Square Garden of the big prizefights between the nation's most powerful interest groups.

On June 13, notwithstanding the low public support for his initiatives,

Schwarzenegger officially called the expected special election for November 8, 2005. Given his repeated threats (or promises) that he'd do so, the fund-raising he'd been doing for much of the spring, and the elaborate campaign organizations around him, there was almost no way he could not have called it. While it gave him some leverage with the Democrats in the battle over the budget, and possibly the chance to declare victory if he could get Democrats to agree to some sort of compromise on his truncated agenda, even his handlers knew that his initiatives generated little interest among the voters. He thus went on the stump warning that, if his measures weren't passed, the left would go after Proposition 13 or raise other taxes—even though none of that could be accomplished without a two-thirds vote of the electorate and had no direct connection with his proposals.

Nonetheless there was an ironic underlying truth in the warning. If his spending cap passed, the chances for any future tax increase would be greatly circumscribed—as would the chances for any upgrading of state programs, education particularly—since the state would be constrained from spending it. If Uhler's initiative passed, moreover, the power of the public sector unions to push for any expansion of programs would be severely curtailed as well. Indeed, it was probably the Uhler initiative that would be the biggest substantive issue, not just for California but also for the nation. Even if Schwarzenegger won on reapportionment and budget reform, he would do little more than reinforce the state's dysfunctional status quo and its below-average public sector investment. A victory for Uhler's paycheck protection would be a blow to the political power of public sector unions everywhere. In September, in what was at least in part an attempt to shore up his financial support, Schwarzenegger told cheering Republicans at their state convention that he'd run for re-election in 2006, a decision that surprised almost no one. He also endorsed Proposition 75, the Uhler initiative, leaving no doubt about his determination to turn his year of sniping into a no-holds-barred fight against the unions.

What was certain was that the special election, the sixth statewide election in California in less than four years, had become part of a permanent campaign of round-the-clock politics. It would further poison the political waters and further alienate voters. It would, said Jean Ross of the liberal but nonpartisan California Budget Project, "set the chances of consensus back by a decade." California's fundamental disconnects—the challenge of the New California, the crumbling infrastructure, the frayed civic culture—were not on any ballot or any other official agenda.

IV

In the days before the special election, the governor, knowing that his measures were in trouble, changed tone again. The ad hominem references to "girlie men," "losers," and the "three stooges" were jettisoned and replaced by a posture of honorable dedication. There was nothing personal, he said, in his campaign. He liked nurses, teachers, and firefighters. He had learned from his mistakes. "The best thing for the state is for everyone to work together," he told reporters on his campaign bus two days before the election: "Democrats, Republicans, the unions." He was just working for California. Nonetheless, his campaign appearances continued to be dogged by those same nurses, firefighters, teachers, and, latterly, by actors Warren Beatty and Annette Bening, who tried to crash one of his events, and, in a clash of Hollywood celebrities, became as big a draw outside the hall as Schwarzenegger was inside.

When the pollsters asked the voters whether they'd be more inclined or less inclined to support a measure if they knew Schwarzenegger was behind it, a plurality made it clear that Arnold was now a liability in his own campaign. On the eve of the election, a Public Policy Institute of California poll found that only 33 percent of voters approved of his job performance; 58 percent disapproved.

For the governor the election was a rout. Every one of his initiatives—indeed, everything on the ballot—was rejected, in some cases by significant majorities. The centerpiece of Schwarzenegger's agenda, Proposition 76, the complex spending-cap measure, was voted down by a margin of

62–38; the proposal to take redistricting powers away from the legislature failed by 59–41. Even Proposition 73, the initiative that would have required parental notification before a physician could perform an abortion on a minor, which had nothing to do with the governor's reforms and which had been heavily favored in early surveys, was rejected 53–47.

Schwarzenegger, hoping to draw religious conservatives to his own agenda, had endorsed the abortion measure. Republicans hired Gary Marx, a Christian conservative political consultant who had worked for Bush in 2004, to get fundamentalists to the polls. But Proposition 73, too, was caught in the wake of a set of proposals and a special election that few voters wanted. Instead of it helping Schwarzenegger, *he* seemed to have hurt *it*. In this leg at least, hybrid democracy had hit a bad bump. Worse, the state had lost a year that could have been spent addressing its problems.

The big winners, if there were any, were the public employee unions, which had again defeated proposed restrictions on the use of union dues for political purposes; the education lobby, which had thwarted the governor's attempt to change California's school spending mandate; and the pharmaceutical industry, which had poured money into the campaign to crush Proposition 79, the initiative that would have required the state to negotiate prescription drug discounts for low- and moderate-income Californians. Because Proposition 79, like Proposition 80, the proposal to reregulate electricity in California (it lost by nearly 2–1), was part of the game of initiative chicken, a strategic effort to draw corporate money from the governor's measures, it might even be argued that Proposition 79 served its purpose.

For Gale Kaufman, the Sacramento consultant who ran the $100 million "no" campaign of the Alliance for a Better California, a coalition of unions and Democrats, it was an exquisite victory. Aided by Schwarzenegger's hubris, Kaufman had countered the governor's attacks on unions with the sympathetic faces of firefighters, cops, nurses, and schoolteachers; had driven off some of his corporate support with her initiative chicken countermeasures; had helped turn Schwarzenegger into what pollster Mark DiCamillo called "an extremely partisan figure"; and had weakened his support to the point where little more than his Republican base was left. Two weeks before the election, the Field Poll found that only 36 percent of voters were inclined to reelect him in 2006, while 55 percent were not. "This exercise in direct democracy," said DiCamillo, "was a bad idea."

But if any of that deeply troubled the governor, who was the biggest loser of all, he showed few signs of regret. Two days after the election, he compared his defeat to a movie "that goes in the toilet." For him, said Kaufman, it was just another piece of show biz; if one failed, there would be another. "But this election wasn't just some joke. . . . How did they throw this shit on the ballot? How can have they have so little respect for the process?" (Kaufman acknowledged that she hadn't done badly herself in the course of the nine-month campaign; but she, of course, was not the one who launched this fight.)

Even before the election, Schwarzenegger had declared that his initiatives were only the beginning—he could have put "fifteen more ideas" on the ballot. On election night, as his proposals were going down, he smiled and joked as if he'd won and again invoked his new-old theme of common ground and cooperation. Together with the people he had demeaned not many weeks before, he would pursue "big ideas, radical ideas" to "make California again the great state it once was."

Sounding like a New Deal Democrat, an echo, almost, of Pat Brown (and like a candidate for office), he said he wanted to rebuild the state's infrastructure—more roads, schools, hospitals. "We need more nurses, teachers, firefighters, and police officers. We need more affordable housing, more energy, and more water. We need more of everything, and I recognize that we also need more bipartisan cooperation. I promise I will deliver that." He'd already been extended an offer "to start working together again" by Senate President Pro Tem Don Perata. But a lot of others, among them Kaufman, Assembly Speaker Fabian Nunez, and Democratic Party chairman Art Torres, were wary and a lot less giving. Schwarzenegger had sounded, and unsounded, similar themes before. On behalf of the unions that Schwarzenegger had so relentlessly attacked, they wanted both a concession and an apology. They got a belated concession, but no apology.

If the election and the accompanying surveys revealed anything, it's that the voters didn't much like either Schwarzenegger or the legislature, whose collective approval numbers were even lower than his. But with a year to go before Schwarzenegger's term ran out, his low numbers hardly precluded reelection. Other governors, including his immediate predecessors, had come back from low poll ratings. In general, first-term California governors get reelected. And, as GOP consultant Dan Schnur said, the Democrats were likely to overreach with yet another gay marriage bill, or some other reform that voters strongly opposed. The Democrats themselves weren't sure that either of their announced candidates, Treasurer Phil Angelides or Controller Steve Westly, could beat Schwarzenegger, and they had started looking at Beatty as a possible alternative. Four days after the special election, Schwarzenegger, endeavoring to recover some gubernatorial luster, took an entourage of officials and corporate executives on a well-publicized trade mission to China. The reelection campaign would begin in Beijing.

For the governor and legislature there was plenty to work on. But the biggest challenge the state's leaders faced was to persuade California voters to allow the state's dysfunctional system to work. Californians, Schwarzenegger said, "are sick and tired of all the fighting," which they probably were, but if they voted *for* anything on November 8, it was the status quo. Californians seemed deeply committed to the supermajority requirements to pass budgets and raise taxes, they liked stringent legislative term limits, and they would rise up in rage if anyone seriously tried to loosen the constitutional restrictions on local government's ability to raise taxes, and thus increase local control. In their deep distrust of government, they refused to give any branch of it more authority to address the problems that they continually told pollsters they were concerned about. Maybe California voters, fearful of the new society growing up around them, really liked their dysfunctional system.

5

FRAGILE EXPERIMENT

In 2003, Steve Murdock, a Texas A&M University sociologist and the official Texas state demographer, and a group of colleagues published a book called *The New Texas Challenge: Population Change and the Future of Texas.*[1] Along with making many other demographic, economic, and fiscal projections through the year 2040, Murdock and his coauthors tried to calculate what the long-term consequences would be if Texas, which, like California, has since become a majority-minority state, educated its poor and non-Anglo students to the same degree that it educated its Anglo children. Not surprisingly, the differences in raising state income and consumer expenditures and in lowering prison populations and costs in human services were enormous. By 2040, under the Murdock projections, aggregate income would be half again as high as it would be if current levels of education achievement remained constant; prison costs would be 60 percent lower; Medicaid costs 65 percent lower. Conversely, under baseline conditions of population change, meaning without substantial improvement in the education of the state's rapidly growing ethnic minorities,

Texas would have a population that not only will be poorer, less well educated and more in need for numerous state services than its present population but also less able to support such services. It would have a population that is likely to be less competitive in the increasingly international and other markets.

At the same time, our analysis has shown that if socioeconomic differentials between demographic groups were to be reduced through increased education and other means, Texas population growth could be a source of increased private and public sector resource growth. Coupled with such growth would be increased competitiveness and a population whose diversity may create a competitive advantage relative to that of other states in competing in international markets.[2]

Late in 2005, in a study modeled on Murdock's, Henry Brady, a political scientist at Berkeley, issued a similar study showing that California, where average personal income had been far higher than the nationwide average forty years earlier, was now just above the median and still going down. Much of that decline, not surprisingly, was attributed to the growing numbers of low-wage immigrants. To arrest the decline and, if possible, reverse it, Brady said, would require higher levels of education and training for those immigrants. As in the Murdock study, the issue was not merely economic competitiveness but also reduction in the need for costly social services.

Such projections, needless to say, aren't hard science. Even if the Murdock and Brady goals could be achieved, which is highly unlikely, particularly in a state as tax-averse as Texas—or, given the cultural hurdles, maybe anywhere—would the jobs be there? And who would do the dirty, menial jobs that low-skilled workers now do? Would that suck in yet more low-skilled immigrants? If the economic projections discussed in the first section of this book are correct, moreover, the growing sectors of the economy might not offer pay, on average, that's nearly as high as the jobs in shrinking industries. By 2005, the gap between the average earnings of college graduates and high school graduates, while still at an all-time high (of 45 percent) had stopped growing, raising the possibility that, with higher high school graduation standards and the uncertain fluctuations in the labor market, the gap might actually shrink.[3] In California, moreover, and probably in Texas as well, the academic achievement of the average white Anglo student was nothing to cheer about either.

Whatever the future of the economy, however, a state of immigrants could never continue as a progressive democracy with decent lives for its people without high standards of education and the social and civic capital it created. "We are not the problem," said University of California president Robert Dynes during the budget crisis of 2004. "We are the solution. Whatever makes California special, creative—its risk-taking mentality—UC is at the center of it." The Master Plan, which guaranteed every student a place somewhere in the state's higher education system, had served the state well for nearly a half century. "But it's not free." Conversely, every time California cut its university and school budgets, said economist Steve Levy, director of the Center for the Continuing Study of the California Economy, "they cheer in Texas, they cheer in China." California can't grow great trying to be like Mississippi. "While we're screaming about education, we're shutting out students."[4] California was living off the huge investment it had made in its education system and infrastructure in the postwar generation. That didn't mean that the high-flying days of the late 1990s would ever return, but without further investment the prospect would certainly be worse.[5] If California were to succeed, it would never succeed at the low end—it could never, as Treasurer Phil Angelides said in 2004, outcompete Malaysia or Indonesia.

What was particularly significant about the Murdock book and the Brady report, however, was that, in trying to look at their states' futures in a systematic way, they underscored one of California's continuing failures: the absence of any comprehensive planning and data analysis capacity. Patrick Callan, president of the National Center for Public Policy and Higher Education, had pointed out again and again, as did the late Clark Kerr, that California began retrenching in its support of higher education—indeed all education—just as the state's school enrollment, including its high school graduating classes, was becoming increasingly nonwhite.

With the exception of the Legislative Analyst's Office, whose staff had been decimated by the effects of voter-mandated budget cuts fifteen years before, there was virtually no capacity in state government to analyze long-term issues, much less any agency attuned to the political and policy implications of the New California. There was a so-called Office of Planning and Research, but it had long been a parking lot for the governor's political hacks during the periods when they weren't needed for more crucial campaign and related work. Under Schwarzenegger, it was headed by Sean Walsh, who had been one of his press people in the recall.[6]

The absence of comprehensive planning and coordination, or even adequate data on many issues, left almost everything to the political struggle and the initiative: between the University of California and the California State University over petty turf issues—who gets to give doctoral degrees in education, for example—or over major questions such as criminal sentencing and class size reduction, both of which have enormous fiscal and social consequences, or between large political and economic interests over the budget. On one side stood Schwarzenegger and his backers in the state's business community, on the other stood the legislature's majority Democrats; the public sector unions, including the teachers' union, with which he had made his friendly deal in his first year; and other backers of higher public spending. A decade earlier, leaders of conflicting interest groups in the capital had met regularly in a "consensus project" to generate some understanding, seek out some common ground, compromise on some issues, and keep the channels of communication open. By the time of the 2005 election, however, that political civility was long gone, and the special election threatened to stifle its return indefinitely. While the state urgently needed to plan for its future—housing, transportation, schools, growth—its leaders, like members of a dysfunctional family, were fighting over shreds of power and buckets of blame, further eroding public trust in government. When they agreed, as they did on the budget, it was only on deferring the tough decisions once again.

Early in 2004, in a "graffiti" session at a meeting in Oakland of the League of Women Voters, arguably still the ultimate good government group, the attendees were asked to post their ideas for making California government more effective and rational. Among the postings: raise the state gasoline tax to bring revenues from auto use into line with the wear on highways and the environmental effects of auto use; bring back the vehicle license fee for similar reasons; restore some financial independence to local governments; close corporate tax loopholes, which, by some calculations, were costing the state over $7 billion a year without any commensurate returns in jobs or business activity;[7] raise taxes on high-bracket incomes; decriminalize marijuana; end the inequities in property taxes under which "my neighbor (who bought her house earlier than we did) pays much less"; repeal the two-thirds-vote requirement to approve the state budget; institute public financing of elections as Arizona had done; stop subsidizing low-wage jobs (presumably referring to allegations that workers at big-box retailers like Wal-Mart who weren't getting health benefits were encouraged by their bosses to get on the Medi-Cal rolls); end the fiscalization of land use under which residential property taxes are so low that new housing doesn't pay for the costs its residents—and especially schoolchildren—impose on local services, and under which local jurisdictions battle each other for sales-tax-paying retailers and auto malls.

Most of the proposals were familiar (some would probably have compounded the state's fiscal problems). Most were arguably moderate to liberal, echoing a long list of previous reform proposals from a spectrum of official and semiofficial commissions: on constitutional revision; on reform of the state-local fiscal relationship; and on requiring more deliberation, study, and public information in the initiative process. In 1996, a state Constitution Revision Commission appointed (albeit reluctantly) by Governor Pete Wilson and chaired by the ubiquitous Bill Hauck, who subsequently served on a variety of other commissions, had come up with many of the items that would appear on the League's graffiti boards eight years later.

The Hauck commission, composed of a spectrum of distinguished government, business, and community leaders, also proposed to restore more fiscal authority to local governments, reduce the long and confusing number of elected public officials, and revise the initiative process to give the legislature some power to amend measures after they pass, which, in one form or another, was the rule in all other initiative states. California is alone in not permitting some form of legislative revision or amendment of statutory initiatives. In one draft, the commission even proposed a unicameral legislature of 120 members, which would make each of California's impossibly large districts somewhat smaller and thus slightly increase the chances voters would know who their member was. By 2005, when Hauck cosponsored the state's budget-cutting California Live Within Our Means Act, most of the commission's old agenda had been forgotten. That was perhaps less a sign of how much Hauck, now pushing the kind of autopilot budget formulas his commissions had deplored, had changed, and more a sign of how much the world had changed around him.

In 1995, another commission of business executives and education leaders had warned that California "can no longer ignore investment in public infrastructure and human capital and maintain a strong economy."[8] For a time in the late 1990s and the first years of the new century, every assembly Speaker seemed to have a commission on some broad array of reforms. But most of all, the "graffiti" sounded like nothing so much as the old civics textbook, founded on the traditional state-local divisions of governmental responsibility, majority rule on policy and fiscal issues, and clear accountability for governmental officials. In another time, most would have been regarded as self-evident. That they were now controversial, if not entirely unattainable, was a measure of how far government, the state's fiscal system, and public attitudes had wandered in the preceding forty years.

Nearly all of the proposals—the League's and the commissions'—had been ignored or explicitly rejected. In 1996, after business interests engaged in a dubious set of fund transfers to bolster their No campaign, voters narrowly rejected a ballot measure (Proposition 217) increasing the marginal tax rate for upper-income earners. In the first years of the twenty-first century, voters turned down one ballot measure easing legislative term limits; rejected another lowering the legislative margin to pass budgets and raise taxes, from 67 percent to 55 percent; and defeated the proposed "blanket primary"—essentially a nonpartisan primary. They also rejected the initiative slightly modifying the mandatory three-strikes sentencing law to require that the third offense be a violent felony, not just any felony. The three-strikes law, which sharply reduced judicial discretion, arguably was precisely the kind of autopilot spending law that Schwarzenegger had complained about. But he opposed the reform.

With the exception of one short-lived flurry of interest among Democrats, two of the most promising ideas were hardly considered. One was to expand the scope of the sales tax to cover services, now the fastest growing sector of the economy, and to Internet and catalog sales, which were unfairly competing with traditional retailers. It was the in situ local businesses—electronics retailers, bookstores, department stores, appliance and specialty stores—that paid local property and sales taxes, supported the Boy Scouts, Little League, and other community activities, and created local jobs, and thus unfairly bore the burden, while most E-tailers paid nothing. More generally, as the Legislative Analyst pointed out, the state was too dependent on revenues from high-income taxpayers and thus on the volatile income from capital gains and stock options. It needed a broader base. The second promising idea was requiring reassessment of business property when control was transferred through a shift in majority stock ownership and/or instituting a "split roll," whereby business, which had been paying a decreasing share of all taxes,

would be assessed at market valuations and/or pay property tax at a different rate from that paid on residential property.

But all reform was effectively blocked by (in the first case) an increasingly costly federal moratorium on taxation of Internet sales as well as by
understandable apprehension about the political and administrative
(though not unmanageable) complexity of taxing services; in the second
case, the problem was the by-now familiar paralysis engendered by anything that came near Proposition 13, the permanent "third rail" of California politics. Worse, both proposals involved wonky process issues that,
even in the best circumstances, the vast majority of voters didn't understand or care about. In 2002, the CTA, the California Teachers Association, came close to running an initiative that would have tied a change in
the business property tax rate to increased education funding, but in the
face of adverse polls, the high cost of the campaign, and competing concerns, the CTA dropped it.

The reform proposals and the commissions that made them, however,
left an ironic legacy, as so many actual reforms had as well: they helped
persuade much of California, and certainly its more publicly engaged citizens, about the state's increasingly dysfunctional fiscal and governmental system and the inability of government to address it. *Sacramento Bee*
political columnist Dan Weintraub was convinced that the recall in 2003
either constituted or symbolized the collapse of an old order in California politics and the coming of some new system—akin perhaps to Elizabeth Garrett's hybrid democracy. But hybrid democracy as practiced by
Arnold Schwarzenegger, while it would almost certainly weaken the legislature even further if it continued, may turn out to have been unique to
an individual who possessed Schwarzenegger's first-year popularity, sales
skills, financial assets, ambitions to power, and inherent belief in his own
destiny. It could not be successfully used by most other politicians—and,
as it turned out, not very much even by Arnold.

Either way, the outcome was unlikely to address most of California's
pressing problems. Given the ongoing domination of the statewide electorate by middle- and upper-income whites and the power of big money,

the old order was still very much in charge, both at the ballot box and, more generally, in California's public life. Its collective preference seemed to be the status quo—or perhaps more accurately, the stasis between the desire for better schools and roads and the unwillingness to pay higher taxes. When Schwarzenegger began to talk about the threat of tax increases in his effort to sell his reforms, it was the status quo he was selling. The conviction that the system wasn't working helped drive the recall and sustain Schwarzenegger's successful efforts in the year following. But the system was largely a creature of the voters themselves.

II

The late U.S. senator Daniel Patrick Moynihan, for many years a close student of urban issues, and coauthor of the classic *Beyond the Melting Pot*, used to say that the best predictor of students' math scores in the United States was the proximity of their schools to the Canadian border. For all its facetiousness, it had a certain accuracy in the national geography of test scores, which tend to be higher in the Northeast and upper Midwest than in the Southeast and Southwest. In part, that may be due to generally more rigorous school systems, in part to lower proportions of minority students, in part to less sunshine and more severe climates. More pertinently, public services, both in their efficiency and in the level of support they get, tend to be inversely proportional to the degree of ethnic and economic diversity of the communities they serve. If the studies are correct that, in the words of the Harvard economist Alberto Alesina and two colleagues, "shares of spending on productive public goods—education, roads, sewers and trash pickup—in U.S. cities (metro areas/urban counties) are inversely related to the [area's] ethnic fragmentation,"[9] then they explain a lot about contemporary California politics and about the deterioration of California's public services since the mid- or late 1970s.

There are no data that apply specifically to California, and there are a great many thoughtful people, ranging from liberal economists like

Stephen Levy of the Center for the Continuing Study of the California Economy to moderate conservatives like Hauck, who emphatically reject the connection. Hauck, perhaps correctly, attributed the largest share of the growing reluctance of voters to support more generous public spending to their distrust of government, particularly state government. Levy, sharing Richard Rodriguez's perception, believes that the changing face—the browning complexion—of the average Californian will gradually eliminate the "us and them" dichotomies of ethnic fragmentation. But the most systematic comparative studies—both at the local level and among nations, and through history—reinforce the commonsense notion that, the more similar the beneficiaries and the voters are, the more likely the latter will be to provide generous support for schools, roads, social services, and other programs and the more likely (for similar reasons) that these programs will be efficiently run. In a major study published in 2004, economist Peter H. Lindert concluded that "the net national costs of social transfers, and of the taxes that finance them, are essentially zero," meaning such spending tends to contribute to a good society regardless of who spends it. Thus, while "no Darwinian mechanism has punished the bigger [public] spenders" in costs to economic growth, both low voter turnouts and ethnic diversity in the population dampen social spending.

> The more a middle-income voter looks at the likely recipient of public aid and says "that could be me" (or my daughter, or my whole family), the greater that voter's willingness to vote for taxes to fund such aid. Affinity would be fostered by ethnic homogeneity between middle-income voters and the perceived recipients. Conversely ethnic division would create suspicions that taxpayers' money will be turned over to "them." So would durable divisions between middle and lower income classes, because such divisions undermine the political demand for safety-net programs. In the other direction, affinity between the middle-income and rich groups, and a greater sense of upward mobility, is traditionally thought to promote the conservative view that taxes and safety nets are bad for economic growth and moral discipline.[10]

Those observations closely track California's history in the two-plus generations since World War II: the high levels of social optimism, even exuberance, and spending in the first generation; then, in step with the rapid growth of the state immigrant population, the tax revolt in 1978 and its progeny in the ongoing series of measures restricting taxes, fees, and spending; and the initiatives further restricting the powers and tenure of legislators and the growing shift from the communitarian ethic to what Philip Chase Bobbitt of the University of Texas called "the market state."[11] There's no direct causal link between the two sets of events, but there's ample anecdotal evidence in the stream of letters and e-mails that follow almost every published statement about overcrowded schools or environmental stress. Lindert's observations are also reinforced by the fact that the New Deal and the development of the social programs of the American welfare state took place almost entirely during the forty-year period after 1924, when federal policy drove immigration to its lowest levels in history. Was that merely coincidence?

The point is made politely by groups like Californians for Population Stabilization, which declared, among other things, that "California cannot be expected to educate millions of children brought here by untold numbers of illegal aliens and millions of legal immigrants. Schools have reached the crisis point." The argument is echoed almost daily even by public employees. "There are 1.5 million illegal immigrants in our school system costing the state $15 billion a year to educate alone," said one Sacramento teacher. "Until they are removed from or charged for the space they take up, we will have a run down, broke education system." Said another e-mail, "If the taxpaying public was to be spared illegal immigration and some other outside influences on the state's financial affairs, they might more willingly submit to a tax increase at some point."[12]

The point is made much less politely by other e-mail writers and angry radio-talk-show callers who say they'll be damned if they'll pay one more cent to educate the kids of people who have no right to be in this country in the first place. Virtually every poll in the past decade confirms this, as do the votes on Proposition 187 in 1994 and on Arizona's Proposition 200 in 2004, which requires proof of legal residency to vote and to receive all public benefits, excepting only those, like emergency health care and schooling, that are guaranteed by federal law or federal constitutional decisions. Proposition 200 passed by a vote of 56–44, including the support of 47 percent of Latino voters. A generation earlier, Howard Jarvis himself made the connection in a newspaper column, published a few months after the passage of Proposition 13, when he wrote about "illegal aliens who just come here to get on the taxpayers' gravy train."[13]

By now, even virulent opponents of immigration no longer contend that people come to this country to get on the taxpayers' gravy train. With the changes in welfare eligibility, and the generally limited access of undocumented immigrants to social services other than schooling and emergency health care, there's not much of a gravy train left. There may still be Mexican women who try to have their babies in the United States so that their children are automatically citizens, but even most immigration absolutists have abandoned the contention (often made by Governor Wilson in the early 1990s) that California is a "welfare magnet" either for immigrants, legal and illegal, or for residents from other states. Most acknowledge that immigrants, legal and illegal, come to work, and often work harder at awful jobs than natives do.

Conversely, there's not much question about the social and economic burdens imposed by low-skill immigrants—as by all low-skill residents—on state and local governments and particularly on clinics, hospitals, and schools, a fact acknowledged privately by even the most liberal school officials. In 2003, the Los Angeles County Health Department estimated that it spent approximately $340 million per year on emergency and follow-up health care for undocumented immigrants. The county also said that 11.5 percent of people seeking care at county-run emergency rooms are illegal (and uninsured) immigrants. The figures were disputed by others who argued—correctly—that a far larger part of the burden was uninsured citizens, a contention that the county's own data bore out.[14]

But, whatever the proportions, the politics are the same. A sizeable percentage of Americans resent those burdens, particularly those resulting from illegal immigration, and, like their predecessors of a century or a century and a half ago, they're aware of the new tones of skin, language, and culture rising around them. And the signs were hard to miss: in 2005 there was that new round of proposals pending both in Congress and in California (by way of a ballot measure being circulated for signatures) designed to further tighten immigration controls; to increase employer sanctions and create a tamper-proof Social Security identification system; to bar all illegal aliens from qualifying for in-state tuition at California colleges; to put into the state constitution a permanent ban on driver's licenses for undocumented residents; to require all claimants for medical and social services to show evidence that they're legal residents; and to impose penalties on all public employees who fail to report illegals to immigration authorities. The reason that "the problem of public goods in America appears so intractable," said the Alesina study quoted above, is that "the public goods problem is linked to another problem that also appears intractable: ethnic divisions."

Nearly one in five California adults, many of them undocumented—some 4.6 million people—is not a citizen and thus not entitled to vote, and of the Latinos who are eligible to vote, less than half do so. Those facts alone help explain the growing gap between voters and the people most reliant on schools and other public programs, which in turn closely tracks the history of Proposition 13 and other tax cuts, the increasing curtailment of legislative discretion through term limits and various other ballot measures, and the concomitant retrenchment of support for those programs. "Brown kids in the schools," said Harry Pachon, who runs the Tomas Rivera Center, a major think tank focusing on Latino issues, "dampen the support for public education," even though Latinos badly want better schools.[15] That's not necessarily evidence of racism. For most foreign visitors, as Leo Estrada, a professor of urban planning at UCLA, pointed out, the wonder is why, "with California's culture of diversity, there isn't more racial tension. They're impressed by our multiculturalism."[16]

But the correspondence between rising immigration and declining services certainly reinforces the research and simple logic which indicate that, when the beneficiaries are the voters or their children, voters are likely to be more enthusiastic about services than when the beneficiaries are someone else's children, especially if the someone else is an illegal alien. As noted earlier, while Anglo whites (in 2004) represented roughly 46 percent of the population and less than a third of California's school enrollment, they still constituted some 70 percent of the voters. Conversely, Latinos, now 35 percent of the population (and nearly half the state's K–12 school enrollment), constitute only 14 percent of voters. In short, the children in the schools, on the playground, in the parks, and in the clinics tend to be "other people's children." And so also are many of the first-generation students in the community colleges. And since they and their parents also tend to be poorer, less well educated, and less skilled in negotiating the official systems, their collective influence is further attenuated. When the gerrymandered liberal legislature blocks crime bills or the power of the Latino caucus threatens to give driver's licenses to the undocumented, the initiative is there to trump them.

This process is hardly new in U.S. history. At the turn of the century, the Yankee voters of Massachusetts enacted a string of laws to remove fiscal authority and other local powers from Boston, then being taken over by new immigrants, the Irish in particular, and transferred those powers to a collection of "nonpolitical" boards and committees chosen by outsiders—to the point where city voters had no control over the Finance Commission, which had the power to scrutinize all city affairs. California Progressivism had inherited a good strain of xenophobia, racism, and suspicion of cities as hotbeds of crime and corruption, as well as its antipathy toward partisan politics, from its Populist forebears.[17] And like other American progressives, California progressives always considered clean government to be government as free as possible from urban-interest-group politics, partisanship, or, when you came down to it, very much in the way of politics of any kind. On the one hand, they embraced direct democracy; on the other, like the Yankees of Boston in the same era, they tried to spread power as far and wide, and into as many non-partisan entities, as possible. It's no accident that California is laced with some seven thousand governmental entities, few of them contiguous with any others.

But California's latter-day governmental discontinuities and dysfunctions are far larger in degree and very different in kind from any in the past. In essence the state is trying to confront and manage a twenty-first-century economy and culture with a rigid adherence to the nation's residual nineteenth-century ideas of nationality, citizenship, and good government, patched with an overlay of ad hoc fixes. The resulting gaps are increasingly apparent in the huge discontinuity between population and voters, which, combined with supermajority requirements on everything from state budgets to raising local parcel taxes, is itself enough, as California Budget Project director Jean Ross has pointed out, to "create a major crisis for democracy."[18] There's the alienation of local voters from a governmental system, state and local, that's ever more incomprehensible and remote; the chasm between declared demands for high-quality services and the unwillingness to pay the taxes to fund them; and the growing gap between the state's wealthiest and its poorest. And then there are the gaps between the globalized market, corporate structure, and labor force movements that honor few national borders, and the industrial-age political system which refuses to recognize them and pretends that just a few more fixes will restore us to some pristine condition. It's more than conceivable that the conditions of the global economy and labor markets in which California is a major player, and the technologies California has done so much to invent and promote, make the state's institutions and its Rube Goldberg political machinery increasingly insufficient to address its problems. For a generation, the state enacted reform after reform, recalled a governor, installed a larger-than-life hero figure, only to find that as a society it seems no nearer to solving these problems.

Because of those gaps, this unique but foreshadowing majority-minority state, with its huge population of immigrants and its high-tech energy, imagination, and ambitions, was stuck in an ambivalent policy no-man's-land. In the summer of 2004, Assemblywoman Loni Hancock, former mayor of Berkeley and a former official of the Clinton administration, and thus hardly a novice in the business, was complaining that, eighteen months into her first term as a member of a term-limited legislature, she was still being forced to try to learn "at a pace the human mind can't absorb."[19] (And of course, by the time she knew much of it, she'd be termed out.) At that moment she was trying to block the planned expansion of a card room in the East Bay city of San Pablo into a giant Indian casino with five thousand slot machines that the governor had approved in a closed-door deal. At the same time, she was fighting for continued state funding of a costly, long overdue (and much mismanaged) earthquake retrofit of the Bay Bridge, part of whose cost the governor wanted to foist on the locals. Did the system, as Hancock said, badly need to become more deliberate? Or was the real problem, as David Broder believed, that voters used to click-of-the-mouse speed were frustrated with precisely the slow pace at which government moved and responded?

Could both of them be right? Five years after the energy crisis and blackouts of 2000–01, the state was still stuck with essentially the same misbegotten regulatory structure that had opened the doors to the price and supply manipulation by Enron and others that caused the crisis in the first place. The governor was talking grandly about hydrogen highways and a million solar homes, neither of which was likely to make much of a dent in the state's problems (and which, in the case of solar energy, was far more expensive than wind). Southern California Edison was encouraging users, including residences, to take advantage of a real-time-pricing metering system that offered lower rates for off-peak use, but in 2005 state policy was still stuck between the advocates of old-fashioned rate and supply regulation and "direct access" free marketers, including the governor, who wanted users to be able to negotiate their own deals on the open market. Politicians, said Severin Borenstein, director of the University of California Energy Institute, "hate the energy issue."[20]

Steve Peace, the assembly member who in 1996 had rammed California's deregulation scheme through a legislature that didn't understand it, later said that when the California energy crisis arose in 2000 his successors never understood that the problem was caused in Washington. "A more mature legislature, with more than six people who had been there at the time the work product was passed, would have had enough institutional memory to fight back."[21] But he might have just as persuasively said that a legislature that was not term-limited might have had enough concern for the future consequences of the original scheme to have looked at it a lot more carefully.

A great many of the political tensions, both in California and nationally, tensions regarding economic development, job protection, immigration, ethnicity, government programs, civil rights, education—the list runs on—arise in the gaps between dysfunctional political institutions and new world technology and economics. If government, state or federal, denies low tuition or financial aid to students who are themselves undocumented aliens, even those who were brought here as young children and have known no other country, isn't the country locking itself into a permanently undereducated workforce—a workforce that will most likely remain forever in this country and on whose skills our economy will depend? If driver's licenses are denied to undocumented workers, many of whom were eligible for them for virtually the whole of the twentieth century, whose life is being eased?

Where's the benefit in a system in which tens of thousands of unlicensed illegal aliens, fearing the moment when the police catch them in their uninsured cars, drive disposable junkers—mobile salvage—that can be cheaply replaced if they're impounded by the cops?[22] If the perverse side effects of ever stricter and more costly border controls result in escalating numbers of semipermanent, low-skilled illegal residents, is anything being served other than some cut-your-nose-off-to-spite-your-face sense of satisfaction? Are current policies in effect trapping increasing numbers of aliens in the shadows of the economy and the common culture and, despite their centrality to the state's economic future, locking millions of them into menial jobs—or worse? And if the state's voters and taxpayers become increasingly reluctant to fund a rich array of public programs—roads, universities, health care, parks—because they benefit immigrants, are they curtailing every citizen's future? Do such policies perversely assure that the rigid class divisions found in Latin American societies will, ironically, take permanent root north of the border—as immigration opponents like Victor Davis Hanson fear?

None of those questions can be effectively addressed, however, until there are institutions in place to make certain that, if the crossborder flow of labor is regularized and controlled, and the nation's de facto permanent immigrants are recognized, there won't again be a secondary wave of undocumented immigrants, as there was after the Immigration Reform and Control Act's amnesty of 1986, only larger this time. There also has to be recognition that, by definition, latter-day immigrants cannot be counted as victims of historic U.S. discrimination, as blacks and, in a different way, American Indians have been.

In many sectors, American policy—and California state policy—has implicitly accepted the fact that, with their educational and economic successes, most Chinese Americans and Japanese Americans (and many other Asians) no longer qualify as underrepresented minorities. At many American universities—and certainly at the University of California—they're overrepresented by a considerable margin.[23] What's politically untenable and self-defeating is the insistence of some activists, flying the flag of multiculturalism, that ethnic or cultural minorities are entitled to taxpayer-supported programs to foster their separate identity as a culture apart, including segregated classrooms, while simultaneously demanding the full panoply of American constitutional rights. One of the reasons affirmative action came crashing down in California is that it became overloaded with claimants, including millions of new immigrants, for whom it was never intended.

In the course of his first term, recognizing both the problem and the growing voting power of Latinos, George W. Bush twice proposed some combination of regularization for illegal immigrants and a guest worker program.[24] Both times the proposals encountered a fusillade of opposition from members of the president's own party. But if Republicans are sharply divided between the *Wall Street Journal* free marketers (and the business and agriculture groups aligned with them) who support the free flow of cheap labor, and the cultural conservatives who want the nation to give no quarter to illegals and, in many cases, demand tighter immigration quotas in general, the left, and the various civil rights groups that the left is allied with, is crippled by ambivalence as well. As discussed above, it's hard to contend that California's changing demographics—and perhaps the nation's—have had no bearing on wages or on the eroding support for K–12 education and social welfare programs. Notwithstanding the need for immigrant labor, no one questions that California's classrooms are crowded with immigrants' children, many of them children of illegal immigrants, providing conservative taxpayers with an argument for nonsupport and giving at least some teachers an explanation, sotto voce, for academic failure.

Yet, despite the rhetoric of immigration opponents, the vast majority will remain here. The United States, said Harvard economist George Borjas, one of the most vocal of those opponents, "is not going to deport ten million people."[25] What makes it particularly difficult is that a high proportion of immigrant households are composed of both legal and illegal immigrants and, because of children born in the United States, of citizens as well.[26] Short of something approaching a pogrom, they can't be driven back. But until the voters are assured that immigration is under control, it's unlikely that California's illegal aliens will be allowed out of the shadows. The resulting policy no-man's-land is not a formula for a healthy democracy.

And yet every discussion among liberals about immigrant rights falls silent when questions are raised about immigration controls. Do the panelists favor open borders? Well, no, not quite. But the borders certainly must not be controlled by creating the inhumane conditions under which countless illegal crossers die in the heat of the desert, or suffocate in coyotes' trucks, or freeze in the Arizona mountains, or are subject to indiscriminate *migra* searches for illegal aliens on the streets or shop floors of Los Angeles. Then how should the borders be managed? What about a guest worker program, combined with tamper-proof Social Security cards and rigorous enforcement of employer sanctions? (Sorry, ID cards are un-American violations of individual privacy.)

What about Mark Krikorian's argument that, if pay were higher, there would be American workers for most of the jobs that people say only immigrants are willing to do? Who did the work in the restaurant kitchens, made the hotel beds, hauled the cement on construction sites, mowed the lawns, cleaned the houses, and did the child care before the great immigrant surge began two decades ago? Who does this work even now in places like Iowa or Nebraska or the thirty other states that, according to the U.S. Census, and notwithstanding the growing dispersion of immigrants, collectively are home to no more than 13 percent of immigrants?

Does any industry, possibly excepting only agriculture, even need guest workers? With fewer immigrants, Borjas said, U.S. workers "would be slightly wealthier and the employers would be slightly poorer, but everything would get done."[27] Conversely, if the labor laws were more rigorously enforced, and if the minimum wage were higher, and if the United States made greater efforts to spur Mexican development—both with pressure for political reform and with investment funds, as the European Union did when it admitted Spain and Portugal—would that reduce both the supply and the demand for immigrant workers? But whenever the tough questions are raised about the nation's immigration dilemma, said Berkeley historian David Hollinger, "everybody leaves the room."[28]

Because most of those questions concern federal policy, they're beyond the state's direct control; but they're not beyond state influence, particularly if the most intensely affected border states made joint efforts to develop a rational immigration reform proposal that combined amnesty for those already here, a guest worker program, a tamper-proof identification system, and effective employer sanctions. All were elements of the Immigration Reform and Control Act of 1986, but in allowing almost any document to be submitted as proof of legal residency, and in failing to enforce employer sanctions, the act legalized millions who were already here without in any way controlling illegal immigration. Instead it opened the doors to the secondary inrush of spouses, children, and others that continues to this day. The state—and the nation— have been enormously successful in assimilating immigrants, but the economic capacity to assimilate them, and more important, the political willingness to do so, is not unlimited. The welfare of the immigrants already here, and of their children and grandchildren, depends in large measure on how national policy treats the millions more who want to come but are not yet here.

III

It's long been a cliché that California is to America what America is to Europe, or maybe now, what America is to the rest of the world—America squared. At least in folklore, it was a place of double immigration: Californians were immigrants first as Americans, after they had ventured across the Atlantic. And then they were immigrants again, during the gold rush, after they rounded the horn—or after they sailed down the Atlantic Coast, slogged across Panama, and then sailed up the other side, or after they crossed the plains, two ranges of mountains, and the deserts in between. They were thus a people with an enhanced claim to a special destiny. Most, of course, only made one crossing—they were children of Iowans or Vermonters or Kansans, who were born in the United States, or they were Asians who crossed the Pacific, or they were Chileans or Peruvians who came up from South America. But the reality never stood in the way of the belief of each generation in its unique role as the special possessors of the place, its history, and its traditions. "The phrase 'these new people,' " wrote Joan Didion, Sacramento's "native daughter," "generally signified people who had moved to California after World War Two, but was tacitly extended back to include the migration from the Dust Bowl during the 1930s, and often further. New People, we were given to understand, remained ignorant of our special history, insensible to the hardships endured to make it, blind not only to the dangers the place still presented but to the continued responsibilities its continued habitation demanded."[29]

With those beliefs came a sense of entitlement: As most Americans (excepting only southerners) believed they were somehow exempt from tragedy, so Californians once believed they were blessed by a special destiny. Maybe it was the weather or the scenery, or Hollywood, or the sales job the railroads and real estate promoters had done in shaping the state's image, or the certainty that, as the ultimate America yeomen, they or their forebears had created the place. "Good times today and better times tomorrow," said Didion, "were supposed to come with the territory, roll in with the regularity of the breakers on what was once the coast of the Irvine ranch and became Newport Beach, Balboa, Lido Isle. Good times were the core conviction of the place, and it was only their gradually apparent absence, in the early 1990s, that began to unsettle California in ways that no one exactly wanted to plumb. The recognition that the trend was no longer reliably up came late and hard in California."[30]

In her pointedly titled little book, *Where I Was From,* published in 2003, Didion repudiated her earlier sentimentality about the old (and presumably vanished) California, a sentimentality that she contended underlies much of the state's confusion about itself. But what she regarded as the telling fact—that in 1993 California was for the first time spending more on its prisons than on higher education (in fact, not a fact at all, despite the growth in spending on the one and the relative decline in spending on the other)—now no longer seems like evidence of change but rather evidence of some larger, darker continuity.

At about the same time, the ever ebullient Kevin Starr, author of far and away the best social history of California (a now classic series about the California Dream) was working on a book that would be called *Coast of Dreams: California on the Edge, 1990–2003*, and that, as its title indicates, was more tentative about the state's future than anything Starr had said or written before. Starr is forever on the lookout for the positive. "It would be seductively easy," he said in the preface to this seven-hundred-page survey of almost everything California,

> to join the naysayers and see California as one vast failed experiment. Do this and I would be considered a deep thinker, like so many others of my tribe, called upon repeatedly by the press and television to say that California was over. But if I succumbed to this temptation, I would not be seeing the full truth about California and its people. And so, motivated in part by a fear that it was all going wrong, I was actively on the lookout for signs that it was also going right: this California of mine, where I was born as a fourth-generation citizen.

But he was forced to acknowledge that the issue remains unresolved. "California continues," he wrote. "But where it is going and what it will become—how, that is, it will handle the diversity of its people, the confusions of its values and culture; the global-colonial nature of its economy, the trade-offs between its militant environmentalism and concern for local well-being [and] the demands of its industrial infrastructure, and, most important, how it deals with the possible loss of one California and the ambiguous imposition of a new and uncharted identity—remains, like this book, on the edge, an open question."[31]

How could it all be put together? Starr applauded the Schwarzenegger election, but the questions seemed to pile up. California had "grown incredibly complex, competitive and cold in comparison to the dreamy lotus land that had once been imagined, even believed in, by many." People were still arriving to "take their chances with life on the edge[, but] for many the edge was dropping off into nowhere." The state was increasingly divided "among the very rich, the merely rich, the affluent, the embattled middle and blue-collar classes, a growing number of the downwardly mobile, the poverty stricken, the marginalized, and those who had fallen completely below the graph." He was cheered by the new generation of immigrants with their capacity for hard work, their commitment to family, their determination to fit into American society, their willingness, whether legal or illegal, to risk so much to pursue the American dream and to raise "American culture to new levels of effective ecumenism." By 2003, he said at the very end of the book, "if and when the United States wanted to see and know itself as a successful world commonwealth, an ecumenopolis, all it had to do was look to California as it remained the coast of dreams, even if so many of the dreams were, increasingly, on the edge."[32]

Starr believed that, after seventy years of progressive governmental programs, both the country and the state were taking a "time-out," a breather to adjust, correct, and absorb the programs that had been created in the previous three generations. There was a "fatigue among Americans about money programs," he said in an interview. "This covenant with the New Deal was up for renegotiation." But he also understood that, for California, the real question was how to reassemble a vast, enormously complex society that had no real model either in its own history or in any other society and that was suffering a serious case of "intellectual impoverishment." Who, he asked, was doing the thinking? Was the California Democratic Party brain dead? Stanford University pretended it was not even in California. Where were leaders like Pat Brown or Clark Kerr or Phil Burton, the San Francisco congressman who saw the grand possibilities of the Golden Gate National Recreation Area and brought it to realization? Where were visionaries like the great Harvard philosopher Josiah Royce, born in 1855 in the foothill community of Grass Valley to a family of California pioneers, who believed that Californians—"persistently cheerful, energetic, courageous and teachable"— would always understand that their interests lay in community and not in narrow self-aggrandizement? California, said Starr, was the "epicenter of a new Mexican American civilization." In people like Richard Rodriguez and David Hayes-Bautista, it had its articulate voices; its Latino leadership showed surprising political maturity.[33] But it badly lacked clear alternative voices and visions.

What was needed, Starr said, was to "rebuild the California narrative"—create a compelling new metaphor—and, though he didn't say it, maybe rebuild the American narrative along with it. Maybe Arnold would do something to help that along: "Everyone is aware of what could be lost." The state was not as divided as its politics seemed to be; it was becoming acclimated to the fact that there "weren't many all-white places anymore." As the official California state librarian, who participated in many local library events, Starr had seen the pride of people in their communities. New people, Latinos particularly, were inheriting the nation's political genes. Still, as a native San Franciscan who, in the face of the privations of his childhood, "had struggled for an optimistic view of life that was nurtured by the larger California impetus," he confessed that he was sometimes lonely and "less optimistic than I used to be."[34]

The idea of California, as Treasurer Phil Angelides said, was "still very powerful."[35] Indeed, for the nation as a whole, the only other possible model, in size or demographics or its economy and education system, was Texas, which had never had magic and was always likely to be a distant second. There was even a story in the *New York Times* about Floridians who, in view of all the crazy things that were happening there, decided that Florida had become the new California.[36]

The problem was that California, perhaps like the nation itself, now had so many particularistic narratives—social, economic, political. This diverse state did not live and die by bushels of wheat or the price of corn or the Oklahoma Sooners or the Boston Red Sox, or even, perhaps, by Hollywood and Silicon Valley, much less by financial services, which was its biggest industry. In the noir versions offered by writers like Mike Davis and Joan Didion, in its new multiethnic incarnation, its hyper-American disregard of history, and its disorienting sense of direction (disorienting in more senses than one), California often seemed increasingly disconnected even from America's own predominant myths. It was Arnold who, in his first year as governor, was the nearest thing to Starr's unifying California narrative—the perfect body, the Hollywood celebrity, and action hero, the accidental moderate Republican with the Kennedy wife, the unifier, the bringer of yet another golden promise to fix it all and restore everything to its pristine perfection. But that was the first year.

The unifying narrative, if it were created, would have to transcend California's hard realities—the endemic distrust of state government and, in the big cities, of municipal government as well; the regional particularism of the media markets and the failures of the media generally; the great ethnic gaps between the coming Latino majority and the residual WASP electorate; the growing gap between rich and poor and the eroding middle between them; the disconnect between the inexorable power of global markets, with their transnational workers and their ability to move jobs within days and capital within seconds, and the old economic and political institutions; between native Mexican Americans and immigrant Mexicans; and, of course, between the (more or less) blue coast and the red inland. It was indeed hard to be middle class in California, as Republican senate leader Jim Brulte said just before his term ended, and the migration patterns of middle-class families to other states showed it. Even as Schwarzenegger was launching his campaign to end partisan gerrymandering of legislative and congressional districts and create more competitive districts, which in turn might produce more moderate legislators, the polls were reporting that the electorate itself had become more partisan and divided than ever. "The voters," said Mark Baldassare, director of research at PPIC, the Public Policy Institute of California, "can't agree on issues any more than the legislature can."[37]

That was hardly an uncontroverted fact. Scholars like Morris P. Fiorina of the Hoover Institution were arguing that most Americans were more centrist than their representatives, less divided even on hot-button, culture-war issues like abortion, and certainly less locked into their redness and blueness. By 2004, the bluest states in the 2000 election, those that voted heavily for Al Gore and against George W. Bush—California, of course, among them—all had Republican governors. The culture war thesis, said another scholar, was mostly the invention of intellectuals.[38] California was always mutable. The five-year swing from the Davis landslide in 1998 to the recall of 2003 proved that. The results of the 2004 presidential election even provided some indications that, the culture war thesis notwithstanding, Californians, to use urbanist Joel Kotkin's words, "prefer pastels over the darkest shades of red and blue. . . . With the exception of the disgracefully overhyped stem-cell initiative, voters [in 2004] generally opted for moderately conservative positions on everything from health-care mandates to tort reform and changing the 'three strikes' law. In most cases, they follow not the loony left in the Legislature, but Bush's biggest California backer, Governor Arnold Schwarzenegger."[39]

The president, though he lost California again, had made inroads in what Kotkin called the "Third California," as he had in similar places: ex-urban and rural areas, a "geographic and democratic triumph of the land of McMansions, Target and new office parks over the hip sophisticates of the older cities . . . areas [that] are now the focus of American middle class aspiration, not only for Anglos but also for growing numbers of Asian and Latino voters."[40] Five years after other conservatives pronounced California the hopelessly left-out coast, here was a very different reading about the state's direction, based yet again on one election.

Given the increasing polarization of the parties, the media, the churches, and a long list of other social institutions, and the enervation of the traditional mediating instruments of public discourse, the increasingly divided electorate, state and national, seemed hardly inconsistent with the rest of the culture. At the same time, Californians themselves seemed unsure of what they wanted. Yes, according to the polls, for better schools, better roads, and better services generally, but no, not if it costs me. On the question of higher taxes and better services versus lower taxes and poorer services, the score was nearly tied. The common joke around Sacramento (and no doubt in most other capitals) was that people thought there was an item in the budget called "waste, fraud, and abuse." All you had to do was cut that and there'd be plenty of money for everything without new taxes.

Meanwhile, what PPIC's Mark Baldassare called the "growing and solidifying gaps" between Democratic and Republican voters showed no sign of closing.[41] Given the requirements of the federal Voting Rights Act—the imperative that electoral districts respect communities of interest wherever possible—and the state's political demographics, it was highly unlikely that even the most determined effort to create competitive districts would significantly moderate the divisions in the legislature. What the polls consistently showed was that the state's likely voters were more conservative than its residents generally, which in turn reinforced the general presumption that, while native and assimilated Latinos tended to become somewhat more conservative on economic issues than new arrivals were, their growing numbers in the voting population were likely to nudge the electorate to the left.

IV

And yet, so much of California was so new, unfamiliar even to itself, that it was surprising that the state was holding together as well as it was. By the beginning of the twenty-first century, it was hardly a stretch to say that all Californians were immigrants to the new society growing around them, whether they were newly arrived illegal aliens from Mexico or El Salvador or sixth-generation Daughters of the Golden West whose forebears had crossed the plains in pioneer wagons. It was that new new-world condition, far more than tax policy or California's direction on the privatization of pensions, influential as they might potentially be, and much less the Schwarzenegger celebrity sideshow, that now made California the bellwether for a nation whose population forty years hence was predicted to look almost like California's did just before the year 2000. The nation would still have a white Anglo majority, but hardly an overwhelming one, and in many crucial places, minority-majorities.

In effect, the state had become the test case for something that no nation had ever attempted before: to forge and maintain a modern, prosperous high-tech democracy out of the great ethnic and social diversity of people, many of them from the Third World, that California had attracted. The test entailed, not least, taking people from that enormous spectrum of California backgrounds and cultures and educating them all to the high level of proficiency that those ambitions required, not only for the world's economy but also for effective citizenship and cultural competence in this new society. Simultaneously, California was also testing the power and adaptability of classic Western constitutional principles of limited government—individual liberty and the right to dissent, equal protection, due process, minority rights, separation of powers, civic participation and responsibility in that new environment—something that people like Huntington and Hanson believed couldn't successfully be done.

The political safety of any social diversity and multiculturalism, regardless of their nature or extent, indeed of all domestic tranquility in a diverse society, rested squarely on those Western principles. The one was impossible without the other because no one had yet invented—or was likely to invent—any other rulebook to govern and manage such a society. Thus those principles remained the best hope for reducing, if not closing, the gaps and fissures that seemed to be opening under the stress of latter-day life and politics. Yet wherever thoughtful people discuss the problems of contemporary society, they seem to be talking about distances—the distance of voters from state policy making, or even from their local schools; the disbelief, as one longtime Republican legislative staff member put it, that people's commitment (say in supporting additional taxes) "would do any good"; the question about how to re-create and reengage communities, how to empower parents or citizens generally. "Bowling alone" might not in fact be statistically persuasive, but as a metaphor it worked pretty well.

With the near certainty that California's residents—the children of the new immigrants and of the old, the first generation and the sixth, the whole New California—would gradually be absorbed into the new society they were themselves creating, and that the imbalance between residents and those eligible to vote would begin slowly to close, a new equilibrium was almost certain to emerge. By the year 2030, according to the

best estimates, the state would still have as large a percentage of immigrants as it had in 2005, but fewer than 7 percent of California residents
would be "new arrivals"—immigrants who'd been in the country ten
years or less—compared to about 8.5 percent in 2005.[42] But whether the
emerging equilibrium would come to rest in equity, a high standard of
living and generous public services, a strong middle class, a civically engaged electorate, and a progressive, stable government, or whether the
whole society would be further divided across a great socioeconomic gap
between an affluent upper class and a large, predominantly Latino and
black underclass, and whether some communitarian ethic could be restored, all depended crucially on decisions that the voters and their leaders would make in the interim.

In the early years of the new millennium, neither the job indicators,
nor the housing market, nor the political system was encouraging. Kevin
Starr told stories of frustrated former Californians returning to the
Golden State: "You can't get good take-out in Idaho," one returnee told
him.[43] But ever since the early 1990s, as manufacturing jobs disappeared
and living costs were going up, the white native-born middle class had
been moving elsewhere. Was the state growing a permanent two-tier
economy that also foreshadowed something for the nation? Increasingly
California seemed like one of the nation's older cities, a place for either
affluent high-tech people living in modest million-dollar homes or the
working poor who serviced them and lived four to a room. Meanwhile,
the economy, the tax structure, and the regulatory policy nearly insured
a perpetually tight and increasingly unaffordable housing market. In
2002, California home ownership (57 percent) was near the bottom
among the states and ten points lower than the U.S. average.

In the larger context, California, with its diversity of cultural backgrounds and languages, had extraordinary advantages both as a beacon
to, and as the nation's preeminent economic and cultural link with, the
rest of the world. It was a global society with comfortable connections to
almost every culture on earth. But the good news also brought bad news.
The Indian Silicon Valley engineer, the Japanese Hollywood computer-

designer, and the Mexican restaurant worker in the kitchens of Palo Alto or Brentwood who'd never gone past the sixth grade had more offshore connections—more links with family and peers, in Taiwan, Mumbai, New York, London, Michoacan, or Zacatecas—than they had with each other. Could the society create institutions to bridge the gaps and bring them together in a single vital political and social community? Here, too, California was likely to be a national trendsetter not only in its demographics but also in the choices it made, the institutions it created, the programs it maintained—even the sacrifices it was willing to make, or not make—in the face of an increasingly globalized economy. Again and again, through more than a century, the state had been the nation's economic and cultural leader. This made the fearful, mincing steps California was taking to address its governmental dysfunction, its deteriorating infrastructure, and its neglected public services even more troubling.

A half century ago, Harvard political scientist Louis Hartz observed that the U.S. Constitution was created out of the founders' mistaken belief that they had to deal with "frightful [political and economic] conflicts," when in fact the nation enjoyed a fundamental consensus. In response to those imagined conflicts, they devised "a complicated scheme of checks and balances which it is reasonable to argue only a highly united nation could make work at all." It was a system made for delay and confusion—was, in short, designed to work as little and as slowly as possible.[44]

The system that has evolved in California is both similar and different. Designed by the Progressives in the first decades of the last century as a check on unresponsive or corrupt government, it now makes government even more unworkable, in part at least because California is not a "highly united" state and hasn't been for more than a generation. The national constitutional consensus, as Hartz said, broke down when it faced the slavery crisis but otherwise worked reasonably well, at least until recently. But in California, the checks and balances—the supermajority requirements, the spending mandates, and tax limitations—are more restrictive than those in the federal constitution, and they're supposed to apply to a society that's more divided than the one Hartz wrote about. And unlike Hartz's assumptions about eighteenth-century America, the latter-day impulse to write ever more checks and commandments into the state constitution may rest not on a mistaken belief about social and economic conflict, as the impulse did in 1787, but on accurate, if unstated, assumptions about the state's diversity.

Californians get constant queries from out-of-state scholars, consultants, and journalists asking whether the state is governable. It's the subject of conferences and Sunday supplement pieces and no end of late-night conversations among California's policy wonks. But in the context of Hartz's analysis of the federal constitution, the more pertinent question may be whether California really wants to be governable.

The challenges are both frightening and awe-inspiring, each carrying opportunity within it, even as the opportunities bring new challenges. In trying to forge a modern postindustrial democratic society not only from its cultural diversity but also from a population consisting in considerable part of Third World immigrants, California was undertaking something that had never been done in human history, and trying it at a time of growing overseas competition in industries and technologies that this country had once regarded as its own. Even under the best of circumstances, as planner William Fulton said, it was "disconcerting that the best possible result might not be as good as it used to be."[45] Much of public policy, state and national, was restrictive and fearful—basically un-American in the historic sense. But there were plenty of ideas, and the state's history and traditions of adventure and optimism were always there for those who cared to recall and honor them. The question is which way California—or the nation, for that matter—really wants to go.

NOTES

Introduction

1. The initiative, referendum, and recall were all written into the California constitution in 1911. To qualify for the ballot, a popular initiative to put a law on the books, or a referendum challenging a law recently approved by the legislature, requires signatures of registered voters equal to 5 percent of the total vote cast in the last regular governor's election. A proposed constitutional amendment has an 8 percent threshold. A recall requires 12 percent. Once on the ballot, each requires a simple majority to pass.

2. Arnold Schwarzenegger, at a meeting with the editorial board of the *Sacramento Bee*, January 18, 2005.

3. David Firestone, "Does Pain Make States Stronger?" *New York Times*, April 27, 2003. "Gov. Bob Riley [the Republican who supported the Alabama tax increase]," Norquist said, "is going to serve as a bad example. Years from now, little baby Republican governors will be told scary stories late at night . . . about the sad fate of governors who steal a billion dollars from their people. . . . This is a shot across the bow. Every Republican governor who thinks of raising taxes next year will walk past Traitors Gate and see Bob Riley's head on a pike. The voters of Alabama have saved taxpayers from California to Maine billions of dollars."

4. Larry M. Bartels, "Homer Gets a Tax Cut," August 2003, www.princeton.edu/~csdp/research/pdfs/homer.pdf (accessed on May 10, 2004).

5. In the 1980s, California voters passed an initiative ending the state's inheritance taxes, with the exception of the amount that federal law allowed as a

credit against the federal estate tax (and which therefore cost the estate nothing). The payment to California—nearly all paid only on very large estates—was thus pinned directly to the federal tax.

6. Stanley B. Greenberg, *The Two Americas: Our Current Political Deadlock and How to Beat It* (New York: St. Martin's Press, 2004), pp. 110–14, 126–28. Most areas of the country, as a lot of critics have pointed out, are shades of purple, which will be discussed below, but that doesn't change the general California political landscape. On governability, see, for example, Sara Miller, "Tough Job: Can Anyone Govern California?" *Christian Science Monitor,* July 11, 2005.

7. See, for example, Ruth Ellen Wasem, "Naturalization of Immigrants: Policy, Trends, and Issues," Congressional Research Service Report to the Congress, February 21, 1995. 107th Cong., 1st sess.

8. The complex question of intergenerational comparisons is discussed more fully in part 1.

9. Public Policy Institute of California, *Public Policy Institute of California Statewide Survey* (San Francisco: PPIC, April 2005).

10. Joan Didion, *Where I Was From* (New York: Alfred A. Knopf, 2003).

11. Carey McWilliams, *California: The Great Exception* (Santa Barbara, CA: Peregrine Smith, 1976).

12. The phrase was coined by demographer William Frey. "Charticle," *Milken Institute Review,* 3rd quarter (2003): p. 7.

13. Bill Hauck, interview by author, February 18, 2004.

14. A more detailed, though now dated, version of the same story is told in Peter Schrag, *Paradise Lost: California's Experience, America's Future,* with a new preface (Berkeley: University of California Press, 2004).

15. Robert Reich, remarks at the Public Policy Institute of California, April 25, 2005, and conversations with author, various dates.

16. Ellen Hanak and Mark Baldassare, eds., *California 2025: Taking on the Future* (San Francisco: Public Policy Institute of California, 2005), p. iv.

17. Hauck, interview by author, February 18, 2004.

1. The New California

1. The other states (2000) were Hawaii and New Mexico, plus the District of Columbia.

2. All population data are from the U.S. Census Bureau or the Demographic Unit of the California Department of Finance, www.dof.ca.gov. It should be clear that I'm using *non-Hispanic white* and *Anglo* interchangeably. The same

goes for *Latino* and *Hispanic*. *Asian*, of course, comprises a wide range of ethnic groups.

3. David Hayes-Bautista, interview by author, September 13, 2004; Jorge Ferraez, "David Hayes-Bautista: The End of California as We Know It—Q&A," *Leaders: The National Magazine of the Successful American Latino* (April–May 2003). Also see David Hayes-Bautista, *La Nueva California: Latinos in the Golden State* (Berkeley: University of California Press, 2004). The data on births to immigrant mothers was supplied by the Center for Immigration Studies in Washington, D.C., which is dedicated to restricting immigration, but whose data on this issue, based on health statistics, are probably as reliable as any. Steven Camarota, "Births to Immigrants in America, 1970–2002," Center for Immigration Studies, July 2005, www.cis.org.

4. William H. Frey, "Charticle," *Milken Institute Review*, 3rd quarter (2003): 7–10. In California more than one marriage in eight is a mixed marriage. See also Jerry A. Jacobs and Teresa A. Labov, "Gender Differentials in Intermarriage among Sixteen Race and Ethnic Groups," *Sociological Forum* 17, no. 4 (December 2002): 630–33.

5. Gregory Rodriguez, "Mongrel America," *Atlantic Monthly* (February 1, 2003).

6. Jeffrey S. Passel, Randolph Capps, and Michael E. Fix, "Undocumented Immigrants: Facts and Figures," Washington, DC: Urban Institute, January 12, 2004, www.urban.org/url.cfm?ID=1000587.

7. Dowell Myers, John Pitkin, and Julie Park, *California Demographic Futures: Projections to 2030, by Immigrant Generations, Nativity, and Time of Arrival in the U.S.* (Los Angeles: School of Policy, Planning, and Development, University of Southern California, January 2005), www.usc.edu/schools/sppd/research/popdynamics; "Fact Sheet on the Foreign Born: California," Migration Policy Institute, www.migrationinformation.org.

8. The source for cities populated by foreign-born residents is researcher Paul Lewis of the Public Policy Institute of California, in conversation with the author. Also Jeffrey S. Passel, interview by author, September 9, 2004; and Passel, "Immigration Today: Emerging Patterns, U.S. and California" (data prepared for the Conference on Immigration and the Changing Face of Rural California, Parlier, CA, September 9, 2004).

9. Rafael Alarcon, a researcher at the Colegio de la Frontera Norte, Tijuana, interview by author, September 13, 2004. More than likely, the Pakistani business person or the Mexican professional or the Indian engineer will belong to one of several professional associations composed of fellow Mexican professionals or

Indian engineers or Pakistani business people. Americans, as Tocqueville pointed out long ago, are great joiners.

10. Pao Fang, interview by author, April 12, 2004. The story of the Hmong in Fresno is told eloquently in Anne Fadiman's *The Spirit Catches You and You Fall Down* (New York: Farrar, Straus, and Giroux, 1997). The largest Hmong community in the United States is in St. Paul, Minnesota. California's Central Valley is second.

11. U.S. Census 2000: Table DP-1, Profile of General Demographic Characteristics: 2000. Geographic Area: Santa Ana, California, censtats.census.gov/data/CA/1600669000.pdf.

12. Ben Fox, "New Legislator Basks in a First for Vietnamese-Americans," Associated Press, *San Diego Union-Tribune*, November 4, 2004.

13. Alice Petrossian and others at Glendale Unified School District, interviews by author, April 27, 2004. Also see www.glendale.k12.ca.us/.

14. And not surprisingly, it also has its Armenian immigrant crime gangs, one of which was suspected of running a credit card racket out of a Glendale pickle factory. Richard Fausset, "Possible Hit-Man Ring No Surprise," *Los Angeles Times*, June 1, 2004.

15. "L.A. Koreatown Business Catering to Booming Latino Population," *Korea Times*, May 29, 2004.

16. Author's garment district tour and interviews, September 14, 2004. The owners, of course, are themselves under enormous economic pressure from the chain marketers, who are at the top of this exploitative food chain. See, for example, Andrew Gumbel, "Fashion Victims: Inside the Sweatshops of Los Angeles," *The Independent* (UK), August 3, 2001.

17. Peter Schrag, "Charney's Sweatshop-Free T-Shirt Kibbutz in L.A.," *Sacramento Bee*, September 22, 2004.

18. Gil Cedillo, interviews by author, April and September 2004.

19. "Fact Sheet on the Foreign Born," Migration Policy Institute, June 1, 2004, www.migrationinformation.org/USfocus/statemap.cfm#.

20. Erika Hayasaki, "Cultural Divide on Campus," *Los Angeles Times*, December 3, 2004.

21. Dov Charney, interview by author, September 14, 2004. American Apparel had a clip of the event on its company Website, www.americanapparel.net/films/filmsCulture.html.

22. Juan Arambula, interview by author, September 7, 2004; Randolph Capps, Michael Fix, Jeffrey Passel, Jason Ost, and Dan Perez-Lopez, "A Profile of the Low Wage Immigrant Workforce," *Urban Institute*, September 27, 2003, www.urban.org.

23. Arturo Rodriguez, interview by author, April 28, 2004; Paul Chavez, interview by author, April 28, 2004; Marc Grossman, UFW attorney, interview by author, July 1, 2004; Matt Weiser, "UFW Membership Remains a Disputed Issue," and "Pay Raises in a Time of Poverty," *Bakersfield Californian*, May 8, 2004; Philip L. Martin, "Promise Unfulfilled: Why Didn't Collective Bargaining Transform California's Labor Market," Center for Immigration Studies Backgrounder, January 2004, www.cis.org/articles/2004/back104.html.

24. Kenji Hakuta, interview by author, April 11, 2004. At least in its first years, UC Merced will be torn between fulfilling its boosters' expectations that it will have a regional focus and its own ambitions to be, as its administrators like to say, "world class" and play on the national and international scenes. But as a beacon of possibility, it's likely to be a major positive force in a region that has few others.

25. Mechel Paggi, interview by author, September 8, 2004. Data generated by the Agricultural Coalition on Trade, a growers' lobby, show large growth in imports of foreign fruits, nuts and vegetables between 1995 and 2003, and very small growth in exports.

26. David Mas Masumoto, interview by author, September 8, 2004. Masumoto is the writer of a series of lovely books about his relationship with his place—with place—and about the fruit he grows. See www.masumoto.com/about-mas.htm.

27. Mark Drabenstott, "Exploring Agriculture's New Frontier," *AgDM Newsletter* (July 2002). A similar piece appeared in the *Main Street Economist* in February 2002.

28. William H. Frey, *Census 2000 Reveals New Native-Born and Foreign-Born Shifts across U.S.*, PSC Research Report No. 02–520 (Ann Arbor, MI: Population Studies Center, Institute for Social Research, University of Michigan, August 2002).

29. Iowa Center for Immigrant Leadership and Integration. http://www.bcs.uni.edu/idm/newiowans/ (accessed in January 2005).

30. Jeffrey S. Passel, *Unauthorized Migrants: Numbers and Characteristics*, Pew Hispanic Center, 2005, http://pewhispanic.org/reports/report.php?ReportID=46. Passel estimates that, between 2000 and 2004, the number of illegal residents in the United States has been growing at a rate of 700,000 a year. In the five previous years, it was 750,000 a year. In the 1980s, it was 130,000 a year.

31. Jeffrey S. Passel and Wendy Zimmermann, *Are Immigrants Leaving California? Settlement Patterns of Immigrants in the Late 1990s* (Washington, DC: Urban Institute, 2000), pp. 1–2, www.ui.urban.org; quote about dependency on

foreign workers is from "New Report Reveals Nation's Growing Dependence on Foreign Immigrants since 2002," press summary for Andrew Sum, Neeta Fogg, Ishwar Khatiwada, and Sheila Palma, *Foreign Immigration and the Labor Force of the U.S.: The Contributions of New Foreign Immigration to the Growth of the Nation's Labor Force and Its Employed Population, 2000 to 2004*, Center for Labor Market Studies, Northeastern University, July 2004, www.nupr.neu.edu/7–04/immigration_july04.shtml; "Employment Up, Wages Flat, for Hispanic Workers," Pew Hispanic Center, June 16, 2004, http://pewhispanic.org/newsroom/releases/release.php?ReleaseID=12.

32. Daniel Carroll, "Immigration and Integration of Hired Crop Workers: Findings from the National Agricultural Workers Survey" (paper presented to the Tenth Changing Face Seminar on Immigration and Rural California, Parlier, CA, September 9, 2004). Quote about the binational nature of the farm workforce is from Edward Kissam, Jo Ann Intili, and Anna Garcia, "The Emergence of a Binational U.S.-Mexico Workforce: Implications for Farm Labor Workforce Security" (paper presented to the America's Workforce Network Research Conference conducted by the U.S. Department of Labor, Washington, DC, June 26–27, 2001).

33. Philip L. Martin, remarks at the Conference on Immigration and the Changing Face of Rural California, Parlier, CA, September 9, 2004; Martin, interview by author, September 9, 2004. In California, 27 percent of the native-born children of immigrants have at least one undocumented parent, according to Michael Fix of the Urban Institute in his remarks at the same conference.

34. Governor Schwarzenegger was treated like a head of state on his visits abroad, but Schwarzenegger, of course, is a special case. After the reelection of George W. Bush in 2004, there were even Californians who talked, only half facetiously, about secession.

35. "Income Inequality among Families in California Has Increased since the 1970s," chart in Jared Bernstein, Heather Boushey, Elizabeth McNichol, and Robert Zahradnik, *Pulling Apart: A State-by-State Analysis of Income Trends*, Economic Policy Institute and Center on Budget and Policy Priorities, April 23, 2002, www.cbpp.org (accessed on April 30, 2004).

36. Malibu Parks and Recreation Department, "Have you ever seen a child in a commercial and thought, 'My child could do that!'? Your child will have loads of fun . . . " Malibu Parks Department, flyer, n.d.; "Malibu Keeps Pace with Region, State," *Malibu Times*, December 6, 2004.

37. Heather Knight, "Teachers Could Get Break on Housing If Plan Gets Go-Ahead," *San Francisco Chronicle*, October 8, 2004; Dowell Myers and Xin

Gao, "Trajectories of Home Ownership in California: 1980 to 2000 and 2000 to 2030" (working paper no. PDRG 0403, Population Dynamics Research Group, Los Angeles: School of Policy, Planning, and Development, University of Southern California, November 2004).

38. William J. Kelly, "Noxious Neighborhoods," *California Journal* (May 2003): 20–26.

39. Carol Whiteside and others at the Great Valley Center, Modesto, interviews by author, April 2004.

40. In Alpaugh, a private water company agreed to bring in a five-thousand-gallon tank to provide safe drinking water until new wells were dug. Luis Hernandez, "A Cool Drink for Alpaugh," *Tulare Advance-Register,* November 15, 2003; Diana Marcum, "Leaving Alpaugh," *Fresno Bee,* May 6, 2004.

41. Stephen P. Erie, interview by author and talk at the Public Policy Institute of California, San Francisco, March 4, 2004. Erie, *Globalizing L.A.: Trade, Infrastructure, and Regional Development* (Stanford, CA: Stanford University Press, 2004). Erie's analysis of how Los Angeles developed into a vital port city while San Diego nestled comfortably into a federally subsidized navy town is itself a telling story.

42. "Dumping without Borders: How U.S. Agricultural Policies Are Destroying the Livelihoods of Mexican Corn Farmers," Oxfam International, August 2003, www.oxfam.org.uk.

43. Los Algodones, a town of fifteen thousand located forty miles from Mexicali, is said to draw some five hundred people daily who come to buy medical services and products, nearly all of them retirees from the United States and Canada. Rosa Maria Mendez Fierros, "U.S. Health Crisis Fuels a Border Boom Town," *El Universal,* June 25, 2005.

44. Because the parent companies tend to lay off first at the maquiladoras when demand declines, in recessions the job picture tends to be "chronically volatile." William C. Gruben, "Beyond the Border: Have Mexico's Maquiladoras Bottomed Out?" *Report of the Federal Reserve Bank of Dallas* (January–February 2004). On crossborder trade, see Howard Shatz and Luis Felipe Lopez-Calva, *The Emerging Integration of the California-Mexico Economies* (San Francisco: Public Policy Institute of California, August 2004).

45. Among them: the California-Mexico Commission on Science, Education, and Technology, headed by the president of the University of California and the director of Mexico's National Council on Science and Technology, and its operational spin-off, UC MEXUS, which is conducting research on issues such as the strained Colorado River resources, health and migration issues, and other matters. See http://ucmexus.ucr.edu/.

46. Warren Vieth, "He'll Take Your Job and Ship It," *Los Angeles Times*, April 27, 2004; Amy Waldman, "Indians Go Home, but Don't Leave U.S. Behind," *New York Times*, July 24, 2004; AnnaLee Saxenian, "Silicon Valley's New Immigrant Entrepreneurs" (working paper no. 15, Center for Comparative Immigration Studies, La Jolla, CA., May 2000); Saxenian, *Local and Global Networks of Immigrant Professionals in Silicon Valley* (San Francisco: Public Policy Institute of California, 2002); Karl Schoenberger, "Indo-American in Maelstrom of Offshoring Controversy," *San Jose Mercury News*, September 6, 2004.

47. Aneesh Aneesh, remarks at the Conference on Diaspora and Homeland Development, Berkeley Center for Globalization and Information Technology, April 13, 2004, Berkeley, CA. "Brain circulation," he said, also permits "a specific segment of NRIs (Non-resident Indians) to address inter-community racial politics in the U.S. while simultaneously justifying intra-community class and caste politics across national boundaries." Paula Chakravartty, "The Emigration of High Skilled Indian Workers to the United States: Flexible Citizenship and India's Information Economy" (working paper no. 19, Center for Comparative Immigration Studies, La Jolla, CA., August 2000); Saxenian, *Local and Global Networks*, p. vii.

48. Inter-American Development Bank, *All in the Family: Latin America's Most Important International Financial Flow: Report of the Inter-American Dialogue Task Force on Remittances, 2004* (Washington, DC: Inter-American Development Bank, January 2004); Ginger S. Thompson, "Mexico's Migrants Profit from Dollars Sent Home," *New York Times*, February 23, 2005. Some critics, however, contend that the migrants would be better off investing in their American communities rather than repatriating their surplus funds.

49. Manuel Orozco, interview by author, June 29, 2004; Orozco, *Remittances, the Rural Sector, and Policy Options in Latin America* (Washington, DC: Migration Policy Institute, June 1, 2003, http://migrationinformation.org/USFocus/display.cfm?ID=128; Pew Charitable Trusts, *Immigrants Send Billions to Families Back Home in Latin America and Caribbean* (Washington, DC: Pew Hispanic Center and the Multilateral Investment Fund, November 24, 2003); Kevin O'Neil, *Remittances from the United States in Context* (Washington, DC: Migration Policy Institute, June 1, 2003); Manuel Orozco, *Hometown Associations and Their Present and Future Partnerships: New Development Opportunities?* (Washington, DC: U.S. Agency for International Development, September 2003).

50. Roberto Suro, *Remittance Senders and Receivers: Tracking the Transnational Channels* (Washington, DC: Pew Hispanic Center and the Multilateral Investment Fund, November 24, 2003), pp. 4, 5.

51. Ernesto Ruiz, director of the California Region II Migrant Education Program, interview by author, February 8, 2005. According to Mexican reports, in border cities like Juarez, across the Rio Grande from El Paso, "remittances are plowed back quickly into the U.S. economy [because] many Juarez residents spend their money in El Paso stores which offer cheaper products. Since many of the El Paso shops frequented by Juarez consumers are owned by Korean immigrants, the ultimate destination and impact of border remittances becomes a broader, global question." Summary by the Center for Latin American and Border Studies, New Mexico State University, Las Cruces, N.M., May 14, 2005, www.nmsu.edu/~frontera/.

52. Rafael Alarcon, interviews by author, April 8, 2004, September 13, 2004.

53. Douglas S. Massey, Luin Goldring, and Jorge Durand, "Continuities in Transnational Migration: An Analysis of Nineteen Mexican Communities," *American Journal of Sociology* 99, no. 6 (May 1994): 1500.

54. Rick Mines, California Institute of Rural Studies, interview by author, August 10, 2004; Douglas S. Massey, interview by author, July 2, 2004; Douglas S. Massey, Jorge Durand, and Nolan J. Malone, *Beyond Smoke and Mirrors: Mexican Immigration in an Era of Economic Integration* (New York: Russell Sage Foundation, 2002), 132–33; Hans Johnson and Belinda Reyes, *Holding the Line: The Effect of the Recent Border Build-up on Unauthorized Immigration* (San Francisco: Public Policy Institute of California, 2002).

55. Efrain Jimenez, interview by author, September 13, 2004. Rick Mines of the California Institute of Rural Studies is among those who believe that, in general, migration freezes development in Mexico.

56. Matt Bakker and Peter Michel Smith, "El Rey del Tomate: Migrant Political Transnationalism and Democratization in Mexico," *Migraciones Internacionales* 2, no. 1 (January–June 2003): 73, 79. Bermudez ran twice; after he won the first time, in 2002, he was disqualified. He then ran again and won under revised rules. The quoted piece is about the first campaign. On the second campaign, see Emily Bazar, "Homecoming: Yolo Grower Leaves U.S. to Lead Village," *Sacramento Bee*, September 29, 2004.

57. Jesus Martinez-Saldana, interview by author, September 7, 2004; "Fresno State Professor Selected for State Legislature Seat in Mexico," California State University, Fresno, press release, July 23, 2004.

58. Jeffrey S. Passel, "Estimates of the Size and Characteristics of the Undocumented Population," Pew Hispanic Center, March 21, 2005, http://pewhispanic.org/reports/report.php?ReportID=44. What may have been most significant is that the percentage of undocumented individuals in the United States who

were living in California was just over half the percentage of those who were living there in 1990. Their numbers were dispersed far more widely around the country. Richard Rodriguez, *Brown: The Last Discovery of America* (New York: Viking Penguin, 2003), pp. 160–61.

59. Kevin Starr, *Coast of Dreams: California on the Edge, 1990–2003* (New York: Alfred A. Knopf, 2004), p. 300.

60. George J. Borjas, "The Labor Demand Curve Is Downward Sloping: Re-examining the Impact of Immigration on the Labor Market," *Quarterly Journal of Economics* (November 2003): 1335–74.

61. For example, James P. Smith, "One More Embrace, Then Slam the Door," *Los Angeles Times*, May 1, 2005.

62. Steven A. Camarota, *A Jobless Recovery? Immigrant Gains and Native Losses* (Washington, DC: Center for Immigration Studies, October 2004), www.cis.org/articles/2004/back1104.html; Sum et al., *Foreign Immigration and the Labor Force*, p. 27. Employers, sociologist William Julius Wilson has often said, prefer to hire immigrants or women over blacks, but they often prefer to hire almost anybody over blacks.

63. Quotations from a letter to the author, August 2004.

64. Harry Holzer, "New Jobs in Recession and Recovery: Who Are Getting Them and Who Are Not?" Testimony of Harry J. Holzer before the Subcommittee on Immigration, Border Security, and Claims, U.S. House of Representatives, 109th Cong., 1st sess., May 4, 2005, www.urban.org/url.cfm?ID=900808; Carolyn Lochhead, "Immigration Hurts American Workers, Lawmaker Says," *San Francisco Chronicle*, May 5, 2005.

65. "Average Wages in Growing and Contracting Industries, End of Recession through November 2003," Economic Policy Institute, analysis of data from the Bureau of Labor Statistics, January 21, 2004, www.epinet.org.

66. Lawrence Mishel, Jared Bernstein, and Sylvia Allegretto, *The State of Working America, 2004–2005* (Ithaca, NY: Cornell University Press, ILR Press, 2005), 5. The Labor Information Division of the California Employment Development Department has projected similar data. See www.projectionscentral.com/projections.asp. The Public Policy Institute of California has published data showing that the percentage of high-skill jobs is increasing compared to lower-skill jobs, but in terms of absolute numbers the largest growth is still disproportionately in low-skill jobs. David Neumark, "California's Economic Future and Infrastructure Challenges," in *California 2025: Taking On the Future.*, ed. Ellen Hanak and Mark Baldassare (San Francisco: Public Policy Institute of California, 2005), pp. 69–82.

67. Daniel H. Pink, "The New Face of the Silicon Age," *Wired* (February 2004), www.wired.com/wired/archive/12.02/india.html.

68. "NAFTA has not helped the Mexican economy keep pace with growing demand for jobs; NAFTA-led productivity growth in the past decade has not translated into increased wages; NAFTA has not stemmed the flow of Mexican emigration to the United States; the fear of a 'race to the bottom' in environmental regulation has proved unfounded; Mexico's evolution toward a modern, export-oriented agricultural sector has failed to deliver the anticipated environmental benefits of reduced deforestation and tillage." John Audley, Sandra Polaski, Demetrios Papedemetriou, and Scott Vaughan, *NAFTA's Promise and Reality: Lesson from Mexico* (Washington, DC: Carnegie Endowment for International Peace, 2003); Celia W. Dugger, "Report Finds Few Benefits for Mexico in NAFTA," *New York Times*, November 19, 2003.

69. James P. Smith et al., *The New Americans: Economic, Demographic, and Fiscal Effects of Immigration* (Washington, DC: National Academies Press, 1997), pp. 8, 281, 333.

70. Michael S. Clune, "The Fiscal Impacts of Immigrants: A California Case Study," in *The Immigration Debate: Studies on the Economic, Demographic, and Fiscal Effects of Immigration*, ed. James P. Smith and Barry Edmonston (Washington, DC: National Academies Press, 1998), p. 167.

71. Eduardo Porter, "Illegal Immigrants Are Bolstering Social Security with Billions," *New York Times*, April 5, 2005. Interestingly enough, many of the same people who defend illegal immigration as a consequence of economic necessity are in the forefront of the attack on Wal-Mart for loading the burden of employee health care on the taxpayers.

72. Frey, *Census 2000;* William H. Frey, "Charticle," *Milken Institute Review*, 4th Quarter (2003): 5.

73. Dowell Myers, John Pitkin, and Julie Park, "California's Immigrants Turn the Corner," *Urban Initiative Policy Brief* (March 2004), www.usc .edu/schools/sppd/research/popdynamics/; Dowell Myers and John Pitkin, *Demographic Futures for California* (Los Angeles: Population Dynamics Group, School of Policy, Planning and Development, University of Southern California, 2001).

74. Contreras himself died unexpectedly, apparently of a heart attack, in May 2005, at the age of 52.

75. Steven Levy, *Expanding Economic Opportunity for California and Californians* (Palo Alto, CA: Institute of Regional and Urban Studies, June 16, 2004), www.ccsce.com/pdf/bseries10-expanding.pdf; Western Interstate Commission

for Higher Education, *Knocking at the College Door: Projections of High School Graduates by State, Income, and Race/Ethnicity* (Denver: WICHE, 2003), www.wiche.edu/policy/knocking/1988–2018/.

76. Arthur M. Schlesinger Jr., *The Disuniting of America* (New York: Norton, 1991); Victor Davis Hanson, *Mexifornia: A State of Becoming* (San Francisco: Encounter Books, 2003); Samuel P. Huntington, "The Hispanic Challenge," *Foreign Policy* (March–April 2004), p. 37, www.foreignpolicy.com. The article is based on Huntington's *Who Are We? The Challenges to America's National Identity* (New York: Simon and Schuster, 2004).

77. Jim Sleeper, "The Last Throes of Patriotism," *Los Angeles Times*, May 2, 2004.

78. Hanson, *Mexifornia*, p. 149.

79. Summary of Mexican news reports by Frontera NorteSur, June 19, 2005, www.nmsu.edu/~frontera/.

80. See, for example, Daniel Hernandez, "Spanglish Moves into Mainstream," *Los Angeles Times*, January 11, 2004.

81. David Abraham, "Citizen Solidarity and Rights Individualism: On the Decline of National Citizenship in the U.S., Germany, and Israel" (working paper no. 53, Center for Comparative Immigration Studies, University of California, San Diego, May 2002). "Transnationalism," said a French scholar writing about European transnationalism, "leads to an institutional expression of multiple belonging where the country of origin becomes a source of identity, the country of residence a source of rights[,] and the emerging transnational space a space of political action combining the two or more countries." Riva Kastoryano, "Settlement, Transnational Communities, and Citizenship," *International Social Science Journal* 152, no. 165 (2000): 311.

82. "Fifty Years after *Brown v. Board of Education*," National Public Radio Series, March 8, 2004, www.npr.org.

83. David A. Hollinger, *Postethnic America: Beyond Multiculturalism* (New York: Basic Books, 1995), pp. 152–53. The data are from Stephen Thernstrom, ed., *The Harvard Encyclopedia of American Ethnic Groups* (Cambridge: Harvard University Press, 1980), pp. 798, 1036.

84. Henry Cabot Lodge, "The Restriction of Immigration," *North American Review* 152, no. 410 (January 1891): 32, 34; Lodge, "Lynch Law and Unrestricted Immigration," *North American Review* 152, no. 414 (May 1891): 608, 609.

85. Daniel J. Kevles, *In the Name of Eugenics: Genetics and the Uses of Human Heredity* (New York: Alfred A. Knopf, 1985), pp. 114–16.

86. Huntington, *Who Are We?* p. 170. Huntington here is quoting the *New*

York Times quoting Callaghan; *Public Policy Institute of California Statewide Survey* (San Francisco: PPIC, April 2005).

87. Despite his complaint that Latinos were persuaded to vote against Proposition 227, he also says that "many" voted for it. Huntington, *Who Are We?* p. 169.

88. Pew Hispanic Center and Kaiser Family Foundation, *National Survey of Latinos*, December 2002, www.pewhispanic.org; Richard Alba, "Language Assimilation Today: Bilingualism Persists More Than in the Past, but English Still Dominates" (Albany, NY: Lewis Mumford Center for Comparative Urban and Regional Research, December 2004), www.albany.edu/mumford.

89. Pew Hispanic Center and Kaiser Family Foundation, *National Survey of Latinos*.

90. Leonicio Vasquez, interview by author, April 13, 2004; Rodriguez, *Brown*, pp. 94, 108.

91. In some cases, this may not be altogether desirable. David Hayes-Bautista at UCLA points out that, despite their poverty, the health of new immigrants tends to be better than that of other immigrants, apparently in large part because of better personal habits.

92. Gregory Rodriguez, "Mexican Americans Are Building No Walls," *Los Angeles Times*, February 29, 2004.

93. John Pitkin and Dowell Myers, "Immigrants Get Ordinary in Old Age," *Los Angeles Times*, June 12, 2005.

94. On Ruiz Foods, author visit and interviews with workers and Ruiz executives, September 2004. On the vintners, see Eric Asimov, "Pickers to Vintners: A Mexican-American Saga," *New York Times*, October 17, 2004. Although jobs at Ruiz pay decent wages and benefits compared to other work in the valley, and the company treats its people fairly, the work—rolling enchiladas on an assembly line, or cutting excess dough off tortillas—is boring, repetitive work.

95. Passel, *Unauthorized Migrants*; Suro quote is in "Pew Hispanic Center Offers Fuller Portrait of Unauthorized Migrants," press release, June 14, 2005, www. pewhispanic.org/newsroom/releases/release.php?ReleaseID=33.

96. Monica Lozano, interview by author, September 13, 2004.

97. Sandy Close, interview by author, July 22, 2004; Marcelo Ballve, Rene P. Ciria-Cruz, Martin Espinoza, Teresa Moore, Benjamin Pimentel, Sandip Roy, and Sandy Close, *Profiles of Ethnic Media: California's New Civic Communicators* (San Francisco: New California Media, 2002).

98. "California's Expanding Electorate," Field Institute, May 2000, http://field.com/fieldpollonline/. In 2004, the National Association of Latino Elected Officials calculated that Latinos represented 16.5 percent of registered

California voters, but Latinos have never voted in this proportion. National Association of Latino Elected Officials, "2004 Primary Election Profiles: California Primary: March 2, 2004," NALEO Educational Fund, 2004, www.naleo.org.

99. For further elaboration of this point, see Gregory Rodriguez, "Mexican-Americans and the Mestizo Melting Pot," in *Reinventing the Melting Pot: The New Immigrants and What It Means to be American,* ed. Tamar Jacoby (New York: Basic Books, 2004), pp. 125–38.

100. Barbara Hagenbaugh, "U.S. Meatpackers Make Deal on Immigration Crackdown," Reuters, May 7, 1999. "The unstated subtext," wrote Wayne Cornelius, director of the Center for Comparative Immigration Studies at UC San Diego in 2001, "is that most members of Congress are not concerned about the absence of workplace enforcement; indeed, many of their constituents and campaign contributors would become very upset if the INS ever became serious about worksite inspections." "Death at the Border: Efficacy and Unintended Consequences of U.S. Immigration Control Policy," *Population and Development Review* 27, no. 4 (December 2001): 678. Also, Louis Uchitelle, "Plan May Lure More to Enter U.S. Illegally, Experts Say," *New York Times,* January 9, 2004.

101. Massey, Durand, and Malone, *Beyond Smoke and Mirrors,* p. 120.

102. Among SAW's chief sponsors was Senator Pete Wilson of California, who, as governor, later campaigned on the illegal immigration issue and became a chief backer of Proposition 187.

103. James Sterngold and Mark Martin, "Governor Signals He'd Welcome Minutemen on California Border," *San Francisco Chronicle,* April 30, 2005; Wyatt Buchanan, "Volunteers Start Patrol of Border," *San Francisco Chronicle,* July 17, 2005.

104. Fred Alvarez, "A Street-Fighter Mentality on Illegal Immigration," *Los Angeles Times,* June 27, 2005.

105. Interviews and border tour with U.S. Border Patrol agents, San Ysidro, September 16, 2004. All Border Patrol agents are required to learn Spanish, and many, like Santa Ana (an ironically appropriate name), are Hispanics themselves. Richard Marosi, "Border Jumpers Leave Their Imprint on a Besieged Town," *Los Angeles Times,* June 3, 2004. On Border Patrol staffing, see also Douglas S. Massey and Chiara Capoferro, "Measuring Undocumented Migration" (working paper #03–09i, Center for Migration and Development, Princeton University, 2003). A subsequent version is in *International Migration Review* 38, no. 3 (2004): 1075–102.

106. Wayne Cornelius, "Evaluating Enhanced US Border Enforcement," Migration Policy Institute, May 1, 2004, www.migrationinformation.org/; Chris

Hawley, "Mexico Publishes Guide to Assist Border Crossers," *Arizona Republic* (January 1, 2005).

107. Jorge Durand, Douglas S. Massey, and Emilio A. Parrado, "The New Era of Mexican Migration to the United States," *Journal of American History* 86, no. 2 (September 1999). Also see Massey, Durand, and Malone, *Beyond Smoke and Mirrors*, p. 133.

108. Massey, Durand, and Malone, *Beyond Smoke and Mirrors*, pp. 136, 140.

109. Ibid., p. 158.

110. Richard Alba and Victor Nee, *Remaking the American Mainstream: Assimilation and Contemporary Immigration* (Cambridge: Harvard University Press, 2003), pp. 281–86.

111. Hayes-Bautista, interview by author, September 13, 2004; David Glenn, "Scholars Cook Up a New Melting Pot," *Chronicle of Higher Education* (February 13, 2004); Margaret Gibson, e-mail to author, December 15, 2004. Gibson is a professor of education and anthropology at the University of California, Santa Cruz.

112. Robert Hughes, *Culture of Complaint: The Fraying of America* (New York: Oxford, 1993); Peter Skerry, "Mexican Immigration: A Special Case of What?" Center for Immigration Studies, July 2000, www.cis.org/articles/cantigny/skerry.html. Also see Skerry, *Mexican-Americans: The Ambivalent Minority* (Cambridge: Harvard University Press, 1993); Victor Nee and Richard Alba, "Toward a New Definition," in *Reinventing the Melting Pot: The New Immigrants and What It Means to be American*, ed. Tamar Jacoby (New York: Basic Books, 2004), p. 95. For a very different view, see George J. Borjas, "Economic Assimilation: Trouble Ahead," in *Reinventing the Melting Pot*, pp. 199–210.

113. Donald E. Miller, Jon Miller, and Grace R. Dyrness, *Immigrant Religion in the City of Angels* (Los Angeles: Center for Religion and Civic Culture, University of Southern California, 2001), p. 4.

114. Ibid.

115. Francis Fukuyama, "Identity Crisis: Why We Shouldn't Worry about Mexican Immigration," *Slate* (June 4, 2004), www.slate.msn.com.

116. Rodriguez, *Brown*, p. 31.

117. Victor Valle, remarks made at the "Conference on the New Metropolis," Berkeley, April 16, 2004. The comment is reminiscent of similar remarks made about the function of black maids, nannies, and cooks through much of American history as the common carriers of the recipes, manners, styles, and traditions of the dominant white society.

118. Mireya Navarro, "Mad Hot Reggaeton," *New York Times*, July 17, 2005.

119. Peter Schrag, "California, Dreamed," review of Made in California: Art, Image, and Identity, 1900–2000, an exhibit at the Los Angeles County Museum of Art, *American Prospect*, January 29, 2001.

120. Esa-Pekka Salonen, interview by Jeffrey Brown, *PBS NewsHour*, June 30, 2004.

121. Carolyne Zinko, "Vivid Images Challenge Status Quo," *San Francisco Chronicle*, August 9, 2004.

122. Rodriguez, *Brown*, pp. 121–22.

123. Ibid., p. 35. In an interview in 1997 with Scott London, host of a radio series called *Insight & Outlook*, Rodriguez said he keeps telling kids that when they fill out forms they should answer yes to everything—"Yes, I am Chinese; yes, I am African; yes, I am white; yes, I am a Pacific Islander; yes, yes, yes—just to befuddle the bureaucrats who think we live separately from one another." See www.scottlondon.com/insight/scripts/rodriguez.html.

124. But he also expresses consternation that the faces on contemporary Mexican television soap operas are almost indistinguishable from those in Sweden. "Now with Bill Moyers," transcript of PBS interview, February 14, 2003, www.pbs.org/now/transcript/transcript_rodriguez.html. Also see Richard Rodriguez, "Magic's Deductive Hold," *Salon* (June 17, 1999), www.salon.com/news/feature/1999/06/16/magic/.

125. Richard Rodriguez, remarks at the "Convocation on Providing Library Service in California's Twenty-first Century," California State Library, Sacramento, May 23, 1997.

126. Alba and Nee, *Remaking the American Mainstream*, pp. 275, 282.

127. The exceptions, as most Americans know, were Japanese Americans who served in segregated units that fought in Europe with great distinction despite the internment of their fellow Nisei at home, and blacks, often relegated to duty as cooks and mess boys or segregated into all-black units, like the Tuskegee airmen.

128. Alba and Nee, *Remaking the American Mainstream*, p. 276; Juan Onesimo Sandoval, Hans P. Johnson, and Sonya M. Tafoya, *Who's Your Neighbor? Residential Segregation and Diversity in California*, California Counts: Population Trends and Profiles, August 2002, www.ppic.org.

129. School dropout and high school completion numbers are famously squishy, depending on how the count is done, whether transfers are recorded, and how dropouts are categorized (or miscategorized).

130. Jeffrey Grogger and Stephen J. Trejo, *Falling Behind or Moving Up? Intergenerational Progress of Mexican-Americans* (San Francisco: Public Policy Institute of California, 2002), p. 79; Lozano, interview by author, September 13, 2004; Pia Orrenius, "Immigrant Assimilation: Is the U.S. Still a Melting Pot?" *Southwest Economy* (Federal Reserve Bank of Dallas) (May–June 2004): 5.

131. James P. Smith, "Immigrants and Their Schooling" (working paper no. 108, Center for Comparative Immigration Studies, La Jolla; University of California, San Diego, October 2004), p. 25; James P. Smith, "Assimilation across the Latino Generations," *American Economic Review* 93, no. 2 (May 2003): 315–19; Walter A. Ewing and Benjamin Johnson, "Immigrant Success or Stagnation?" Immigration Policy Brief, Immigration Policy Center, American Immigration Law Foundation, October 2003, www.ailf.org/ipc/; Deborah Reed, Laura Hill, Christopher Jepsen, and Hans Johnson, *Educational Progress across Immigrant Generations in California* (San Francisco: Public Policy Institute of California, 2005). Like Smith, they find that third-generation Mexican Americans (and Latinos generally) have many more years of schooling than their immigrant grandparents, but because those grandparents had so little education, the grandchildren still lag well behind the third generation of groups that immigrated with higher levels of schooling.

132. Victor Davis Hanson, "Do We Want Mexifornia?" *City Journal* (Manhattan Institute) (Spring 2002), www.city-journal.org/html/12_2_do_we_want.html.

133. Peter Andreas, "The Escalation of U.S. Immigration Control in the Post-NAFTA Era," *Political Science Quarterly* 113, no. 4 (October 1998): 605; Massey, Durand, and Malone, *Beyond Smoke and Mirrors*, p. 88. Much of this story is based on the reporting of *Los Angeles Times* reporter Sebastian Rotella.

134. Massey, Durand, and Malone, *Beyond Smoke and Mirrors*, p. 129.

135. Ibid., p. 161.

136. Robert A. Pastor, *Toward a North American Community: Lessons from the Old World for the New* (Washington, DC: Institute for International Economics, 2001), pp. 18, 186–88.

137. Philip L. Martin, interview by author, March 8, 2004.

138. The Bush proposal was almost certainly a preelection come-on for Hispanic votes, but even that was a sign of change. On Rohrabacher, see Ashley Collins, "ERs to Stay out of Immigration Checks," *Los Angeles Times*, May 19, 2004.

139. Zachary Coile, "Hospitals Won't Be Required to Report Illegals," *San*

Francisco Chronicle, May 19, 2004; Miriam Jordan, "Driver's Licenses for Illegal Immigrants Divide Congress," *Wall Street Journal*, December 6, 2004.

140. James Brulte, interview by author, March 9, 2004.

2. Dysfunction, Disinvestment, Disenchantment

1. Lou Cannon, *Governor Reagan* (New York: Public Affairs Press, 2003).

2. Quoted in "California," *Look* (September 18, 1962): 30.

3. George B. Leonard, "California," *Look* (September 18, 1962): 31.

4. *Newsweek* (September 10, 1962); *Life* (October 19, 1962); *Ladies' Home Journal* (July 1967); *Time* (November 7, 1969); *Saturday Review* (September 23, 1967). (As an editor of *Saturday Review*, I was one of those who came to join in the wonder.)

5. Carey McWilliams, "Cults of California," *Atlantic Monthly* (March 1946): 108. As in much of Southern California, where a lot of retired people had moved in the Depression, a large proportion of Long Beach's population was elderly.

6. *Modern Crusader*, October 26, 1934. This was the newsletter of the Townsend movement.

7. Statement confirmed in personal conversation with the author, 1979.

8. Brown oral history project interview with Amelia R. Fry, *Years of Growth, 1939-1966: Law Enforcement, Politics, and the Governor's Office* (Berkeley: Regional Oral History Office), p. 284; "Political Giant 'Pat' Brown Dies," *Sacramento Bee*, February 17, 1996.

9. Clark Kerr, interview by author, May 26, 1995; Kerr, *The Uses of the University* (Cambridge: Harvard University Press, 1963), p. 67.

10. "Grading the States 2005," Government Performance Project, http://results.gpponline.org/.

11. Ry Cooder, John Hiatt, Jim Dickinson, "Across the Borderline," *Music by Ry Cooder*, Warner Bros./WEA.

12. The Rumford Act was repealed by a ballot measure in 1964, which was itself subsequently declared unconstitutional by the courts. On Watts, see State of California Governor's Commission on the Los Angeles Riots, *Violence in the City— an End or a Beginning? A Report by the Governor's Commission on the Los Angeles Riots*, (Sacramento, 1967), pp. 1, 3. The report is commonly known as the McCone Report.

13. Cannon, *Governor Reagan*, p. 272.

14. Joan Didion, *Slouching toward Bethlehem* (New York: Delta, 1968), pp. 220–21.

15. Kerr said at the time that he had ended his tenure as UC president just as he began it, "fired with enthusiasm." It was clear that some regents had been uncomfortable with Kerr since the beginning of the Free Speech Movement in 1964; some, most notably oil millionaire Ed Pauley, were chafing to be rid of him. Pauley, who contended that "Kerr was either a communist or a communist follower and should be fired," had initiated contact with the FBI in 1965, which subsequently launched an extensive investigation of Kerr. (That story is extensively documented in Seth Rosenfeld, "Reagan, Hoover, and the UC Red Scare," *San Francisco Chronicle*, June 9, 2002.) But in his determination to have a showdown with Reagan, who was threatening to cut UC's budget, Kerr tried to order the UC chancellors to stop accepting new students until the budget issue was resolved—and in asking for what was, in effect, a vote of confidence from a board that wanted to keep the peace with the new governor, he helped seal his own fate. Cannon, *Governor Reagan*, pp. 274–78; Clark Kerr, *The Gold and the Blue: A Personal Memoir of the University of California, 1949–1967* (Berkeley: University of California Press, 2003), 2:61–74, 283–324, 331–65.

16. Cannon, *Governor Reagan*, pp. 359, 388.

17. A much more extensive account can be found in Peter Schrag, *Paradise Lost: California's Experience, America's Future*, with a new preface (Berkeley: University of California Press, 2004), pp. 129–87. Also see Robert Kuttner, *Revolt of the Haves* (New York: Simon and Schuster, 1980).

18. California State Senate Forum on the Future of California, California State Archives, Senate Videos, March 21, 1996, Show 492 (Tape 2).

19. Alexander Pope, "The Assessor's Perspective," *University of Southern California Law Review* 53 (1979): 155.

20. *Serrano v. Priest*, 5 Cal 3d 600 (1971).

21. "California Schools: Resources and Results in K–12," *Cal-Tax Research Bulletin* (June 1988).

22. National Education Association, *Rankings and Estimates, 2003–04* (Washington, DC: National Education Association, 2004). Highlights are Table 2: Summary of Selected Estimates Data, 2003–04; Table C-11: Average Salaries of Public School Teachers.

23. Paradoxically, Proposition 13 also helped give the state's public sector unions, including teachers, much of the clout they've developed since its passage. By effectively barring local governments from raising property taxes, the proposition eviscerated much of the interest the local business community had in run-

ning or financially supporting moderate and fiscally conservative candidates for city councils, school boards, and other entities, making the public employee groups—teachers, community college employees, cops, and firefighters—far and away the largest contributors of local campaign money and often the most important sponsors of candidates, who were often union members in nearby districts themselves.

24. *CA Rankings*, 2003–2004 (Palo Alto, CA: EdSource, January 2005), p. 2.

25. The irony, of course, is that, in trying to punish the California Teachers Association by refusing to give the schools the money without restrictions (and thus adding it to the salary pot), Wilson added thousands of new teachers—the greatest percentage of them new association members—to the rolls.

26. *Williams et al. v. State of California*, Superior Court, City and County of San Francisco, No. 312236 (2000). The case was settled in 2004 with some nominal state commitments to remedy the most egregious problems. But under the agreement, Los Angeles and other districts didn't have to phase out the Concept 6 schools until 2012. Many other states have similar problems, though few of them had been regarded as exemplary a generation before. Most of the documents in the Williams case are available at http://decentschools.com/. Also see Peter Schrag, *Final Test: The Battle for Adequacy in America's Schools* (New York: New Press, 2003).

27. On the provision of better teachers, the settlement relied primarily on the state's promise to abide by the No Child Left Behind Act, the Bush administration's sweeping school reform law, which required every school to have a "highly qualified" teacher in every classroom by 2005–06, something that, if it was to have meaning, would be virtually impossible. *Williams v. California*, Superior Court of California, No. 321236, Notice of Proposed Settlement, August 13, 2004. The full text of the settlement and many related documents are available at the Decent Schools for California Website maintained by the plaintiffs' law firm, Morrison and Foerster, www.decentschools.org/settlement.php.

28. Heather Rose, Jon Sonstelie, Ray Reinhard, and Sharmaine Heng, *High Expectations, Modest Means: The Challenge Facing California's Public Schools* (San Francisco: Public Policy Institute of California, 2003).

29. Stephen J. Carroll, Cathy Krop, Jeremy Arkes, Peter A. Morrison, and Ann Flanagan, *California's K–12 Schools: How Are They Doing?* (Santa Monica: Rand Corporation, 2005). The quotation is from Rand Press Release, January 3, 2005, www.rand.org/news/press.05/01.03.html; NAEP data is from the National Center for Education Statistics, U.S. Department of Education, http://nces.ed.gov/nationsreportcard/. The questions regarding the accuracy of

the tests, the effects of variations in state testing protocols (and on occasion official fudging), and the varying demographics of the students being tested fill volumes. I've included Texas and North Carolina to indicate that even some southern states with significant numbers of minority students do considerably better. In any case, few people contend that California students are doing well. The College Board, which runs the SAT testing program, warns the SAT should not be used for state-by-state comparisons. The scores and other data are at http://www.collegeboard.com.

30. Mark Baldassare, Mino Yaroslavsky, and Paul G. Lewis, *The State Budget and Local Health Services in California: Surveys of County Officials* (San Francisco: Public Policy Institute of California, May 2004).

31. Centers for Medicare and Medicaid Services, *Program Information on Medicaid and State Children's Health Programs (SCHIP)* (Washington, DC: Centers for Medicare and Medicaid Services, 2004), pp. 34. This report is better known as the Medicaid Chartbook.

32. Colleen Moore and Matthew Newman, *Variation in Funding and Service Levels among California Public Libraries,* CICG Research Brief (Sacramento: California Institute for County Government, 2001).

33. Maria Alicia Gaura, "Beleaguered Salinas Plans to Close Its Libraries," *San Francisco Chronicle,* November 18, 2004; David L. Beck, "Salinas Libraries to Stay Open," *San Jose Mercury News,* April 8, 2005.

34. Jeffrey L. Rabin and Sue Fox, "63,332 Inmates Were Released Early, Los Angeles Sheriff Says," *Los Angeles Times,* October 28, 2004.

35. Mark Baldassare, *When Government Fails: The Orange County Bankruptcy* (Berkeley: University of California Press, 1998).

36. Davan Maharaj, "Bankruptcy Judge Approves Complex O.C. Recovery Plan," *Los Angeles Times,* May 16, 1996; Matt Lait, "Bankruptcy Over, Recovery Not," *Los Angeles Times,* June 9, 1996.

37. David T. Hartgen, "The Looming Highway Condition Crisis: Performance of State Highway Systems, 1984–2002," manuscript, February 10, 2004, www.johnlocke.org/policy_reports/2004020943.html; The Road Information Program, *Bumpy Roads Ahead: Cities with the Roughest Rides, and Strategies to Make Our Roads Smoother* (Washington, DC: The Road Information Program, April 2004).

38. California Business, Housing, and Transportation Agency, *Final Report of the Commission on Building for the 21st Century: Invest for California—Strategic Planning for California's Future Prosperity and Quality of Life* (Sacramento: California Business, Housing, and Transportation Agency, February 27, 2002), ex-

ecutive summary, pp. 5, 8; California Business Roundtable, "Building a Legacy for the Next Generation" (Sacramento: California Business Roundtable, n.d. [ca. 1999]).

39. Norm King, interview by author, April 28, 2004. Also see Peter Schrag, "On the Road: Asthma, Gridlock, and Dumb Policies," *Sacramento Bee*, May 19, 2004.

40. *Portable School Buildings: Scourge, Saving Grace, or Just Part of the Solution?* (Palo Alto, CA: EdSource, April 1998). The preeminent symbol of that mismanagement was almost certainly the debacle of the Belmont Learning Center, a $200 million high school construction project first planned in 1993. In 1999, when it was half completed, authorities discovered that the project was sitting on a toxic site, an old oil field emitting poisonous hydrogen sulfide and methane gas, creating the possibility that the place could blow up. The project was stopped while the school board decided what to do. Ultimately, the board, desperate for space, opted for a multi-million-dollar cleanup and completion of the school, which would bring the price to $220–$240 million, making it the most expensive school ever built in this country. In 2002, before that work was finished, engineers discovered that the place was also sitting on an earthquake fault, and again the work was suspended. In the spring of 2003, the site was finally deemed safe and the project approved for completion. Andrew Trotter, "Los Angeles Revives Beleaguered Belmont Project," *Education Week*, March 20, 2002; Joetta L. Sack, "Romer Puts New Hold on Troubled Belmont Site," *Education Week*, January 9, 2003; Cara Mia DiMassa and Erika Hayasaki, "L.A. Board Votes to Finish Troubled Belmont Project," *Los Angeles Times*, May 23, 2003.

41. University of California officials and professors, interviews by author, Spring 1993; David Gardner, *Earning My Degree: Memoirs of an American University President* (Berkeley: University of California Press, 2005), pp. 341–52; "Report on Voluntary Early Retirement Incentive Program for Faculty and Its Effect on Academic Programs," *Report of the [UC] Regents Committee on Education Policy*, University of California, Berkeley, May 19, 1994. Guthrie went to Vanderbilt, where he still teaches. The pension deal had been part of a larger and very generous compensation package when Gardner was appointed. Kerr, *The Gold and the Blue*, p. 188.

42. Callan, interview by author, April 15, 2004; Clark Kerr, various interviews by author, 1997–2002; Kerr, *The Gold and the Blue*, p. 188.

43. Gender was never a real issue at UC, which, like other universities, had long admitted more undergraduate women than men. No one suggested they were getting preferred treatment.

44. Eric Brazil and Tanya Schevitz, "Chang-Lin Tien, 1935–2002: Former Cal Chief Dies—Proponent of Diversity," *San Francisco Chronicle*, October 31, 2002.

45. See, for example, Richard Sander, "Commentary: College Will Just Disguise Racial Quotas," *Los Angeles Times*, June 30, 2003.

46. Jeffrey Rosen, "Damage Control," *New Yorker* (February 23, 1998): 58. In a significant gesture, though one without practical effect, in 2001 the regents, under pressure from faculty and students, also rescinded their 1995 resolution against affirmative action. By then Wilson was gone, Gray Davis was governor, and Proposition 209, which wrote a broader affirmative-action ban into the state constitution, had been passed.

47. Data from official UC enrollment figures, "Student/Workforce Data," 1995–2005, University of California, Office of the President, www.ucop.edu/news/studstaff.html. In 2002, 12 percent of new enrollments in the five UC medical schools were "underrepresented minorities" (African Americans, Indians, Latinos); in the three law schools, the figure was 11 percent. That compared to a consistent average of over 20 percent for both categories before the end of affirmative action. "Memo to the Committee on Educational Policy," from University of California, Office of the President, July 10, 2002.

48. Moores said their failures were double those of others. The university said that those who left did so for financial or other personal reasons and that, in this case, the "double" was the difference between a 5 and a 10 percent attrition rate. More than 90 percent of the students in Moores's group returned in the fall of 2003 for their second year, which was when he issued his complaint. John Moores, e-mail exchanges and interview by author, May 27, 2004; John Cummings, UC Assistant Chancellor, and others, interviews by author, November 7, 2003; letter from Robert Berdahl, chancellor of the University of California, Berkeley, to Robert Dynes, president of the University of California, October 7, 2003, UC Berkeley News Center, www.berkeley.edu/news/media/releases/2003/10/06_admit_rmb.shtml; "UC Responds to Regent Moores' Report on Admissions," UC press release, October 31, 2003; Eleanor Yang, "Independent Review of UC's Admissions Is Sought by Moores," *San Diego Union Tribune*, March 27, 2004.

49. Gerald C. Hayward, Dennis P. Jones, Aims C. McGuiness Jr., and Allene Timar, *Ensuring Access with Quality to California's Community Colleges* (San Jose, CA: National Center for Public Policy and Higher Education, May 2004). The numbers were based on the community colleges' data for the decline in enrollment in combination with their (somewhat more hypothetical) estimates of the

additional number of students who would have enrolled. "2003–4 Budget Signed into Law," California Budget Project, August 6, 2003, www.cbp.org; "Budget Watch: The 2003–4 Budget and Beyond," California Budget Project, September 2003, www.cbp.org.

50. *Policy Alert: The Educational Pipeline: Big Investment, Big Returns* (San Jose, CA: National Center for Public Policy and Higher Education, 2004). As noted earlier, the problems of tracking students who move out of state or even from district to district, the ninth grade classes swollen by students who are in effect being held back because they're not considered ready for high school, and other imponderables make graduation rates notoriously difficult to calculate, especially in the absence of universal student identifiers. Thus the numbers generated by different studies may vary widely.

51. "Academic Senate Recommendations Regarding Freshman Eligibility Requirements," memo from President Robert Dynes to the Committee on Educational Policy of the UC Regents, September 20, 2004, www.universityofcalifornia.edu/regents/regmeet/sep04/304.pdf; Tanya Schevitz and Lynda Gledhill, "State University Deal a 'Shocker' to Critics," *San Francisco Chronicle*, May 12, 2004; Tanya Schevitz, "UC, CSU Funding to Be Spared; Reversal: Junior College Deferrals Averted," *San Francisco Chronicle*, July 28, 2004; Schevitz, "Why UC, CSU Chiefs Kept Quiet on Cuts: They Accepted Governor's Promise of Future Funding," *San Francisco Chronicle*, August 10, 2004.

52. Murray Haberman, interview by author, November 30, 2004. Also see Suzanne Pardington, "A Gold Standard, Dulled," *Contra Costa Times*, September 14, 2004; Rebecca Trounson, "Lean Times Foreseen for U.C. System," *Los Angeles Times*, September 22, 2005.

53. Steven M. Sheffrin, "State Budget Deficit Dynamics and the California Debacle," *Journal of Economic Perspectives* 18, no. 2 (Spring 2004): 217.

54. "Terminating the Deficit: Does the Governor's 2004–5 Budget Restore California's Fiscal Health While Restoring Public Services?" (Sacramento: California Budget Project, January 2004), p. 32.

55. "Perspective on the Vehicle License Fee," in *LAO Analysis of the 1998–99 Budget Bill: Perspectives and Issues* (Sacramento: Office of the California Legislative Analyst, February 18, 1998), www.lao.ca.gov/.

56. "California Schools: Resources and Results in K–12," *Cal-Tax Research Bulletin* (June 1988); "Comparing the 50 States' Combined State/Local Tax Burdens in 2004" (Washington, DC: Tax Foundation, April 2004), http://www.taxfoundation.org/statelocal04.html; "Who Pays Taxes in California?" California Budget Project, April 15, 2004, www.cbp.org.

57. Jean O. Pasco, "O.C.'s Reserve for Pension Payments Is $1 Billion Short," *Los Angeles Times*, July 19, 2004.

58. Philip J. Levelle, "Staggering Cost Seen for S.D.'s Pension Fix," *San Diego Union-Tribune*, September 16, 2004; John Ritter, "San Diego Now 'Enron by the Sea,' " *USA Today*, October 24, 2004.

59. The Pacific Telephone Company got a tax cut estimated at $130 million; Pacific Gas and Electric got $90 million; Standard Oil $13 million in Contra Costa County alone. Significantly enough, whereas Jarvis, as director of an apartment house owners' group, was attacked as a shill for commercial property owners, most of the state's business establishment, fearing that the backlash against Proposition 13 would bring a move to tax commercial property at higher rates, opposed the measure.

60. Kenneth T. Rosen, "The Impact of Proposition 13 on House Prices in Northern California: A Test of the Interjurisdictional Capitalization Hypothesis," *Journal of Political Economy* 90 (1982): 200.

61. "Buffett Suggests Calif. Property Tax Too Low—Report," Reuters, August 15, 2003, www.forbes.com/business/services/newswire/2003/08/15/rtr1058689.html. On Nordlinger's comparison, see "Life and Times Transcript," KCET, Los Angeles, August 27, 2003, www.kcet.org/lifeandtimes/archives/200308/20030827.php.

62. *Nordlinger v. Hahn*, 505 U.S. 1 (1992).

63. Ibid.

64. Joel Fox, various interviews by and conversations with the author, 1996–2005.

65. Residents in the Willow Glen area and elsewhere in San Jose, interviews by author, August 2000.

66. California Tax Reform Association, *California Commercial Property Tax Study* (Sacramento: California Tax Reform Association, April 2004), pp. 5, 7, 9, www.caltaxreform.org/cpts.pdf; Lenny Goldberg, interviews by author, 1996, 1997, 2004; Goldberg, *Taxation with Representation: A Citizen's Guide to Reforming Proposition 13* (Sacramento: California Tax Reform Association and New California Alliance, 1991), pp. 69–70.

67. John Decker, interview by author, January 22, 2004.

68. William Fulton, "Another Legacy of Proposition 13: A Crazy Quilt of 'Cocoon' Citizens," Opinion, *Los Angeles Times*, December 1, 1991, p.1.

69. Data provided at request of the author by School Services of California, www.sscal.com.

70. Edward J. Blakely and Mary Gail Snyder, *Fortress America: Gated Com-*

munities in the United States (Washington, DC: Brookings Institution Press and Lincoln Institute of Land Policy, 1997), p. 60; Edward J. Blakely, interview by author, July 1996; Tom Gorman, "It Has It All—Even a Wall," *Los Angeles Times*, August 19, 1996. In a more recent study of planned communities generally, including condominiums and cooperatives, published in 2004, Tracy Gordon of the Public Policy Institute of California found that these are "the dominant source of new housing in California," and that their residents are less diverse in race, age, and income than are people from similar economic and social classes outside of such communities. But according to Gordon, voting trends within such places don't differ significantly between the two groups. *Planned Developments in California: Private Communities and Public Life* (San Francisco: Public Policy Institute of California, 2004).

71. Robert B. Reich, "Secession of the Successful," *New York Times Magazine* (January 20, 1991): 16. "In many cities and towns," wrote Reich, "the wealthy have in effect withdrawn their dollars from the support of public spaces and institutions shared by all and dedicated the savings to their own private services. As public parks and playgrounds deteriorate, there is a proliferation of private health clubs, golf clubs, tennis clubs, skating clubs and every other type of recreational association in which costs are shared among members. Condominiums and the omnipresent residential communities dun their members to undertake work that financially strapped local governments can no longer afford to do well—maintaining roads, mending sidewalks, pruning trees, repairing street lights, cleaning swimming pools, paying for lifeguards and, notably, hiring security guards to protect life and property. (The number of private security guards in the United States now exceeds the number of public police officers.)"

72. William Fulton, "In Their Race for Sales Tax Income, Cities Often Wind Up as the Losers," *Sacramento Bee*, September 4, 1995, p. B7.

73. Jarvis and Gann had a famous falling-out after the passage of Proposition 13. "I don't give a damn," Jarvis said when Gann was running his Proposition 4. "Gann is trying to promote something to make money. For Gann." Gann replied, "Howard has a very difficult problem with the English language. It's hard for him to get above a two letter word." "Jarvis, Gann Split Bitterly Over Follow-up," *Sacramento Bee*, November 17, 1978, p. A1.

74. David Gardner, president of the University of California, interview by author, November 1988. Gardner considered it an unfraternal act by others in the education community. In fact, Gardner had no right to complain. Honig, along with some public employee groups, had sponsored an initiative the previous June to loosen the Gann spending restrictions, which Gardner and the uni-

versity regents, trying to court the conservative Deukmejian, who had treated the university well, refused to support.

75. State of California, "Governor's Budget Summary, 2004–05," California Department of Finance, www.dof.ca.gov/HTML/BUD_DOCS/Bud_link.htm.

76. Kings County local officials and merchants, interviews by author, April 2004; Peter Schrag, "The Central Valley—California's Gulag Archipelago," *Sacramento Bee*, May 5, 2004; Sarah Lawrence and Jeremy Travis, *The New Landscape of Imprisonment: Mapping America's Prison Expansion* (Washington, DC: Urban Institute, April 29, 2004), p. 32.

77. Carol Whiteside, interviews by author, October 2003, April 2004; Matthew Heller, "The Prison Prosperity Myth," *Los Angeles Times Magazine* (September 1, 2002). Another effect is that, in being located in isolated communities, the prisons are less likely to be subject to any stringent oversight. In a state like California, which has been wracked by prison scandals and brutality, this may not be a negligible factor.

78. R. Michael Alvarez, William Deverell, and Elizabeth Penn, "The 'Ham and Eggs' Movement in Southern California: Public Opinion on Economic Redistribution in the 1938 Campaign" (working paper no. 12, Center for the Study of Law and Politics, USC Law School, and California Institute of Technology, February 21, 2003).

79. Quoted in Franklin Hichborn, *Story of the Session of the California Legislature of 1911* (San Francisco: James H. Barry Company, 1911), appendix, p. v.

80. See, for example, "Drug Policy Measures on the 2004 Ballot," National Conference of State Legislatures, October 18, 2004, www.ncsl.org/programs/legman/statevote/drugpolicy.htm; Peter Schrag, "A Quagmire for Our Time," *American Prospect* 12, no. 14 (August 13, 2001); and, more generally, the Website of the Drug Policy Alliance, www.drugpolicy.org.

81. The Supreme Court decision is *Gonzalez v. Raich*, USSC: No. 03–1454, (2005). Hawaii and Vermont have also enacted medical marijuana laws by the conventional legislative route.

82. All California vote results and campaign expenditure data, here as elsewhere, are from the secretary of state's Website, www.ss.ca.gov.

83. Her brother Jerry had never fully shed his "Governor Moonbeam" reputation—a man more interested in state space programs and other flights of vision than in hands-on governance. She called herself "a different shade of Brown," as indeed she was.

84. Pete Wilson, interview by author, July 19, 2001.

85. Robert Salladay, "Mormons Now Target California," *San Francisco Chronicle*, July 4, 1999.

86. Transcript from the National Press Club Newsmakers Luncheon: "Transcript: National Press Club Q&A with President Gordon B. Hinckley," March 8, 2000, *Deseret News*, March 9, 2000, http://deseretnews.com/dn/print/1,1442,155008723,00.html. Also see David E. Campbell and J. Quin Monson, "Following the Leader? Mormon Voting on Ballot Propositions" (manuscript, n.d.), www.nd.edu/~amdemoc/Campbell_Mormon_Voting.pdf.

87. Dean E. Murphy, "Some Democrats Blame One of Their Own," *New York Times*, November 5, 2004.

88. Daniel Lowenstein, "Campaign Spending and Ballot Propositions: Recent Experience, Public Choice Theory and the First Amendment," *UCLA Law Review* 29 (February 1982): 29.

89. On the term-limits issue, the voice of "the people" probably would never have been heard had it not been for some deep-pockets who paid for the term limits initiative that became Proposition 140: Pete Schabarum, who was retiring after twenty-four years in public office—nineteen as a Los Angeles supervisor and five as a state legislator (no term limits for him)—and who had $1 million in his campaign fund that the law wouldn't allow him to spend on himself; some out-of-state term-limits groups; and the pair of secretive Kansas oil billionaires, Charles and David Koch, who reportedly funded those groups. The real objective of the groups, later succeeded by the Washington-based organization U.S. Term Limits, was to impose term limits on Congress, then controlled by Democrats, but that would have been a far more difficult—and ultimately impossible—project.

90. Kelly Kimball, chief executive officer of Kimball Petition Management, interview by author, March 18, 1997; Charles M. Price, "Signing on for Fun and Profit: The Business of Gathering Petition Signatures," *California Journal* (November 1992): 547.

91. The most important of the think tanks is the Initiative and Referendum Institute, launched by M. Dane Waters, which is now located at the University of Southern California. Among the newer books are David Broder, *Democracy Derailed: Initiative Campaigns and the Power of Money* (New York: Harcourt, 1999); Shaun Bowler, Todd Donovan, and Caroline J. Tolbert, eds., *Citizens as Legislators: Direct Democracy in the United States* (Columbus: Ohio State University Press, 1998); Elisabeth R. Gerber, *The Populist Paradox: Interest Group Influence and the Promise of Direct Legislation* (Princeton: Princeton University Press, 1999); Larry J. Sabato, Howard R. Ernst, and Bruce A. Larson, *Dangerous Democracy?*

The Battle over Ballot Initiatives in America (Lanham, MD: Rowan and Littlefield, 2001); Richard J. Ellis, *Democratic Delusions: The Initiative Process in America* (Lawrence: Kansas University Press, 2002); M. Dane Waters, *The Battle over Citizen Lawmaking* (Durham, NC: Carolina Academic Press, 2001); Daniel A. Smith and Caroline J. Tolbert, *Educated by Initiative: The Effects of Direct Democracy on Citizens and Political Organizations in the American States* (Ann Arbor: University of Michigan Press, 2004).

92. Broder, *Democracy Derailed*, p. 242.

93. Gravel pushed the proposal at a conference sponsored by the Initiative and Referendum Institute in Washington, D.C., in 1999 and in many other venues, https://votep2.us/PhiladelphiaII.html. See also Broder, *Democracy Derailed*, pp. 242-43.

94. Mitchel Benson, "Do Exemptions Threaten State's Sales-Tax Base?" *Wall Street Journal*, Western ed., May 7, 1997.

95. For a quick chronology, see Planned Parenthood Affiliates of California, *Abbreviated History of Abortion Law in California* (Sacramento: Planned Parenthood Affiliates of California, 1998), www.ppacca.org/.

96. California Citizens Budget Commission, *A 21st Century Budget Process for California: Recommendations of the California Citizens Budget Commission* (Los Angeles: Center on Governmental Studies, 1998), p. 3.

97. David Janssen, interview by author, April 26, 2004.

98. Darrell Steinberg, interviews by author, January 29, August 11, 2004.

99. Initiative and Referendum Institute map and state list at www.iandrinstitute.org/statewide_i&r.htm; National Conference of State Legislatures, *Initiative and Referendum in the 21st Century: Final Report and Recommendations of the NCSL I&R Task Force* (Denver: National Conference of State Legislatures, 2002), pp. 11, 63.

100. Arthur Lupia, "Dumber Than Chimps? An Assessment of Direct Democracy Voters," in *Dangerous Democracy? The Battle over Ballot Initiatives in America*, ed. Larry J. Sabato, Howard R. Ernst, and Bruce A. Larson (Lanham, MD: Rowan and Littlefield, 2001), p. 66; Arthur Lupia and Matthew D. McCubbins, *The Democratic Dilemma: Can Citizens Learn What They Need to Know?* (New York: Cambridge University Press, 1998).

101. The only insurance measure that the voters passed, Proposition 103, endorsed by consumer activist Ralph Nader, then a more admired figure than now, toughened auto insurance regulations—it also promised large premium refunds that most people never got—and made the post of insurance commissioner an elective office. Under the first incumbent, John Garamendi (1991-95), this

seemed to work. But his successor, Chuck Quackenbush, elected with huge amounts of insurance industry money—he was described by the nonpartisan *California Political Almanac* as "the insurance commissioner picked and selected by the industry he is supposed to regulate"—ultimately found himself hip deep in charges of kickbacks, fixes, and payoffs, and, after an extended legislative investigation, was forced to resign. (Garamendi, promising to take no money from the industry, was elected again in 2002.) A. G. Block and Claudia Buck, eds., *California Political Almanac, 1997–98* (Sacramento: State Net, 1997), p. 60. The prime issue in the case was the failure of insurers to pay claims in connection with earthquake damage in Southern California and allegations that Quackenbush's office allowed them to get off the hook in return for contributions to a foundation he controlled and which spent a big chunk of the money promoting Quackenbush. Dan Smith, "Quackenbush Mess Lives On: A Year After He Quit in Disgrace, Legal Cases Continue and Quake Victims Still Demand Compensation," *Sacramento Bee*, July 9, 2001.

In the primary election in June 1988, voters had also approved two competing campaign finance reform measures, one of which, Proposition 68, would have provided for public financing for candidates who adhered to certain spending limits. The state supreme court ruled that, because the two measures were irreconcilable, the other measure, Proposition 73, which got more votes, prevailed. But after a federal judge ruled that its campaign contribution limit discriminated against challengers and was therefore unconstitutional, neither reform could go into effect (which probably didn't displease the politicians who were among Proposition 73's chief sponsors). For an overview of this story and other major California campaign law issues, see Charles H. Bell Jr., "California Campaign Finance and Lobbying Regulation: A Summary of Major Initiatives, Litigation, and Current Law," n.d., at the Website of the law firm of Bell, McAndrews, Hiltachk, and Davidian, www.bmhlaw.com/lawsum.htm.

102. Julian N. Eule, "Judicial Review of Direct Democracy," *Yale Law Journal* 99, no. 7 (1990): 1503–90.

103. Greg Mitchell, *The Campaign of the Century: Upton Sinclair's Race for Governor of California and the Birth of Media Politics* (New York: Random House, 1992), p. 546. Dills was, in fact, a fascinating figure, one of two California legislators to oppose the internment of the Japanese in World War II. His slogan in his last campaign for office was "too old to quit." Ralph Dills, interview by author, September 1994; Greg Lucas, "Sen. Ralph Dills—FDR Democrat Who Served 42 Years," *San Francisco Chronicle*, May 17, 2002.

104. Bruce Cain, interview by author, October 14, 2004.

105. Bruce Cain and Thad Kousser, *Adapting to Term Limits: Recent Experiences and New Directions* (San Francisco: Public Policy Institute of California, 2004), p. 38.

106. Bill Bagley, interview by author, March 2004. The Unruh quote is from John Jacobs, *A Rage for Justice: The Passion and Politics of Phillip Burton* (Berkeley: University of California Press), p. 88.

107. Cain and Kousser, *Adapting to Term Limits*, p. 72.

108. Kevin Cody, "Void Electrical Contracts and 'Let Them Sue,' Says Bowen," *Easy Reader*, n.d., http://easyreader.hermosawave.net/news2001/1108/bowen-electicity.asp.

109. John Vasconcellos, remarks at the Public Policy Institute of California, November 22, 2004.

110. Robert Hertzberg, interview by author, January 2002.

111. I owe much of this analysis to Bruce Cain, director of the Institute of Governmental Studies at the University of California, Berkeley.

3. Action Hero

1. I've tortured the definition a bit for my purposes. The full definition, quoted by Robertson Davies in his novel, *Fifth Business:* "Those roles which, being neither those of Hero nor Heroine, Confidante nor Villain, but which were nonetheless essential to bring about the Recognition or the denouement, were called the Fifth Business in drama and opera companies organized according to the old style; the player who acted these parts was often referred to as Fifth Business." *Fifth Business* (New York: Viking, 1970), p. 5.

2. Kathryn Eaker Perkins, "Bitter Battle to Control Gann's Political Legacy; Family Ousted in Fight with Key Backers," *Sacramento Bee*, February 23, 1990; Dale Vargas, "New Suit Filed in Battle over Gann's Group," *Sacramento Bee*, February 27, 1990; Norman D. Williams, "Daughter of Gann Wins $50,000 Suit," *Sacramento Bee*, April 18, 1991. The "shit-kicker" phrase was uttered in a background conversation. Others, like liberal lobbyist Lenny Goldberg, were less generous. Goldberg called him "a right-wing nut case." Patrick May, "Recall Puts Anti-tax Rebel in Spotlight," *San Jose Mercury News*, July 4, 2003.

3. See, for example, William Booth, "California Redistricting Is Off the Ballot," *Washington Post*, December 14, 1999. Under California's constitution, no ballot measure may cover more than one subject. The provision was designed to prevent precisely the kind of stratagem that combined a provision appealing to

voters (legislative pay cuts) with the real objective (reapportionment), but one that voters didn't understand and cared little about.

4. Ted Costa, interview by author, March 4, 2004.

5. *North Dakota Governors, Part 3, 1913–1929* (Bismarck: Historical Society of North Dakota, n.d.), www.state.nd.us/hist/ndgov3.htm. Governor Evan Meacham of Arizona faced a recall in 1987, which was rendered moot when he was impeached. Shaun Bowler, "Recall Elections: The Politics of Spite?" (manuscript, n.d.).

6. Abernathy's remarks were made at a recall postmortem on October 18, 2003, conducted by the Institute of Governmental Studies at the University of California, Berkeley. The quotes are either from author's notes or from the transcript in Gerald C. Lubenow, ed., *California Votes: The 2002 Governor's Race and the Recall That Made History* (Berkeley: Berkeley Public Policy Press, Institute of Governmental Studies, University of California, 2003); Abernathy quotes are at pp. 177, 179.

7. Greg Lucas, "Teachers' Feud with Governor Deepens," *San Francisco Chronicle,* May 2, 2002; Mark Sappenfield, "Governor Tests the Boundaries of Fundraising Zeal," *Christian Science Monitor,* May 20, 2002.

8. Pete Wilson, interview by author at the Public Policy Institute of California, July 19, 2002. He also argued, correctly, that Davis could have averted part of the problem by removing retail price caps and letting the state's utilities negotiate long-term contracts rather than relying on the spiking spot market.

9. Loretta Lynch, interview by author, and Lynch, talk at the Institute of Governmental Studies, Berkeley, May 4, 2005.

10. Paul Maslin, interview by author, December 2000; Gray Davis, at meeting with the editorial board of the *Sacramento Bee,* April 25, 2001; Davis, interview by author, January 16, 2003; "Gray Davis: I Knew Nothing," Associated Press, June 11, 2005. State policy, torn between free market pressures and advocates of reregulation, continued to be stuck in the no-man's-land of partial deregulation. Severin Borenstein, director of the University of California Energy Institute, and other staff members, interviews by author, November, December 2000; March and April 2004. Borenstein later concluded that the "hype" about the California blackouts was more costly to the business climate than the blackouts themselves.

11. The voters in 2002, said Attorney General Bill Lockyer, a Democrat, "started with the opinion 'Anybody but Davis.' God bless him, poor Bill Simon couldn't qualify as 'anybody.' " Lubenow, *California Votes,* p. 261. Riordan's biggest misstep probably was insulting former GOP governor George Deukme-

jian at a candidates' forum. Davis promptly used Deukemjian's return criticism of Riordan in his own ad.

12. The seventy-three-year-old Riordan was vulnerable even without Davis's intervention. Those who saw him in the spring of the primary campaign found him easily distractible, sometimes confused, and famously prone to verbal gaffes. A year later, he would say that the only time he opened his mouth was to put his foot in it. Richard Riordan, interview by author, February 2003. One other governor, Democrat Pat Brown, tried to put his thumb into the opposing party's primary. In 1966, expecting that former San Francisco mayor George Christopher would be a more formidable reelection opponent, his campaign planted some marginally disparaging stories about Christopher with columnist Drew Pearson. But the strategy backfired. Ronald Reagan, who Brown thought would be a pushover for him, beat Christopher in the primary—though not because of Brown's intervention—and then defeated Brown in the general election. Lou Cannon, *Governor Reagan* (New York: Public Affairs Press, 2003), p. 147.

13. Jim Brulte, interview by author, May 2003. Gray Davis, Steve Maviglio, interviews by author, January 16, 2003.

14. Dianne Feinstein, "Californians Should Not Sign the Recall Petition," Feinstein press release and op-ed, from Feinstein Website and e-mails to editors, May 29, 2003, http://feinstein.senate.gov/june-newsletter-smaller.htm.

15. Peter Schrag, "The Political Ops' Full Employments Recall Campaign," *Sacramento Bee*, February 26, 2003. However, the Cox and Parsky misgivings notwithstanding, the state GOP later roundly endorsed the recall. Edward Epstein, "State GOP Strongly Endorses Recall," *San Francisco Chronicle*, July 10, 2003.

16. See, for example, David S. Broder, "Million-Dollar Recall," *Washington Post*, July 31, 2003.

17. Hedgecock, elected in a special election in 1983, resigned the mayor's job in 1985 after a jury convicted him of perjury and conspiracy in connection with a Ponzi scheme run by a pair of close friends. He then turned to talk radio. In 1990, after allegations surfaced that there had been jury tampering, the state Supreme Court reversed most of the convictions. Hedgecock settled the remaining one by paying a $5000 fine. See, for example, Tony Perry, "San Diego–Post Pete, 1983–1988," *San Diego Magazine* (October 1998): 48–57, www.sandiegomag.com/retro/augustretro2.shtml.

18. Lubenow, *California Votes*, pp. 179–80, 189.

19. Dan Schnur, interview by author, July 2003; Lubenow, *California Votes*, p. 193.

20. Lance Williams and Carla Marinucci, "Issa Was Charged in San Jose Car Theft," *San Francisco Chronicle*, June 25, 2003; Jim Puzzanghera and Dion Nissenbaum, "Davis Foe Tangled with the Law," *San Jose Mercury News*, June 26, 2003.

21. For an overview of the California recall process, see, for example, Institute of Governmental Studies, "Recall in California," 2003, Institute of Governmental Studies, University of California, Berkeley, www.igs.berkeley.edu/library/htRecall2003.html.

22. Michael Finnegan, "Big Names Warn of Chaos in a Davis Recall," *Los Angeles Times*, July 10, 2003. The story of the second Texas redistricting after the 2000 census has been told in extensive detail. A state court, in the face of legislative deadlock, reapportioned the congressional districts in 2001. Then, after Republicans gained control of the legislature following the 2002 election, they attempted to reapportion it again with districts far more favorable to themselves. Democrats temporarily blocked the attempt by not showing up and thus preventing a quorum—even leaving the state in order to prevent legislative marshals from rounding them up. DeLay sought to have the FBI find the absentees—and was later admonished by the House Ethics Committee for the attempt. But the Democrats eventually gave up and allowed the vote to go forward.

23. Gary Delsohn, "Davis to Challenge Recall Law," *Sacramento Bee*, August 4, 2003; Harriet Chang, "High Court Refuses to Delay Recall; Setback for Davis," *San Francisco Chronicle*, August 8, 2003. Also see Institute of Governmental Studies, "Recall in California." Davis contended that being excluded from the list of successor candidates was a denial of equal protection under the U.S. Constitution.

24. Garry South, quoted in Lubenow, *California Votes*, p. 217. In 2003, Lieberman was preparing to run for president.

25. Lubenow, *California Votes*, p. 216.

26. Megan Garvey and Peter Nicholas, "The Recall: Front Runner Shifts to Damage Control," *Los Angeles Times*, October 6, 2003.

27. Robert Salladay, "Schwarzenegger Moves Beyond His Father's Nazi Past," *San Francisco Chronicle*, July 13, 2003. Waldheim was put on a Justice Department watch list denying entry into the United States to any foreign national who assisted or otherwise participated "in activities amounting to persecution in World War." Timothy Noah, "Arnold's Nazi Problem," *Slate*, August 7, 2003. *Slate* suggested that Schwarzenegger's reluctance to break with Waldheim was based on his thought that he might someday run for president of his native coun-

try and didn't wish to alienate voters who thought Waldheim was being unfairly attacked by foreigners.

28. George Gorton, in Lubenow, *California Votes*, p. 216. It was on the morning of the taping of the Leno show that Dianne Feinstein, who had seemed to leave the door slightly ajar, announced finally and conclusively that she wouldn't run. This led to speculation that it was her announcement—and thus the withdrawal of the strongest opponent he would have faced—that persuaded Schwarzenegger. Feinstein said the timing of her announcement was purest coincidence. She still expected that her friend Riordan would be the candidate. Feinstein, interview by author, October 13, 2004. On Schwarzenegger's tricks and feints, see Laurence Leamer, *Fantastic: The Life of Arnold Schwarzenegger* (New York: St. Martin's Press, 2005). The statement about Schwarzenegger's destroying his opponents is from Robert Salladay, "Books Explore Schwarzenegger's Psyche, Strategies," *Los Angeles Times*, July 7, 2005.

29. Eleanor Randolph, "Americans Claim Role in Yeltsin Win, Russia: Consultants Say They Spent Months in Moscow Secretly Devising U.S.-Style Strategy," *Los Angeles Times*, July 9, 1996.

30. Lubenow, *California Votes*, p. 225.

31. Jim Wasserman, "Schwarzenegger Unveils Political Reforms as Court Action Nears," *San Francisco Chronicle*, September 18, 2003.

32. Gil Cedillo, interview by author, August, 2004; Garry South, interview by author, March 12, 2004. South, though no longer Davis's official strategist, remained in touch with the campaign. On September 10, 2003, the Field Poll showed that voters opposed the driver's license law 59–34. Field Poll Release #2089, http://field.com/fieldpollonline/subscribers/.

33. Dion Nissenbaum, "Tabloids Starry-Eyed for Schwarzenegger," *San Jose Mercury News*, September 26, 2003; Jim Rutenberg, "Schwarzenegger Prompts Role Reversal Among Media," *New York Times*, October 6, 2003. Some of the story is also summarized in "Drip, Drip, Drip," *Salon*, October 4, 2003, http://blogs.salon.com/0001797/2003/10/04.html; and in Alexa H. Bluth, "Governor Signs On with Two Magazines," *Sacramento Bee*, March 6, 2004; Laurence Leamer, *Fantastic: The Life of Arnold Schwarzenegger* (New York: St. Martin's Press, 2005), p. 275. Also see Peter Nicholas and Carla Hall, "Tabloid's Deal with Woman Shielded Schwarzenegger," *Los Angeles Times*, August 12, 2005.

34. Gary Cohn, Carla Hall, and Robert W. Welkos, "Women Say Schwarzenegger Groped, Humiliated Them," *Los Angeles Times*, October 2, 2003. Garry South, Davis's longtime political strategist, would later talk about his astonishment "that you could have a candidate for governorship of the

largest state in America be hit with serial charges by 16 women, all of them cor-
roborated by other witnesses, that he has been a serial groper and a sexual ha-
rasser for 30 years, and the other side simply wipes that off." Lubenow, *California Votes*, p. 249.

35. Arnold Schwarzenegger, interview by Judy Woodruff, *Inside Politics*,
CNN, December 9, 2003, www.cnn.com/2003/ALLPOLITICS/12/09/elec04
.g.arnold/.

36. In the summer and early fall of 2003, as a writer on California issues, I had
calls and interview requests from reporters and TV crews from Germany, Sweden, Holland, Canada, France, Switzerland, Belgium, and England, as well as
from a long string of American papers.

37. A much more complete story of California's orgy of ballot measures between 1978 and 1998 is in Peter Schrag, *Paradise Lost: California's Experience,
America's Future* (Berkeley: University of California Press, 2004).

38. Paul Maslin, e-mail response to author, July 9, 2003.

39. Lubenow, *California Votes*, p. 238.

40. Marisa Lagos, "Schwarzenegger Will Run in Recall Election," *Los Angeles Times*, August 5, 2003.

41. "Governor Schwarzenegger's Remarks at the Republican National Convention, Tuesday, 08/31/2004," Schwarzenegger Website: www.governor.ca.gov/
state/govsite/gov_speeches_details.jsp.

42. Roland Prinz, "Historians Criticize Schwarzenegger for Austrian History
Gaffes," Associated Press, *San Francisco Chronicle*, September 2, 2004.

43. Lou Cannon, *Governor Reagan* (New York, Public Affairs Press, 2003),
pp. 197–99.

44. Public Policy Institute of California, "Just the Facts: California's Tax
Burden," October 2004, www.ppic.org.

45. Economic Policy Institute, Job Watch, "Unemployment Rate by State,
41 Months After Start of Recession," July 2004, http://jobwatch.org/states/
index.html; Public Policy Institute of California, "Just the Facts: California's
Economy," October 2004, www.ppic.org. Among the California-based Fortune
500 companies: Chevron-Texaco, Hewlett-Packard, McKesson, Safeway, Wells
Fargo, Intel, Disney, Cisco, Northrop Grumman, Apple, Gap, Health Net,
Fluor, Sun Microsystems, Oracle, and nearly one hundred others. "The 2005
Fortune 500," *Fortune* (April 18, 2005), www.fortune.com/fortune/fortune500.

46. California Secretary of State, Campaign Finance Reports, at http://cal-
access.ss.ca.gov/; Lubenow, *California Votes*, p. 232.

47. Gary Delsohn, "Davis Is Told: No Trash Talk," *Sacramento Bee*, August

1, 2003. He also predicted that Bush would resort to "puke politics" in 2004. Lubenow, *California Votes*, p. 262.

48. Gary Gentile, "Recall Election Prompts Review of California's Proposition 13," Associated Press, *San Jose Mercury News*, August 29, 2003.

49. Margaret Talev and Alexa H. Bluth, "Candidates Turn Heat on Schwarzenegger," *Sacramento Bee*, September 25, 2003; Lubenow, *California Votes*, p. 246. Davis, who couldn't succeed himself if the recall passed, and was thus formally a noncandidate, was segregated into his own half hour and wasn't part of the debate.

50. Field Poll, September 9, 2001. Release # 2088.

51. Barry Witt and Howard Mintz, "Bustamante Using Donor Loophole," *San Jose Mercury News*, August 26, 2003. The quote is from Schwarzenegger's political advisor Don Sipple, Lubenow, *California Votes*, p. 241; Arnold Steinberg, "Ninth Recants," *National Review Online*, September 23, 2003. Before the campaign was over, a judge, deeming the donations to be improper, ordered Bustamante to return $3.8 million to the Indian casinos. Bustamante said he'd already spent it.

52. Dan Schnur, interview by author, January 24, 2004; California Secretary of State, "Election Results and Dates," www.ss.ca.gov/elections/elections_elections.htm.

53. *Los Angeles Times* exit poll, October 9, 2003, www.latimes.com/news/local/timespoll/state/.

54. "The Left-Out Coast," *The Economist*, April 10, 2003.

55. Fred Barnes, "Why California Doesn't Matter," *Weekly Standard*, July 31, 2000; Harold Meyerson, "California's Progressive Mosaic," *American Prospect* 12, no. 11 (June 18, 2001).

56. "As Huey Long was once the Kingfish of Louisiana politics," said Pete Schabarum, the initiative's author, "Willie Brown is today's flamboyant symbol of California politics." (He was, said Brown in response, "in a spot where racial minorities are not supposed to be. . . . You could say whatever you wanted about this black man and it was instantly believable.") Peter F. Schabarum, *Enough Is Enough: Term Limits in California* (n.p., Modernage Marketing Services, 1992), p. 21. For a nice illustration of Brown's flamboyance, see James Richardson, *Willie Brown: A Biography* (Berkeley: University of California Press, 1996), pp. 315–17.

57. David Richie, "Anti-tax Advocate Lit Match That Set the Recall Fire," *Sacramento Bee*, July 24, 2003.

58. Robert Salladay, "The Pushed-Around Finally Pushed Back at Ballot Box," News Analysis, *San Francisco Chronicle*, October 8, 2003.

59. Quoted in Jessica Guynn, "California Has a Legacy of Revolt," *Contra Costa Times*, October 12, 2003.

60. Adam Nagourney, "Voter Revolt Could Be Bad for Bush," *New York Times*, October 9, 2003.

61. Lou Cannon, "Elephant Ascending?" *California Journal* (March 2004).

62. Gray Davis, interview by author, January 17, 2003.

63. Steve Lopez, "The Most Fearless Governor in America," *Time* (October 11, 1999).

64. Al Baker, "State Legislature Overrides Pataki on Budget Vetoes," *New York Times*, May 16, 2003.

65. In the "securitizing," the state issued bonds against the expected future annual revenues from the state's share of the settlement from the national suit against major tobacco companies.

66. "Crisis in California," *California Journal* (August 2003).

67. Quoted in George Skelton, "Capitol Journal," *Los Angeles Times*, September 12, 2005.

68. The initiative, Proposition 54, was based on the premise that, as long as government classified people by ethnicity in its official counts (of poverty, school enrollment, etc.), it perpetuated racism.

69. California Secretary of State, "Initiatives in Circulation as of September 27, 2004," www.ss.ca.gov/elections/elections_j.htm.

70. Summaries, ballot arguments, analyses, and full texts of all these measures are at the California Secretary of State's Website, www.ss.ca.gov.

71. Fiona Hutton, spokesperson for the Proposition 71 campaign, and Wayne Johnson, manager of the anti-71 campaign, interviews by author, August 2004. The finance data is from California Secretary of State, www.ss.ca.gov.

72. Laura Mecoy, "Foes: Profit Drives Stem Cell Measure," *Sacramento Bee*, October 16, 2004; Laura Mecoy, "Rivals Charge Prop. 71 Conflict," *Sacramento Bee*, October 20, 2004.

4. Hybrid Democracy

1. See, for example, Mark Gladstone and Ann. E. Marimow, "Rookie Governor Shows His Skill at Cutting Deals," *San Jose Mercury News*, December 13, 2003. The remark about the gaming tribes was made in a broadcast conversation with Leon Panetta at California State University Monterey Bay, Seaside, CA, October 10, 2004.

2. Schwarzenegger Website, "Swearing-in Remarks," Sacramento, November 17, 2003, www.governor.ca.gov/state/govsite/gov_homepage.jsp.

3. Phil Angelides, interview by author, July 1, 2004.

4. All were published on May 16, 2004, and there were others like them.

5. John Vasconcellos, talk at the Public Policy Institute of California, San Francisco, November 22, 2004.

6. "I love him," Janssen said. David Janssen, interview by author, April 24, 2004. Arnold Schwarzenegger, speech at the Sacramento Press Club, January 27, 2004; Darrell Steinberg, interviews by author, January 29 and August 11, 2004; John Burton, speech at the Sacramento Press Club, September 28, 2004; Burton, interview by author, September 28, 2004. Also see Margaret Talev, "Action Figure: Energetic and Charismatic, the State's New Governor Has Earned High Marks from across the Political Spectrum," *Sacramento Bee*, February 22, 2004.

7. Paul G. Lewis and Elisa Barbour, *California Cities and the Local Sales Tax* (San Francisco: Public Policy Institute of California, 1999), p. ix.

8. See, for example, Alexa H. Bluth, "Steinberg Blames Cities for Impasse," *Sacramento Bee*, July 10, 2004; Margaret Talev, "Lines Harden in Budget Fight," *Sacramento Bee*, July 13, 2004.

9. "A Quick Look at California Politics," *Political Pulse*, July 23, 2004, http://www.politicalpulse.com/.

10. Gary Delsohn, "Governor Calls Foes 'Girlie Men,' " *Sacramento Bee*, July 18, 2004.

11. Carla Marinucci, "At Tribute to Women, Schwarzenegger Angers Nurses," *San Francisco Chronicle*, December 8, 2004. Contribution data from the Secretary of State, www.ss.ca.gov or at www.arnoldwatch.org/special_interests/index.html. Schwarzenegger later acknowledged that many of his contributors were also "special interests." "Everybody out there is a special interest," he said. He wasn't against the special interests—"I'm not going after anybody"— only against their power in the Capitol. Schwarzenegger, at meeting with the editorial board of the *Sacramento Bee*, January 18, 2005.

12. California State Auditor, *California Department of Corrections: A Shortage of Correctional Officers, Along with Costly Labor Agreement Provisions, Raises Both Fiscal and Safety Concerns and Limits Management's Control*, report no. 2002–101 (Sacramento, July 2002); Greg Lucas, "State Will Pay Dearly for Davis's Prison Deal," *San Francisco Chronicle*, July 31, 2002.

13. James Sterngold, "Judge Orders Takeover of State's Prison Health Care System," *San Francisco Chronicle*, June 30, 2005; Daniel Weintraub, "Schwarzenegger Loses His Way on Prison Reform," *Sacramento Bee*, July 22, 2004.

14. Dan Morain, "Deal Gives Guards Millions in Benefits," *Los Angeles Times*, July 13, 2004; Kate Folmar, "Concession to Prison Guards Blasted," *San Jose Mercury News*, July 14, 2004.

15. Burton, speech at the Sacramento Press Club, September 28, 2004. The stories of the guard-fostered fights among prisoners for the entertainment of the screws and for the intimidation of honest guards and other personnel to keep them from whistle-blowing, and of the many other scandals and abuses in California's prison system would alone make a volume.

16. Office of the Legislative Analyst, *Overview of the May 2004–05 Revision* (Sacramento: Office of the Legislative Analyst, May 17, 2004), p. 3.

17. See, for example, George Skelton, "Option to Raise Taxes Waits in Wings," *Los Angeles Times*, May 20, 2004.

18. The Master Plan, adopted in 1960, is more fully discussed in part 2, above.

19. Bob Mulholland, interview by author, October 25, 2004.

20. Schwarzenegger, at meeting with the editorial board of the *Sacramento Bee*, January 18, 2005.

21. Laurence Leamer, *Fantastic: The Life of Arnold Schwarzenegger* (New York: St. Martin's Press, 2005), p. 242.

22. Steinberg, interview by author, August 11, 2004.

23. Fabian Nunez, interview by author, September 24, 2004.

24. Kevin Starr, interview by author, March 26, 2004.

25. Bill Hauck, interview by author, January 27, 2004.

26. Mark Baldassare, *Public Policy Institute of California Statewide Survey* (San Francisco: PPIC, October 21, 2004), www.ppic.org.

27. Jean Ross, interview by author, September 28, 2004.

28. Schwarzenegger, at meeting with the editorial board of the *Sacramento Bee*, January 18, 2005.

29. Arnold Schwarzenegger, "Governor Schwarzenegger's State of the State Address," January 5, 2005, www.governor.ca.gov.

30. With better than anticipated revenues, it would later go down.

31. The administration insisted that it was increasing school funding by many billions, the education lobby that he was cutting it. But when all the technicalities of his budget were sorted out, what the schools got were additional funds that covered enrollment growth, increases in the cost of living, and little more. Under the constitution's (Proposition 98) guarantees, they were entitled to $4 billion more, about $700 per child. The governor's acknowledgment of the promise came at a meeting of the *Sacramento Bee*'s editorial board, January 18, 2005. On

the denial, see Gary Delsohn, "Governor: No School Fund Pledge," *Sacramento Bee*, May 18, 2005.

32. He frequently repeated the argument. "I cannot be bought," he told Judy Woodruff of CNN on April 20, 2005. "I have plenty of money myself[,] . . . whereas those guys in our capitol are very vulnerable. They have no money. So they get money from special interests and the unions[,] and then favors go back." Also see Dean E. Murphy, "Donors' Influence on Schwarzenegger Is an Issue," *New York Times*, March 7, 1005. On access, see Robert Salladay, "Candid Talk on the Party Line," *Los Angeles Times*, June 2, 2005. Salladay, who got the number and called in, heard Don Sipple, one of the governor's campaign consultants, lay out an election strategy to create "a phenomenon of anger" at public employee unions.

33. Proposition 77 was also a clunky proposal since the three retired judges who would do the redistricting were likely to be white males (the pool of retired judges was predominantly white and male). The proposition required mid-decade redistricting before the next election, itself an extraordinary process, and it required voter approval of any plan drawn by the panel, even as candidates were running in the new districts.

34. Elizabeth G. Hill, *Overview of the Governor's Budget, 2005–06* (Sacramento: Legislative Analyst's Office, January 2005), p. 1, www.lao.ca.gov; Lynda Gledhill, "The California Budget: Governor's Finance Plan Called Too Restrictive," *San Francisco Chronicle*, January 13, 2005.

35. The whole proposal was some seven thousand words long. Its complicated terms indicated that, even where bonds had been sold for a specified purpose, in a tight year the state might be unable to spend the proceeds, even as it was paying interest on the money. Similarly, fees collected from a business for a project might be frozen. It would also eliminate the legislature's authority in tight times to defer some transportation spending and use the funds for more urgent needs. See, for example, *Limiting the Future? What Would the "Live Within Our Means Act" Mean for California?* California Budget Project, April 2005, www.cbp.org.

36. Carla Marinucci and John Wildermuth, "Campaign Industry Hits the Jackpot," *San Francisco Chronicle*, March 27, 2005.

37. John Marelius, "Petition Hawkers a Breed Apart," *San Diego Union-Tribune*, April 16, 2005.

38. When I quoted the question in a column, I received an e-mail from Oakland mayor and former governor Jerry Brown declaring that "the term *Caesarism* is not appropriate for what the governor is asking. . . . Augustus Caesar trans-

formed the Roman Republic into the Principate. Under this type of regime, the man in charge (the Princeps) had few, if any, of the restraints that a California governor faces and will always face—even if Arnold gets everything he wants." The governor, he told me later, is hemmed in too much. The conversation took place at a book party for Ethan Rarick's *California Rising* (Berkeley: University of California Press, 2005), a biography of his father, Governor Pat Brown, who plainly had no trouble getting things done with the powers he had.

39. Elizabeth Garrett, "Lessons from the California Recall: Remarks for the Workshop on Democratic Governance" (paper presented to the American Association of Law Schools Annual Conference, San Francisco, January 6, 2005); Garrett, interview by author, January 6, 2005. Also see Garrett, "California's Hybrid Democracy," *George Washington University Law Review* (forthcoming, 2005).

40. James Dao, "Virginia Political Shocker: Republicans for High Taxes," *New York Times*, March 26, 2004.

41. John Hein, interview by author, March 4, 2005.

42. See, for example, Jean Ross, "What's the Problem? What's the Solution? Understanding California's Budget Problems and Proposals for Change," California Budget Project, March 2005, www.cbp.org.

43. James Dao, " '55 and Out' Comes Home to Roost," *New York Times*, May 1, 2005.

44. David Firestone, "Does Pain Make States Stronger?" *New York Times*, April 27, 2003.

45. Schwarzenegger, at meeting with the editorial board of the *Sacramento Bee*, January 18, 2005; Gary Delsohn, "Governor: Starve State's Monster," *Sacramento Bee*, January 19, 2005. While the governor avoided all such meetings in his first year—or indeed much other exposure to print media—he began his second year with a round of editorial board interviews at the state's major papers. In the meeting with the *Bee* editors, Schwarzenegger made an odd reference to Nietzsche. *Bee* editorial writer Stuart Leavenworth picked up on it, reminding the governor of Nietzsche's advice to "would be dragon slayers": " 'Whoever fights monsters,' wrote Nietzsche, 'should see to it that in the process he doesn't become a monster.' " "Beware of Monsters," *Sacramento Bee*, January 19, 2005.

46. Carla Marinucci, "Governor Digs Fixing Potholes: As San Jose Crews Destroy Part of Road for Staged Event," *San Francisco Chronicle*, May 27, 2005.

47. Mark Baldassare, *Public Policy Institute of California Statewide Survey* (San Francisco: PPIC, April 2005), www.ppic.org; Field Poll Release #2158, June 21, 2005, http://field.com/fieldpollonline/subscribers/.

48. Dean E. Murphy, "Schwarzenegger's Star Dipping as Californians Feel

Its Singe," *New York Times*, May 2, 2005; "Greater Than Two to One Majority Believe State Is Seriously Off on Wrong Track," San Francisco: Field Poll Release #2162, June 28, 2005.

5. Fragile Experiment

1. Steve H. Murdock, Steve White, Md. Nazrul Hoque, Beverly Pecotte, Xuihong You and Jennifer Balkan, *The New Texas Challenge: Population Change and the Future of Texas* (College Station: Texas A&M Press, 2003).

2. Ibid., pp. 218, 224.

3. Louis Uchitelle, "College Degree Still Pays, but It's Leveling Off," *New York Times*, January 13, 2005.

4. Robert Dynes, interview by author, April 7, 2004; Levy, interviews by author, April, May, September 2004.

5. See, for example, Ross DeVol and Rob Koepp, *California's Position in Technology and Science: A Comparative Benchmarking Assessment* (Los Angeles: Milken Institute, March 2004).

6. Walsh was also a codefendant with the governor in a British libel suit brought by a London TV personality who had accused the governor of groping her after an interview there. When the Schwarzenegger campaign replied that she had initiated it, she sued.

7. See, for example, "Revenue Package for 2003–04," California Tax Reform Association, www.caltaxreform.org/revoptions.htm.

8. John Elwood, Steven Sheffrin, and John J. Kirlin, *California Fiscal Reform: A Plan for Action* (Oakland: University of California Business Higher Education Forum, 1994), p. 4.

9. Alberto Alesina, Reza Baqir, and William Easterly, "Public Goods and Ethnic Division," *Quarterly Journal of Economics* 114, no. 4 (November 1999): 1243. An earlier version was published in 1997 by the National Bureau of Economic Research.

10. Peter H. Lindert, *Growing Public: Social Spending and Economic Growth Since the Eighteenth Century* (Cambridge: Cambridge University Press, 2004), pp. 29, 187. Lindert also observes that voter turnout is positively correlated with social transfers and taxes and observes that Switzerland and the United States, where fewer than half of eligible voters vote, are comparatively low on both counts (p. 181).

11. See, for example, Bobbitt, "Marketing the Future of the State," *New Statesman* (January 17, 2003).

12. Selected from unsolicited e-mails to author, various dates, 2004.

13. Howard Jarvis, "Illegal Aliens Take Free Ride on Gravy Train," *Sacramento Bee*, September 17, 1978, p. F5.

14. Lisa Richardson, "Immigrant Health Tab Disputed," *Los Angeles Times*, May 18, 2003.

15. Joaquin Avila, *Political Apartheid in California: Consequences of Excluding a Growing Noncitizen Population*, Latino Policy and Issues Brief no. 9 (Los Angeles: UCLA Chicano Studies Research Center, December 2003). The turnout of Latino voters is based on the 2000 presidential election. Harry Pachon, interview by author, May 26, 2004.

16. Leo Estrada, remarks at California First Five Conference, Sacramento, April 23, 2004.

17. See, for example, Richard Hofstadter, *The Age of Reform: From Bryan to F.D.R.* (New York: Alfred A. Knopf, 1956), pp. 82–85.

18. Jean Ross, interview by author, October 25, 2004.

19. Loni Hancock, interview by author, August 20, 2004.

20. Severin Borenstein and other staff members at the University of California Energy Institute, interviews by author, August 30, 2004. Nor was it just the big corporate traders who drove up prices. In Long Beach, a natural gas trader "with a fast computer, three telephone lines, and a television tuned to the weather reports" bought and sold natural gas so fast that Federal Energy Commission regulators estimated she singlehandedly cost customers nearly $3 billion in the winter of 2000–01. They called her "the bunny slipper lady." Mary Rivera Brooks, "How a Lone Trader Roiled Energy Market," *Los Angeles Times*, April 20, 2003.

21. "Former State Finance Director Steve Peace Sheds Light on State/Local Fiscal Dysfunctionality," *Metro Investment Report* (June 2004), www.metroinvestmentreport.com/article/173.

22. As many do. Or they drove with licenses obtained in one of the dozen other states that didn't require proof of legal residency. Lydia Chavez, "Immigrants in Game of Musical Cars," *Oakland Tribune*, July 6, 2004.

23. For a fuller elaboration of this point, see, for example, David A. Hollinger, "The One Drop Rule and the One Hate Rule," *Daedalus* (February 2005).

24. See, for example, Elisabeth Bumiller, "Politics at the Border: Bush Woos Both Hispanics and Moderates by Offering Proposal on Illegal Immigrants," *New York Times*, January 8, 2004.

25. Dean E. Murphy, "Imagining Life without Illegal Immigrants," *New York Times*, January 21, 2005.

26. Roughly 85 percent of immigrant families with children are of "mixed" status. Michael E. Fix and Jeffrey S. Passel, "U.S. Immigration at the Beginning of the 21st Century: Testimony before the Subcommittee on Immigration and Claims Hearing on 'The U.S. Population and Immigration' Committee on the Judiciary U.S. House of Representatives," August 2, 2001, Urban Institute, http://www.urban.org/url.cfm?ID=900417.

27. Murphy, "Imagining Life without Illegal Immigrants."

28. David Hollinger, interview by author, February 1, 2005.

29. Joan Didion, *Where I Was From* (New York: Alfred A. Knopf, 2003), p. 95.

30. Ibid., p. 129.

31. Kevin Starr, *Coast of Dreams: California on the Edge, 1990–2003* (New York: Alfred A. Knopf, 2004), pp. xii–xiii.

32. Ibid., pp. 629–31.

33. Kevin Starr, interview by author, March 26, 2004. The Josiah Royce quote is from his *California: From the Conquest in 1846 to the Second Vigilance Committee in San Francisco. A Study of American Character* (Boston: Houghton Mifflin, 1886), p. 2.

34. Phil Angelides, interview by author, July 1, 2004.

35. Ibid.

36. Abby Goodnough, "Strange Brews Are Created in Melting Pot That Is Florida," *New York Times*, April 3, 2005.

37. Mark Baldassare, *California's Partisan Divide* (San Francisco: Public Policy Institute of California, June 2004); Baldassare, interview by author, June 10, 2004.

38. Morris P. Fiorina, *Culture War? The Myth of a Polarized America* (New York: Pearson Longman, 2004). Also see John Tierney, "A Nation Divided? Who Says?" *New York Times*, June 13, 2004.

39. Joel Kotkin, "A Lighter Shade of Blue for California," *Sacramento Bee*, November 7, 2004.

40. In fact, Kotkin didn't have his numbers quite right. He said that Bush had reduced the overall margin in California (compared to 2000) by 300,000. The reduction was from a margin of under 1.3 million votes to just over 1.2 million. Bush got 942,000 more votes than he had in 2000. Kerry got 884,000 more than Gore had.

41. Mark Baldassare, interview by author, February, 2005; Mark Baldassare, *Public Policy Institute of California Statewide Survey: Special Survey on the California State Budget* (San Francisco: Public Policy Institute of California, January 2005), www.ppic.org/main/publication.asp?i=584. Also see "As the Nation Goes, So Goes California? Partisanship Returns with a Vengeance," Public Policy Institute of California press release, January 27, 2005, www.ppic.org/main/pressrelease.asp?i=535.

42. Dowell Myers, John Pitkin, and Julie Park, *California Demographic Futures: Projections to 2030, by Immigrant Generations, Nativity, and Time of Arrival in the U.S.* (Los Angeles: School of Policy, Planning, and Development, University of Southern California, January 2005), Exhibit 2, p. 7.

43. Starr, interview by author, March 26, 2004.

44. Louis Hartz, *The Liberal Tradition in America* (New York: Harcourt, Brace, 1955), p. 85.

45. William Fulton, "The Job Hunt: The Two-Tier Economy Seems More of a Reality in the America of Today Than It Has in Almost a Century," *Governing Magazine* (June 2004), http://governing.com/archive/2004/jun/econ.txt.

INDEX

Abernathy, Mark, 158–59, 164, 294n6
abortion: 1967 state law on, 89, 98;
  parental notification initiative on,
  215, 225, 228; voters' position on,
  182
Abraham, David, 59
Adams, Ansel, 77
affirmative action: ban on, at University
  of California, 112–15, 284n43,
  285n46; initiatives on, 139, 188,
  300n68
Afghan Journal, 67
Afghan Medical Association, 29
African Americans: as affirmative action
  students, 112–14; displacement of,
  from labor force, 51, 272n62; education level of, 82; as elected officials,
  11; as percent of population, 23; UC
  enrollment figures on, 115, 285n47
Agricultural Labor Relations Board, 31
agriculture: in Central Valley, 32; global
  pressures on, 33, 267n25; NAFTA's
  impact on, 40, 273n68; organic
  niche in, 34, 267n26; unionization
  movement in, 31–32. *See also* farmworkers
Aguililla village (Michoacan), 45

Alabama, 9, 263n3
Alarcon, Rafael, 45, 46–47, 265–66n9
Alba, Richard, 62, 73–74, 80–81
Alesina, Alberto, 239, 243
Alien Land Act, 96
All-American Canal, 72
Alliance for a Better California, 217,
  228
Alpaugh (San Joaquin Valley), 39,
  269n40
Altamont Rock Festival (1969), 98
American Apparel (East Los Angeles),
  28
American Civil Liberties Union, 104,
  168
American Council on Education, 93
American Diabetes Association, 191
American Lung Association, 191–92
American Media, 173–74
American Prospect, 182
Americans for Tax Reform, 8–9
Amgen, 224
Anaheim Angels baseball team, 65
Anderson, Glenn, 97
Aneesh, Aneesh, 42, 270n47
Angelides, Phil, 170, 195, 207, 230, 233,
  255

Text:	Janson
Display:	Akzidenz Grotesk Extended
Compositor:	Binghamton Valley Composition, LLC
Indexer:	Patricia Deminna
Printer and binder:	Maple-Vail Manufacturing Group